KT-458-833

THE BEST OF
The Cricketer

THE BEST OF

The Cricketer

1921-1981

THE SIXTIETH ANNIVERSARY SELECTION

Edited by Reg Hayter

CASSELL

LONDON

CASSELL LTD.
35 Red Lion Square, London WC1R 4SG
and at Sydney, Auckland, Toronto, Johannesburg,
an affiliate of
Macmillan Publishing Co., Inc.,
New York.

Copyright © *The Cricketer* 1981
Introduction © Reg Hayter 1981

All rights reserved. No part of this publication
may be reproduced, stored in a retrieval system,
or transmitted, in any form or by any means,
electronic, mechanical, photocopying, recording or
otherwise, without the prior permission of
Cassell Ltd.

First published 1981

ISBN 0 304 30700 9

Printed and bound in Great Britain at
The Camelot Press Ltd, Southampton

HERTFORDSHIRE
COUNTY LIBRARY
796·358
0447801

CONTENTS

ILLUSTRATIONS

INTRODUCTION

The last sixty years of our history may be considered as hardly glorious, apart perhaps from cricket; the great game of country and Empire; the Englishman's second (sometimes 'first') religion.

Where *The Cricketer* is concerned, the longer it flourishes the more difficult and challenging it becomes to produce the ideal representative anthology; and, from an increasing mass of material, to do justice to both past and present, to accommodate the permanent and the ephemeral—whether in prose or in pictures—to keep up with the cricket and cricketers and the changing times, which not only refuse to stand still but rush onwards into the future like an express train—or a jumbo jet.

It is a great enjoyment to edit *The Cricketer*. Even that needs qualifying. 'Enjoyment' not only means responding to the stimulus of a game. It also means the hectic life of an editor; getting the right people at the right time, making the decisions, trying to emulate a prophet of the future and doing, in a sense, virtually everything—apart from printing the words.

One must lay the blame on 'Plum' Warner—Pelham Francis Warner who played cricket for Oxford University, Middlesex and England. He was knighted in 1937 but, long before that, in 1921, he founded *The Cricketer* and bequeathed to all enthusiasts of the game a bible to be collected in instalments. When will it be finished? Never.

Meanwhile, in spite of inflation and high prices, the volume of cricket literature increases yearly. The more leisurely and ruminative writing of the past has declined, succeeded mostly by a crisper, more staccato approach, not always for the best perhaps, but cricket will survive. There is no more ideal subject for nostalgia; the futile, yet fascinating, pastime of comparing past and present achievements is simply an integral part of the mystery of cricket. Some contemporary players are roaming the world who would have given the old players a very good run for their money.

So it goes on: this game of isolated incidents, stops and starts, hours of probe, thrust and parry, then the fireworks which can light up the sky even under a blazing sun.

1981
Reg Hayter
Editor

Publisher's Note: Articles by Reg Hayter, despite the diffidence of their author, are included at our suggestion.

SOME ARTICLES

The year it all began

April 30, 1921. The first issue of The Cricketer, *with a Foreword by the founder and editor, P. F. Warner*

The popularity of, and interest in, cricket, not only here, but in every part of the world where Englishmen are gathered together, was never greater that at the present time. Cricket, indeed, as Tom Brown has told us in the best of all school stories, is an institution and the *habeas corpus* of every boy of British birth, for it is a typically British game.

The Editor believes that there is room for such a paper as *The Cricketer*, which will endeavour to criticise justly and to comment fairly and accurately not only on first-class cricket, which, after all, is but a small part of our national game, but on Club, Services, and School cricket as well. The very essence of cricket is camaraderie and good sportsmanship, and the contributors to *The Cricketer* will strive to write in such a spirit, hoping thereby to spread an even greater love of cricket than exists at present, and, at the same time, to educate the general public in the finer points of the game.

The Cricketer will not confine itself entirely to English cricket, it is catholic in its aims and objects, and will deal with the game in our Overseas dominions; in fact, in every country where cricket is played. News from the outposts of the Empire will be specially welcomed, for it is hoped that the paper will become the recognised medium whereby all players and followers of the game may keep in touch with one another.

The Cricketer makes a special appeal to the boys who are now learning to play the game, in every sense of the phrase. Within its covers will be found instructive articles by famous cricketers whose names are household words, and who from their vast experience will impart knowledge that can be gained from no other source. Young batsmen, bowlers, and fieldsmen will all be considered, and it is hoped that the hints given in these pages will form a valuable adjunct to the general school coaching.

The Editor invites correspondence on any subject connected with cricket, and will gladly do his best to answer questions or to give advice on the game. He is naturally dependent for much information on the goodwill of club secretaries and other enthusiasts, and will always gladly receive suggestions for the benefit of either cricket or *The Cricketer*. He feels that the first number of the paper has scarcely realised his ideal, but he hopes to do better in the future, confident that he will receive the help and sympathy of all lovers of the greatest of English games.

The contributors require but little introduction. Mr MacLaren, who will make a special feature of School Cricket, is one of the greatest batsmen that ever lived. He captained England in no less than twenty-two Test matches, and his record in these great contests has been surpassed by few. He was also a most able captain, with a genius for placing the field and getting the best out of his bowlers. In any history of international cricket Mr MacLaren will always have a foremost place.

Mr Jessop was, in some sense, the greatest genius that cricket has produced, and of him it may well be said that he reduced rustic cricket to a science. He was the idol of every cricket ground, and many of his innings are historic. As a fieldsman at cover point he has had few, if any, equals.

Mr Knight is one of the younger generation, but his batting in 1919 stamped him as a player of rare distinction and class, and as his chapter on batsmanship in the 'Badminton Cricket' proved, he has the power of expressing his ideas on batting with no mean ability.

Mr Altham, who was in the Repton, Oxford, and Hampshire XI's, has long been recognised as one of the greatest authorities on School Cricket, and his style of writing should satisfy even the most critical expert.

Mr G. N. Foster, a fine batsman and a brilliant field, is one of the famous cricketing family, and Mr F. B. Wilson, a former captain of the Cambridge XI, has a sound knowledge of the game, and a keen sense of humour with which to express his opinions.

The Editor considers himself fortunate in enlisting the co-operation of Mr Charles Grave, the famous cartoonist, who makes such a speciality of sporting subjects. In each future number Mr Grave will produce a full page cartoon of a famous cricketer, together with other sketches, and will also have the assistance of other well-known artists. No cricket paper would be complete without photographs, and each issue will be considerably indebted to the work of the camera.

The scores of the Test matches in Australia during the past winter, with critical comments on each, are included from the point of view of statistical record.

A great game, not a business . . .

Defence! Defence! Defence! A protest by L. C. Docker, in 1923, about dull and slow cricket. The argument still goes on today

At the Annual General Meeting of the Warwickshire C.C.C., Mr L. C. Docker, the President of the Club [who played for both Warwickshire and Derbyshire] made so interesting a speech on the present position and condition of English Cricket, that we print it in full. We think that Mr Docker takes too pessimistic a view, but there is force in much that he says:

Last year I stated that I considered there had been a deterioration in English Cricket, and this year I am afraid I cannot alter that criticism.

We did not discover a really good bowler, either fast or slow, and although we sent to South Africa, what everyone will admit with one exception was our best side, we were only just able to get home in the Test matches.

All honour and our heartiest congratulations go out to the team and to Mr F. T. Mann for leading England to victory. I hope this is a happy augury for the future. We had not won a Test Rubber since 1912, and we still have that awful nightmare with us of having lost eight Australian Test matches running, so this win is very refreshing and encouraging.

The match at Durban was a great fight, but the cricket must have been painfully slow, as it lasted six days. I cannot help saying no cricket match ought to last so long, three days should be quite sufficient if there is any enterprise. If you want to win matches you must take risks. I am strongly of opinion matches should begin earlier, finish later, and that the tea interval should be abolished.

There is something wrong with English cricket, and the sooner we find it out and correct it the better.

Since the Australians visited us in 1921, much discussion has centred round the apparent decadence of our players.

The form and methods of our first class cricketers during the past season were, as usual, closely watched by many thousands of onlookers, as well as large numbers of enthusiastic players who, outside the circle of what is called representative or County cricket, possess a sound practical knowledge of the game.

It would be idle to suggest that the present form of our leading cricketers is satisfactory—far from it. I have no hesitation in saying that not only cricketers but the public are anxious and concerned as to the future.

Opinions differ as to the main defects of the present day methods. Too much importance is attached to the position of teams in the championship, with the result that the fear of losing a match becomes an obsession to the exclusion of the everlasting hope that any game may be won.

Defence! Defence!! Defence!!! was the order of the day, without any real effort being made to get runs.

Surely we ought to have profited by the object lessons the Australians gave us in 1921. Do you remember how frequently our men got out because they would not attack the fast bowling by playing forward, or the slow bowling by jumping out at the slightly overpitched ball and driving it?

Last season it was indeed painful to watch many of our best cricketers carefully playing half volleys gently back to the bowler which every time ought to have been driven to the boundary.

The precautionary methods of the opening batsmen may to some extent be justified for the sake of the side, but I hold strongly that every time you are fortunate enough to get a half volley or a badly pitched ball, whether it is the first over or the last, it should be hit, and hit hard.

Whatever justification the opening batsmen may have had it certainly was no reason why such extreme caution should be adopted by many of the succeeding men, and frequently even the ordinary bowler was treated with profound respect to the increasing boredom of the spectators.

In the university match at Lord's last summer on a slow easy-paced wicket against moderate bowling, seven overs and three balls were bowled at the beginning of the match before a run was scored; one run was made in the first 25 minutes and 24 runs in the first hour. I was real glad when the lunch interval arrived.

I am obliged to say that slower and less interesting play has scarcely ever been witnessed at our county ground than on the occasion of the visits from the leading county teams last season, and I will not even except the Champion County [Yorkshire].

No charge could justly be made of poor play as far as defence of the wicket was concerned, but the method of playing the ball and the absolute refusal to get at the bowler before he gets at you, as "W. G." used to say, reduced the play to an aggravating spectacle of over cautious barndoor cricket, pitiable in its inexcusable timidity and utter absence of enterprise.

The man in the crowd is thoroughly fed up with the dull and slow cricket, which is today being played by our best professional batsmen. If these batsmen were only to hear some of the forcible uncomplimentary remarks that are frequently made by onlookers, I cannot help thinking they would realise that they are killing the goose that lays the golden eggs.

Let us have more of the *joie de vivre* in our cricket, and let us never forget that it is a game, a great game, and not a business. Do, please, let us always remember this.

I believe I played my first cricket match when I was twelve years old, and I fancy I have a record of that great event at home. Although that was about 50 years ago, I still believe cricket is the best game in the world if it is only played in the right way.

During my active career as a cricketer, I was fortunate in playing at a time when England possessed some really great exponents at the game. I had the good luck to be closely associated with four great men, and in playing with them and against them, I had many opportunities of closely studying their wonderful play. I am mentioning the names of W. G. Grace, Arthur Shrewsbury, as batsmen, George Lohmann and Dick Pougher, as bowlers, in order to emphasise and justify the opinion I am about to express as to the deterioration in English Cricket.

It is my considered opinion that the two-eyed stance is utterly wrong in theory, method and practice, and it is to a great extent responsible for our feeble batting. It necessitates a clumsy crouching attitude, and frequently one sees a fine batsman place two well-padded legs as a second line of defence, in front of the wicket, as Mr Pardon says in *Wisden*, to play an ordinary plain straight ball. This is all wrong, and yet it is frequently described in some of the newspapers as wonderful footwork. By all means let the batsman use his feet, but let it be to jump out to the pitch of the ball, rather than sit on the splice and let the ball hit the bat. Our batsmen are too mechanical, and there is a strange lack of personality.

I hardly like to say our first-class County batsmen are deficient in scoring strokes, but last season these were few and far between, and after all, the first principle of a batsman is surely to get runs, or at all events to make an effort to do so.

Our young bowlers pay a great deal too much attention to swerve, spin, and the leg theory, with the result that we are lacking in the old fashioned good length bowling. I maintain that length comes first of all and is everything, but ever since the googley bowler appeared, a great deal too much attention has been given in trying to make the ball swerve and turn in an unnatural manner at the entire sacrifice of length.

I say emphatically that the bowler should practise! and practise!! until he can bowl a good length and has obtained control of the ball and forget all about the tricks of flight or break or spin until he has acquired this necessary control.

I devoutly hope this next season we shall turn over a new leaf and get back to the well tried and sound principles under which English cricket scored so many glorious successes.

Those who kept off the hard stuff

From the *New York Herald*, of September 9, 1924:

"TEETOTALING CRICKETERS ARRIVE ON
'LANCASTRIA.'

"INCOGNITI CLUB TO REPRESENT ENGLAND HERE
BECAUSE MEMBERS DON'T DRINK.

"The 'Lancastria' arrived last night from Southampton with thirteen members of the Incogniti Cricket Club of England.

"The cricket players are to play the All-New York team and then will go on to Philadelphia for a match. They said that they were picked to come to the United States, not so much because of their skill at the game as because they were teetotalers, the club being unwilling to violate international courtesy by sending a cricketer who indulged in beer or strong drink."

The benefits of the game

Sir Home Gordon, Bart., a regular contributor between the wars, examines the matter of players' benefits in The Cricketer Annual, *1922–3*

It may be thought that so serious a topic as the benefit of a professional is rather a solid item in the Christmas fare provided in this Annual. Yet let it be borne in mind that winter is the period for reflection on cricket, and that in the off-season are arranged many momentous matters about which there would not be time to deal adequately during the stress of the season. It is with some measure of temerity that I am writing on this topic because the Editor of *The Cricketer* has more than once assured me that it is among the most topical articles he has so far commissioned, and one that is being anticipated, and will be debated. I can only say that in a life devoted to studying cricket I have always been in cordial sympathy with the paid division, and recognise how essential it is that its members should go on the field reasonably relieved of financial anxiety.

His benefit must be the climax of a cricketer's life, the three days of paramount importance in his career. Therefore inevitable regret is felt that it should be so much of a gamble, owing to weather. Even when the receipts are insured, fine weather or the reverse may make a difference of five hundred pounds, or even more. I believe I was the first, when private secretary to my cousin in Lloyd's at the close of the nineteenth century, to introduce the insurance of a benefit, and I remember my chief's disgust at having to pay a pretty substantial claim on the initial occasion—he knew as little about cricket as I do about football. Since then cricket insurance has developed into a recognised branch, and is in process of being accurately dealt with on the law of averages.

The popularity of the individual cricketer undoubtedly affects both the amount of his subscriptions and of the collections on the ground. Be it noted that at the annual Whit-Monday benefit at Lord's no collection is permitted in the pavilion. The player who catches the imagination of the public, one whose name is a household word, reaps pecuniary benefit to an extent that a more stolid and utilitarian comrade does not enjoy. This cannot be helped, because, in what is purely voluntary, hero worship must be a factor, especially when schoolboys may be among the donors.

It is also obvious that there can be no uniformity, or even approximation, in the matter of the amounts of benefits. Those of Yorkshire or Lancashire are out of all proportion, say, to those of Somersetshire or Essex. Nor can this be obviated. One amateur has suggested to me that the ideal system would be to pool two and a half per cent of all the gates in county Championship matches all over the country, and as each man's benefit came give him a fixed sum in lieu of the receipts of a match. I believe this would be as unpalatable to the beneficiary as it would seem cold-blooded to the public. Not only might the outcome not be satisfactory, but there would be no appeal to local enthusiasm, which is worth such a lot.

The old-time plan was simply to hand over the whole proceeds, after deducting expenses—and in those days professionals often did not take remuneration from an old colleague. The man himself might be his own worst enemy—many old-time pro's were—or he might be the victim of sharks, or, for instance, put it into some business for which he himself was unsuited. Therefore cricket history is sadly smudged with sad stories of reckless finance. It is terrible to think that a man who had honourably and skilfully served his county well nigh a score of years, and perhaps figured in representative cricket, should end his days in destitution or sordid poverty after means had been put in his hands to ensure the ease of the the rest of his life.

Of course that has long been altered, and as there are divergent methods of dealing with the important matter, it is of value to indicate some. Naturally, after Lord Hawke had effected such a marvellous transformation from the old-type county pro. to the modern one—and that's another story, as Rudyard Kipling says—one turns to Yorkshire for a lead, and that absolutely invaluable and indefatigable secretary, Mr F. C. Toone, generously writes at length in answer to my interrogations:

'Having accepted the principle of benefits, it is up to each county authority to see that the beneficiare is adequately rewarded for his services. Apart from the authority of the county, the benefit is given in the form usually adopted to enable the general public, who have enjoyed the play of the individual concerned, to contribute. The benefit is for the purpose of establishing the player in business after his cricketing career, or of obtaining sufficient to enable him to live in comfort.

'In Yorkshire it is laid down that a benefit is granted after ten years' service, and this benefit is usually given when the player is at the height of his form, and looming largely in the public eye. No one in this country has studied this matter more closely than Lord Hawke, and no one, to my knowledge, has done more to establish the player on a sound basis, and to see that his future happiness is provided for. Having granted the benefit, organisation and enthusiasm can do the rest.

'We insure the match for £1,150, either with the Yorkshire Insurance or the British Dominions. £150 more than pays the premium, and the £1,000 left is the amount guaranteed to the player. He is given the choice of any match except the Bank Holiday one, pays all the expenses, both home and away, and takes the profits. The percentage to the ground is part of the expenses, and is made easy by reducing it from 25 to 15 per cent on the gross takings (less tax). In Yorkshire nearly forty-sub-committees of interested people are formed to solicit subscriptions, make collections on the ground, and so forth. It is a large county, and no part must be neglected. We make collections at each county ground, two days at the grounds other than where the match is played, and on each of the days during the benefit match. This all requires a lot of arranging, but answers splendidly. All the time, from the head office, people are being invited to subscribe. We always aim at £2,000 net as a good benefit.

'When all is completed, the county committee invest in trustee stock two-thirds of the amount, and hand over the other third at the annual general meeting. The interest on the invested money goes to the beneficiare while he lives. If he dies and his wife survives, the interest goes to her, and when both are dead the stock is sold and divided equally among the children, if any, or given to the next of kin. This is considered a wise policy. It ensures the safe-keeping of money. Those who helped the benefit know that their help is not being frittered away, and that the player will never come to poverty. But, when all is said and done, it is only right that the County Committee should seek to put their players in a position of comfort after many years of service, and their benefits may be regarded as justifiable, and ought, therefore, to be taken up with zeal.'

Mr Toone also encloses the Yorkshire County regulation for players, and there it is further stated: 'Players with county caps who have played regularly for the county for five years shall receive a bonus of £250 if their services are no longer required. When such players have played more than five years and less than ten, bonuses in such cases shall be specially considered by the Committee, who guarantee not less than £50 for each subsequent year above five years.'

From the wealthiest county clubs let us turn to the poorest, Northamptonshire, and there Mr V. W. C. Jupp tells me a provident fund is being formed which will guarantee each beneficiary that, no matter how small the proceeds of the gate, these shall be made up to a minimum of £800, apart from collections and subscriptions.

It would be idle to pretend that the allocation of £850 to Hitch for his benefit match, Surrey v. Kent, 1921, did not create profound surprise to thousands under the impression that he was realising all the proceeds of that crowded match. Therefore, it is of particular interest to obtain the views of Mr H. D. G. Leveson-Gower, that very live member of the Surrey Committee, than whom the professionals never possessed a more affectionate friend. When I was staying with him for the Scarborough Festival in September, I asked him what he thought on the matter. He replied:

'In my opinion, a cricketer's worth and what he has done must be taken into account in selecting which benefit match he should enjoy. What I mean to say is that Y or Z might not have the same claim as Jack Hobbs, who, besides being such a paramount cricketer, has drawn so many thousands to the Oval by his prowess. I do not think, therefore, that it is practicable—nor yet practical county finance—to let a beneficiary choose his match. That should be done by the Committee. For A they might assign the game with Notts, Yorkshire, Middlesex, or Kent. For B, who has done less, either because he could only do his best or else because he has had so few opportunities, a game with Essex, Sussex, or Hants might be selected. As a rule, it is preferable to have one with a neighbouring county, when it is not one with a transcendent opponent. Then it is now possible to obtain the receipts of the match in question for four post-war years. On that an average can be struck, and a round figure approximating to that sum guaranteed to the player. Mind you, I am only giving you my personal view, and not speaking for anybody else; but that is what I regard as the best method of dealing with the all-important yet really delicate matter of a professional's benefit.'

Did space permit, it would be possible to obtain opinions from many other interested parties, and I offer the suggestion for the correspondence pages of *The Cricketer*. Still, it seems to me that the leading points of view are covered. My own opinion is that when a man gets his benefit it is out for the County Committee, and every other individual that the case appeals to, to go 'whole hog' out to make it a success. I would rather see a county lose over that one match than take a surplus sum which would be of such importance to the player. It also stimulates the work of the paid division if they know that by zealous efforts they are laying up for themselves future substantial recognition, rather than an arbitrary guaranteed sum. Of course, in the latter case, the man always knows where he stands, but a sporting risk is what most would prefer. The pressure of popular opinion may well be shown if, as is believed, it is decisive on the matter.

One of the most charming episodes in the career of that grandest of all cricketers, W. G. Grace, was when he transferred the proceeds of a testimonial match to Alfred Shaw because the benefit of the latter had been ruined by rain. Within recent times, Hobbs had two benefit matches, because the first had been spoilt by the declaration of war. There have been other cases of a second game being rightly assigned to a player because the first had been marred. At Lord's, by arrangement with Middlesex, the profits of the gate, not the receipts at the stands, go in rotation to a senior professional on the ground staff of the Club, though I fancy that once in four years a Middlesex man receives a preference—in this I may be wrong; in any case, all the professionals playing for Middlesex are on the ground staff at St John's Wood, 66,923 paid for admission to Walter Lees' benefit at the Oval, Surrey v. Yorkshire, 1906; 78,792 watched George Hirst's match, Yorkshire v. Lancashire, at Leeds, 1904. This latter yielded altogether £3,703, a sum never equalled, though J. T. Tyldesley had an equally deserved and very lucrative result in the Lancashire v. Yorkshire set aside for him. Such plums may not drop into the lap of every county professional, but that he should have the best possible, within necessary limitations, must be the general desire, and this is the due recognition of his services. That the foregoing observations may assist in this direction must be the excuse for putting them forward without prejudice and with every good will.

Dollery's rare feat

'Bold advertisement' deserves to be drawn to the performance accomplished last week by H. E. Dollery for Reading School against the M.C.C., on the former's ground. He went in first and carried his bat through the completed innings of 115 for 104, the next highest contribution being 3 by the tenth man in, G. D. Heath. There were no extras. If he never does anything else worth mentioning that is a feat which should long be remembered, for it is most doubtful where there is a parallel to it in any game, either for the School or against the M.C.C. To say that means much, for the old club is known to have played about nine thousand matches in the United Kingdom since its formation in 1787, and the game at the School can boast considerable antiquity, having been popular there during the time of the Rev. Richard Valpy, who was headmaster from 1781 to 1830. In the circumstances, the score deserves to be printed on satin, framed, and hung in a conspicuous place. The annals of the game, of course, contain particulars of many instances of a player making a hundred or more without any of his companions reaching double figures, but it is very rarely done for a school against a side of much note. One such feat we can recall at the moment, however, in which one who subsequently became a great figure in the game was the chief actor. That was A. J. Webbe, still happily with us, who, playing for Harrow against Prince's Club, on the latter's ground, in 1874, made 102 in his second innings, the next highest contributions being one of 9 and four of 7, one of the latter being supplied by 'Mr Extras'.

(1931)

[Horace Edgar Dollery, known to everyone as Tom, *did* achieve further distinction. He became the first professional ever to captain Warwickshire and in 1951 led the county to their first Championship title for 40 years. He scored 24,413 runs including 50 centuries; held nearly 300 catches and played four times for England.]

No spectator saw the ball

It was, if we remember rightly, the Fat Boy who, in *Pickwick Papers*, wished 'to make your flesh creep'. We are reminded of the benevolent desire of that life-long friend through reports which have come through respecting the wonderful pace of a Queensland aboriginal bowler named Gilbert. His speed has been said to be such that it is impossible for a spectator to see the ball on its way down the pitch. Australia has produced more than one aboriginal speed-bowler in the past, but never one, so far as we are aware, of whom so much has been claimed. Marsh, to whom A. C. MacLaren objected on account of his delivery, and who joined a travelling circus in order to display his skill, was one such. Men of colour, save in the West Indies and India, have rarely made their mark in first-class cricket. Hendricks, of South Africa, however, would probably have done so had he been given the chance.

(1930)

Old-time champion of Surrey

F. S. Ashley-Cooper, essayist and cricket researcher, records the career of 'Silver Billy', the great William Beldham, 1929

All those who are interested in the early history of the game know well that for many years there were few, if any, greater cricketers than William Beldham. Making his first appearance in the best company in 1787, he continued to play for thirty-five seasons, until, in fact, July, 1821, when, being obliged to have the services of a runner, as he had been injured, he carried out his bat for 23 in the Gentlemen v. Players match, at Lord's, which had been arranged in celebration of the coronation of George the Fourth. He was then in his fifty-sixth year, and it was a fitting termination to a career which was as long as it was brilliant.

Beldham, who came of farming stock, was born at Wrecclesham, near Farnham, in Surrey, on February 5, 1766, and succumbed to the great game's spell whilst still a mere boy. In those days there was much excellent cricket in West Surrey, and it seems only natural that a healthy-minded lad, with his older companions gaining triumphs on many fields, should have wished to play a part, and, perhaps, a leading one, in such good sport. How popular the game must have been in the district is attested by the naming of places as Bowler Green, Pitch Place, Balls Corner, Willow Green, and, in Upper Hale, of Ball and Wicket Lane. William's elder brother, George, was a player of some skill, and both were fortunate to receive tuition from one Harry Hall, a gingerbread baker of Farnham, one of whose maxims was the sound one of keeping the left elbow well up. It is a pity that so few particulars of the Farnham matches of that period have survived, for it was as a member of the club that Beldham's earliest successes were obtained. He was certainly a member of the team when only sixteen, and his future pre-eminence must have been foreshadowed when, four years later, Farnham sent a challenge to Hambledon which was declined. One season later still, in 1787 that is, he began to play at Lord's, and, being successful from the start, was soon recognised as one of the best cricketers of the time and was immediately enrolled in the Hambledon team, which was the highest honour which could possibly have been accorded him. He had, however, been engaged by the club, though probably only for practice, since July, 1785.

He was essentially an all-round cricketer, for, besides being a most effective batsman with a free style, he was an excellent fast-medium bowler with a high underhand delivery, a splendid field who could, if necessary, keep wicket well, and also a very successful single-wicket player. He was, too, a capital judge of a short run and had a good knowledge of the game, being, in short, almost a genius of whom it is difficult to write without using superlatives. To all this may be added that he made the Holt Pound ground for Lord Stowell, who was fond of the game. All who watched his play and have recorded their impressions were unanimous as to his greatness. Thus, Mr George Warde Norman said that his batting was 'beautifully skilful', and Fennex, that 'He hit quick as lightning all round him. He appeared to have no hit in particular: you could never place a man against him; where the ball was pitched, there it was hit away.' As there were great men before Agamemnon, so were there brilliant batsmen ere 'W. G.', Trumper, and Hammond began to witch the world with their brilliance. John Nyren, who saw much cricket, summed him up as 'the finest batter of his own, or perhaps of any, age', and he added 'William Beldham was a close-set, active man, standing about five feet eight inches and a half. He had light-coloured hair, a fair complexion, and handsome as well as intelligent features. We used to call him "Silver Billy". No one within my recollection could stop a ball better or make more brilliant hits all over the ground. Wherever the ball was bowled there she was hit away, and in the most severe, venomous style. Besides this, he was so remarkably safe a player; he was safer than the Bank, for no mortal ever thought of doubting Beldham's stability. . . . He was quite a young man when he joined the Hambledon Club; and even in that stage of his playing I hardly ever saw a man with a finer command of his bat; but, with the instruction and advice of the old heads superadded, he rapidly attained to the extra-ordinary accomplishment of being the finest player that has appeared within the latitude of more than half a century. There can be no exception against his batting or the severity of his hitting. He would get in at the balls and hit them away in a gallant style; yet, in this single feat, I think I have known him excelled; but when he could cut them at the point of the bat he was in his glory; and upon my life their speed was as the speed of thought. One of the most beautiful sights that can be imagined, and which would have delighted an artist, was to see him make himself up to hit a ball. It was the beau-ideal of grace, animation, and concentrated energy. In this peculiar exhibition of elegance with vigour, the nearest approach to him, I think, was Lord Frederick Beauclerk.' [His Lordship's style was modelled on Beldham's.] 'Hitherto I have spoken only of his batting. In this department alone, he had talent enough to make a dozen ordinary cricketers.' As a fieldsman, especially at slip, he was very active, and when playing as a given man for Kent v. England at Lord's in 1792, made as many as seven catches.

Quite as interesting and as appreciative was what Mitford wrote after visiting the old player when he was passing the evening of his days in his humble home at Tilford. 'Never was such a player! So safe, so brilliant, so quick, so circumspect; so able in counsel, so active in the field; in deliberation so judicious, in execution so tremendous. It mattered not to him who bowled, or how he bowled, fast or slow, high or low, straight or bias: away flew the ball from his bat like an eagle on the wing. It was a study for Phidias to see Beldham rise to strike; the grandeur of the attitude, the settled composure of the look, the piercing lightning of the eye, the rapid glance of the bat, were electrical. Men's hearts throbbed within them, their cheeks turned pale and red. Michael Angelo should have painted him. Beldham was great in every hit, but his peculiar glory was the cut. Here he stood with no man beside him, the laurel was all his own; it was like the cut of a racket. His wrist seemed to turn on springs of the finest steel. He took the ball, as Burke did the House of Commons, between wind and water; not a moment too soon or late. Beldham still survives. He lives near Farnham; and in his kitchen, black with age, but, like himself, still untouched with worms, hangs the trophy of his victories, the delight of his youth, the exercise of his manhood, and the glory of his age—his BAT. Reader! believe me when I tell you I trembled when I touched it; it seemed

an act of profaneness, of violation. I pressed it to my lips and returned it
to its sanctuary.'

So much for quotation. If Surrey had been playing matches about the
time Beldham was coming to the front, he would have been found in first-
class cricket earlier than was the case. In 1787, the year in which Lord's
and the M.C.C. were founded, he was chosen to play for England against
the White Conduit Club, with six given men, all leading professionals.
His selection for such a side is evidence that his merits were known. In his
first innings he scored only 17, but at the end of the second day England's
second innings read thus:

> W. Beldham, not out 52
> J. Small, jun., not out 31
> Byes 4
>
> Total (no wkts) 87

Rain then stopped play. The runs had taken two and a quarter hours to
make, but the batsmen had to contend with the bowling of David Harris
and Clifford. The pair must, altogether, have made over a hundred before
a wicket fell, for Beldham's score was taken to 63 before he was run out
and his partner's to 42. This was an auspicious start for the newcomer,
and his display on that occasion must be ranked as by no means the least
of his many triumphs. It was at Lord's that he made his highest recorded
score—144, when playing as a given man for M.C.C. v. Middlesex in 1792.
It was there, too, that he carried out his bat for 106 for Surrey v. Hampshire
in 1793 and obtained 72 in his first innings and 102 in his second for the
same side against England a year later. If the truth could be known it
would undoubtedly be found that he made other hundreds—he once
scored 131 at single-wicket against the bowling of his brother-in-law,
John Wells; but, unfortunately, records of many matches in which he
played have been lost beyond recovery. 'For thirteen years,' said Beldham
to Pycroft—and there is no reason to believe that the statement was exaggerated—'I averaged forty-three a match, though frequently I had only
one innings; but I never could half play unless runs were really wanted.'
That he was a man to rise to the occasion was proved repeatedly, such as
in the Surrey v. England match at Lord's in 1801, when he made 82 and
the next highest score in the completed innings of 109, which included
three extras, was Mr G. Leycester's 8. In a single-wicket match on the
same ground five years later he distinguished himself in another way, which
was often recalled as a stroke of genius. Lord F. Beauclerk, having become
set, seemed likely to pull off the game for his side, when Beldham, unseen,

took up a lump of wet dirt and sawdust and stuck it on the ball, which, pitching favourably, made an extraordinary twist and took the wicket.

During Beldham's career, and for long afterwards, all hits had to be run out, and Mitford wrote, in 1833, 'How my heart throbs, and my eyes glisten, and in what fearful suspense I sit, when he [Fennex] calls to life the ghost of a magnificent hit, fresh as the life, though half a century has intervened. I see the ball running at Moulsey Hurst that fetched ten runs off Beldham's bat in 1787, as plainly as if it were in my field.' Another Hambledonian, Noah Mann, once made a similarly productive stroke. 'The roar that followed Mann's celebrated hit never is to be forgotten: it was like the rushing of a cataract; it came pouring from a thousand lungs.' Beldham continued to hit and score well until quite a veteran, and in an England v. Hampshire match at Lord's in 1819 played an innings against Brown, whose bowling was even faster than Osbaldeston's, which has become historic. Let Pycroft tell the story in his own pleasant way. '"We were having a social glass," said Fennex, "and talking with Beldham of the match of the morrow at the 'Green Man', when Brown came in, and told Beldham, with as much sincerity as good humour, that he should soon send his stumps a-flying—'Hold there,' said Beldham, fingering his bat, 'you will be good enough to allow me this bit of wood, won't you?' 'Certainly,' said Brown. 'Quite satisfied,' answered Beldham; 'so to-morrow you shall see.' Seventy-two runs," said Fennex—and the score-book attests his accuracy—"was Beldham's first and only innings"; and Beagley also joined with Fennex and assured us that he never saw a more complete triumph of a batsman over a bowler. Nearly every ball was cut or slipped away till Brown hardly dared to bowl within Beldham's reach. Beldham was at that time fifty-three years of age. Let anyone only picture to himself one of our superannuated players thus doing what he pleased with the fastest bowler ever known, and at his best day.' For all that Pycroft tells us of the famous old cricketer we should be grateful, though it is impossible not to wish that even more had been preserved. Arthur Haygarth also visited the veteran later and persuaded the old man to sit for his photograph, which he did with apologies for the shabbiness of his clothes.

At no time during the period that Beldham flourished were first-class matches numerous, one reason being that travelling was then a vastly different matter from what it became later. The railway was unknown, and on many of the routes which had to be traversed there were no coaches. 'From our parish to Hambledon,' said Silver Billy, 'is twenty-seven miles, and we used to ride both ways the same day, early and late.' In another respect and an important one, custom has changed, for in the old days temptations were put in the way of players which not once, but many times, caused many a good man to fall. The members of the Hambledon Club, one reads, indulged in wine freely, even for such a hard-drinking age, and when a player appeared late on the ground the fine which he was obliged to pay was spent in providing punch for his companions. It was even worse at 'The Green Man and Still', in Oxford-street, where the cricketers used to foregather on the occasion of a big match at Lord's, for there 'drinking, card-playing, betting, and singing' were the diversions indulged in. Roguery was rife, and bookmakers were persistent in their endeavours to bribe men to play false. Some cricketers returned to the country with far more money than they could have received honestly through making six guineas if on the winning side or four on the losing. Beldham himself seems to have withstood the blandishments of the bookies, though he confessed to having sold the game in which XXII of Nottingham beat England by 30 runs in 1817. 'I had been sold out of a match just before, and lost £10,' he explained; 'and, happening to hear it, I joined two others of our eleven to sell and get back my money. I won £10 exactly. . . . I am an old man now, and heartily sorry I have been ever since; because, but for that Nottingham match, I could have said with a clear conscience, "I never sold a match in my life"; but now I can't.' In *The Cricket Field*, Pycroft deals with the subject of bribery in 'A Dark Chapter in the History of Cricket', and a most interesting chapter it is.

Apart from the game, Beldham's life was uneventful. Until he was fifty-five he lived at Wrecclesham, where there was for long an inn known as 'The Rendezvous of the Celebrated Cricketers Beldham and Wells', but in 1821, his last season in great matches, he removed to Tilford, where he farmed on a small scale and for some time kept a public-house. When well advanced in years he revisted Lord's, where he was received as an honoured guest, and whence he was sent home with more guineas in his pocket than he had when he entered the ground. To the end of his long life he took a very great interest in the game, and at the age of eighty-six walked to Godalming, a distance of seven miles, to see the All-England eleven play. When ninety-two he was still accustomed to work in his garden before eight o'clock in the morning. Near the end he became deaf, almost destitute, and quite blind, and was advised by his vicar to give up even thinking about cricket, which, to use his own word, was 'impossible'. The report that he was the father of thirty-nine children was a hoax perpetrated on the compiler of *Scores and Biographies*, for his family consisted of but three sons and one or two daughters. Some of his descendants are to be found in

Surrey today, as are also a few persons who can recall the old cricketer in the flesh. He died at Tilford on February 20, 1862, and is buried there, but no memorial has ever been set up to him.

The night they went to dinner

Farewell to the Australian cricketers: a dinner at the Merchant Taylors' Hall, with some notable contributions from Lord Harris, Jam Sahib ('Ranji') and Sir James Barrie, 1930

On September 8, the President of the M.C.C., Sir Kynaston Studd, gave a farewell dinner to the Australians at the Merchant Taylors' Hall, London. In addition to all the members of the Australian team many famous cricketers were present, and some notable speeches were made by Lord Harris, the Jam Sahib of Nawanagar ('Ranji'), and Sir James Barrie.

In dealing with the Test matches, Lord Harris said: 'I am a little doubtful whether endless matches—matches of five, six or seven days—are likely to attract in this country.

'One match in four years we may be able to survive, but I am doubtful if it would be attractive to the great majority of cricketers if it was proposed to play them all to a finish.

'I am rather apprehensive whether we shall be able to produce bowlers two years hence who will be able on Australian wickets to make a good enough show to satisfy England. I am quite sure we shall try.'

Replying to the toast of 'Cricket', the Jam Sahib made a magnificent speech, which, thanks to the courtesy of the *Morning Post*, we are able to publish as it appeared in that paper on September 9.

'I very much doubt,' 'Ranji' said, 'whether there is any other country in the world today, except Britain, in which a man not belonging to that country would have been selected to reply to the toast of the most characteristic national game.'

In replying to the toast of Cricket, he felt he was replying to the toast of the British Empire.

'The countries which together compose the British Empire,' he continued, 'constitute the greatest cricket team which the world has ever seen. Just as the members of a cricket team differ from each other in stature, in personal characteristics, in ability of one kind or the other, so the various components of the British Empire differ widely among themselves. But, in the one case and in the other, it is not with a series of individual units which we are concerned, but with a great team working for common good by bringing out the best from each component member.

'It is this spirit, I think, which has brought the British Empire through so many trials; certainly it is this spirit which carried us successfully through the greatest war which the world has ever known. But, as it seems to me, warfare and stress are not the greatest trials to which either a cricket team or an Empire such as ours can be subjected.

'The mark of a good team is the manner in which it fights a steady uphill battle; the mark of a great Empire, as it seems to me, is the manner in which it can pull together with all its resources, in order to make good.

'These post-war years are admittedly difficult. There are adjustments to be made in our Imperial team. Some of our players seem dissatisfied with their place in the team; there are some whispers, although of the most irresponsible kind, of resignation. It is occasions such as this, far more than the stress of a crisis, which test both the skill in the captain and the loyalty of the team.

'Every cricketer knows how easy it is on certain occasions to allow himself to become discontented if he starts brooding over his own individual case. Every cricketer knows how strong is the temptation on occasion to criticise the policy of the captain; to blame him for not changing the bowling; and to criticise his placing of the field.

'Yet it is precisely this kind of temptation which cricket teaches us to avoid at all costs. How often have I wished that all the political leaders in all the countries of the Empire were cricketers! For if they had undergone the training and the discipline of the great game, I am sure they would find it easier than they appear to do at present to think first and last of the team.

'I am not a politician myself; and I am well aware that it is an easy thing to criticise the conduct of those whose difficulties one does not understand. But I cannot help thinking that all of us in this great British Empire need more of the spirit which cricket inculcates; we need more team work, more patience, and more unselfishness. To put the matter briefly, we need more of the true spirit of cricket.

'For cricket is more than a game; it is really a manner of living. I am sure it is one of the greatest contributions which the British people have made to the cause of humanity. It is certainly among the most powerful of the links which keep our Empire together. So long as we can maintain in that Empire the spirit of sportsmanship which cricket inculcates, so long shall we be ready, as a team, to meet and defeat any adversity which the future may hold for us.

'If the bowling is difficult, let us present a straight bat with courage and with determination. In the crisis of the Great War, Britain captained the Imperial team to a great victory; I am perfectly certain that in the more difficult times of peace that same captaincy will be characterised by wisdom, patience, and generous good will.

'The Princes of India, to whose Order I have the honour to belong, have been very old members of Great Britain's team; and both on easy and on difficult wickets they have tried their best to play with a straight bat for the Empire.

'In times of peace, as in times of war, you will always find us ready. We are united to you and with you in the bond of devoted loyalty to the King-Emperor. Throughout the period of adjustment of relations between Great Britain and India, upon which we are now entering, I am certain that the Indian Princes will do their best to play a part worthy of their best traditions.

'Like good cricketers, they endeavour to keep up their wickets even under the most difficult circumstances. You can rely upon us in the future, as you have relied upon us in the past, to play the game, and to give every support in our power to the harmony and to the success of the Imperial team.'

At the conclusion of the Jam Sahib's speech Sir James Barrie proposed 'The Australian Team'. He said: 'Sir Kynaston Studd said to me, "If you know nothing about the game it does not matter. We must have a left-handed speaker." '

'It struck me,' Sir James continued, 'that Mr Woodfull might have prepared a few remarks on the assumption that I was going to say the better team had won. Therefore I have no intention of saying that the better side won. Personally, between you and me, I have not the slightest doubt that the better side won. I would go further; I would say that I look upon this team as one of the great Australian teams.

'The next man in is . . . Sir Kynaston made me out a list of the various combatants, and he told me that when I mentioned this name it would be received with hearty but hollow cheers. The name, so far as I can make out, is Mr Badman.

'I feel very sorry for Mr Badman. I do not doubt that he meant to do better. [Laughter.] When the Australian team return home they will be taken to hotels and public places and feasted—all with the exception of "Mr Badman". He has carried this plan of his of not knowing how to get out to such an extent that he now cannot get out of anything. He won't be even able to get out of the ship when all the others are merry and bright.

'I warn you, Kippax, Ponsford, Jackson, I warn you all if you go on as you are doing you will be soon in the same plight..

'Down at the foot of the table there is a small boy—Mr McCabe. I don't know whether as a treat Mr McCabe will be allowed to attend banquets with the men. The nicest thing I have heard about the Australians is that Mr Ponsford and Mr a'Beckett used to sit up every night with Mr McCabe until he fell asleep, because he was afraid of the dark. [Laughter.]

'I know a boy who is a collector of autographs and who has followed the Australian team to every hotel they have stayed at in England collecting McCabe night-lights.

'Mr Oldfield is smiling as if I was not going to say anything about him. The lovely way in which he pulls off those little things on top of the wicket! Without a sound! So courteous! You feel that in the English way he is saying "So sorry." '

W. M. Woodfull, replying, said: 'We have appreciated the wonderful time you have given us all over the Homeland. Naturally we are pleased that we have obtained the Ashes. Neither Australia nor England has been easy to beat in the past. As captain, I can assure you that I have no reason to alter my views in this direction. England has not been easy to defeat. Although we have come out on top, you put a great side in the field.'

Mr P. G. H. Fender

This brief appreciation was written by Nimshi Senior in 1921

Mr P. G. H. Fender was educated at St Paul's School, and before he was twenty years of age he had played for Sussex, but it is as a Surrey cricketer that he has gained fame. He is one of the ablest all-round amateur cricketers in England, and at his best is good enough for an England XI. At present he has some inequalities in his play, but on his day he is a brilliant cricketer, capable of turning a match in a few minutes by a fine piece of hitting or bowling; and he is a beautiful slip fielder.

He is very far from being an orthodox batsman, but he has a fine eye and powerful wrists and forearms, and some of his innings might be called almost 'Jessopian'. He has been a regular member of the Gentlemen XI against the Players at Lord's during the last few years, and he went out to Australia with the last M.C.C. team. He was not selected to play in the first two Test matches, but he showed his value as an all-round cricketer in the last three games of the series, bowling particularly well at Sydney and Melbourne in the fourth and fifth Test matches, and playing three or four useful innings. Many good judges are of opinion that he might with advantage have been played in the first and second Test matches, for he is the sort of cricketer who, if uncertain, is liable to bring off a big performance at any time. As a bowler he can send down both the leg break and the 'googly', which has more of top spin, perhaps, about it than a genuine 'googly', but the real difficulty of his bowling is the peculiar flight he imparts to the ball, which he holds back in the air, making it appear to the batsman farther up than it actually is, with the result that he obtains a great many catches and bowls.

He captained Surrey in the great majority of their matches last year, and earned a well-deserved reputation as a leader, and at the beginning of this season he was appointed the official captain. He is a very intelligent cricketer, and I do not think there is much doubt that he is one of the best county captains in England, if not the best. He gets the utmost out of his men, his enthusiasm and energy are infectious, he changes his bowling and places his field with judgment, and he is always 'out' for a win.

[Percy Fender in fact captained Surrey in 1920-31. Born in 1892, he was England's senior living Test cricketer in 1980.]

Leg before reform

By P. F. Warner, 1926

'I have been all my life a resolute opponent of any such alteration in the laws of cricket as would affect either the implements used or the law of leg before, but I have at last come round to the view that something has got to be done to help the bowler,' said Lord Harris in his address at the Cricketers' Fund meeting at Lord's.

So far as the materials of the game were concerned, he added, the wicket could be heightened or broadened, or the bat reduced in width, but alteration of the leg before rule would unfortunately be more effective when the ball was turning to some extent than when it was not. There had, of course, always been advocates of a reversion to the law which did not require the ball to be pitched between wicket and wicket. He had come to no conclusion himself. He simply advanced the invitation to county cricket clubs and first-class cricketers to give serious consideration to the subject.

In this speech Lord Harris has suggested that some reform is needed to help the bowler, and, so far as my knowledge goes, the active playing cricketer agrees with him. Personally, I am against any alteration in the implements of the game, and I would suggest, with all respect, that the best reform would be to give the benefit of the doubt to the bowler, and not to the batsman, as is the case at present, in appeals for l.b.w. One has heard it said that umpires have negatived appeals for l.b.w. because 'the ball pitched the eighth of an inch off the wicket', or because 'a quarter of the ball pitched off the wicket!'

Further, wickets, and especially wickets for Test matches, are prepared for weeks beforehand. Again, bowlers complain that the balls in use this season are so big that it is impossible to impart spin to them unless one possesses hands of the size of the late Albert Trott, or of A. D. Nourse, the South African cricketer.

Another reform which I would advocate is this, I should like to see a batsman given out l.b.w. after he has hit the ball in the case where the ball has pitched in a straight line between wicket and wicket, and but for the intervention of his leg, or legs, would, in the opinion of the umpire, have hit the wicket. Law 24 of the laws of cricket does not preclude a batsman being given out in the instance stated above, but, as a fact, no batsman is ever given out l.b.w. if his bat has touched the ball.

These suggestions would entail no alteration in the Laws. 'Instructions' to the umpires would be all that would be necessary. Something must be done to help the bowler.

I hope M.C.C. will take the matter up at once, and next season try the above experiments in all cricket, both first and second class. Naturally the great cricket-playing Dominions will have to be consulted.

Recalling the great doctor

Savoy Hill, 1928. The text of a talk on the wireless by P. F. Warner. The subject was W. G. Grace

The first time I ever saw W. G. Grace was at Lord's, in May, 1887, at the match between M.C.C. and Sussex. It was a bitterly cold afternoon, and I sat in the seats directly in front of the old tennis court, and saw C. A. Smith, the well-known actor of today, bowling down the wickets. W.G. was out when I arrived, but during the luncheon interval he passed quite close to me, and I gazed with undisguised admiration, not to say awe, on

the most dominating personality the cricket world has ever seen. Imagine a man of six feet two inches in height, broad in proportion, with a long black beard, swarthy face, rather small but twinkling eyes, and with an M.C.C. cap crowning his coal black hair. His hands were enormous, as were his feet, which evoked the admiration of an Australian squatter, who remarked that he was worth £3 a week and his 'tucker' just to walk about and crush the cockroaches!

The first occasion on which I actually played cricket with him was in the Gloucestershire and Middlesex match at Clifton in August, 1894.

I recollect vividly his arrival on the College ground. He was wearing white flannel trousers, a black cut-away coat, and a black hat—half top hat, half bowler, and his cheery cry of 'Eight o'clock tonight, Webbie; don't forget; it's down the well'; referred to his invitation that the Middlesex amateurs should dine with him that evening, and that the champagne was on ice.

Wherever he went during the intervals of the match, he was followed by an admiring crowd, and I need hardly say how delighted and proud I was when he spoke to me and said that he hoped I would get some runs.

His brother, E. M. Grace (almost as great a personality as W. G. himself) was playing in this match for Gloucestershire, and I had the distinction of being missed by him at point—an unusual bit of luck, for E.M. lives in history as one of the greatest fieldsmen that the world has ever seen. There was a great deal of chattering when he missed me, and cries from W.G. of 'You ought to have caught it, Ted. You know you ought to have caught it.' Jack Board, the wicketkeeper, also joined in the conversation, and I marvelled to myself that so much importance should be attached to the missing of a colt who was playing in only his second match for Middlesex.

E.M. was Coroner for one of the Gloucestershire Divisions, and the story goes that in another Middlesex and Gloucestershire match the batsman was cut over and fell to the ground. E.M., who was batting at the other end, walked up the wicket, and as the fielding side crowded round the injured batsman, a man in the crowd shouted out 'Why don't you hold an inquest on him, Coroner?' whereupon E.M. said to Mr A. J. Webbe (the Middlesex captain), 'Excuse me, Webbie, I can't stand that,' and off he darted, brandishing his bat, to that portion of the ground from which the remark had come. The offender, seeing E.M. in full cry towards him, made post-haste out of the ground, and E.M. returned to apologise, and repeat, 'I can't stand that, I won't stand that.'

But to return to W.G. He first played for the Gentlemen against the Players in the year 1864, when he was only sixteen years old, and in the

course of his career he took part in no fewer than eight-five Gentlemen and Players matches.

He was, of course, always first choice for England, and he played both for the Gentlemen, at Lord's, and for England against Australia when he was over fifty years of age. His last Test match was at Nottingham in 1899. After that game he retired, saying he thought it was time to make room for a younger man.

He made the first 100 in a Test match in England, between England and Australia, in the first Test match ever played in this country, at Kennington Oval, in September, 1880.

There is a good story told about him in the England v. Australia match, at Lord's, in June, 1896. Australia had been dismissed for 53 by Lohmann and Richardson, the great Surrey bowlers, on a splendid wicket, and W.G. and Stoddart came out to open England's first innings. Jones, a man of superb build and physique, and a very fast bowler, opened the bowling from the Pavilion end to W. G. Grace. The first ball was very fast and very short, got up quickly, and went through W.G.'s beard. The wicketkeeper, standing back, lost sight of the ball in W.G.'s beard, and the ball bumped up against the screen with a tremendous thud, 4 byes being scored. W.G. walked up the wicket and, in his well-known voice, said: 'Where the devil are you bowling to, Jonah?' to which Jones made a good reply: 'Sorry, Doctor, she slipped!' I do not know whether the idea was to intimidate 'The Old Man' (as W.G. was affectionately called), but it had no effect on him, for he made 68 of the best before being caught at slip off George Giffen, the W.G. of Australia, who died recently.

It is one of my proudest memories that I had the distinction of going in first with W.G. on more than one occasion—in Gentlemen v. Players at the Oval, North v. South at Lord's, and in M.C.C. matches against the Australians and others.

I can assure you we were a queer pair as we left the Pavilion—he 18 stone, with his black beard and flaming M.C.C. cap. I little more than half his weight, certainly half his width, about three inches shorter, and in a cap—looking, perhaps, many years younger than I really was.

There was nothing W.G. didn't know about the game. He inspired confidence in his team, and, if something of a martinet, had a heart of gold and a most kindly disposition.

At the same time strict discipline existed in any team of which he was captain, and woe betide the man who was in any degree slack in the field or who he thought was slack. I remember him dropping heavily on Wrathall, one of the Gloucestershire professionals, and a member of the

M.C.C. ground staff, in a match between M.C.C. and Australians at Lord's in 1899.

Now Wrathall was an exceptionally keen and hard-working cricketer, a particularly good outfield; but for some reason W.G. thought that a little punishment drill would do him good. So he made him field at long-on to J. T. Hearne's bowling at the Pavilion end, and at long off to C. L. Townsend, who was at the end opposite the Pavilion. This entailed a walk, or, rather, a run of something like 150 yards between the overs, and I ventured to say to W.G., 'Let me go out in the country to Townsend, as Wrathall has a long journey between the overs,' and he replied, 'No, no, Harry is lazy; it will do him good.' It was in this match that he took six wickets for twenty-nine runs. The Australians had something like two hundred and sixty runs on the board with only four men out, but after pulling at his beard—a habit of his when he was worried, W.G. said in his rather high-pitched voice, 'Here, give me the ball,' and almost at once the Australian wickets began to fall in rapid succession.

He used, too, to keep Fred Roberts, the old Gloucestershire fast left hander, a pleasant and amusing character, up to the mark, and the following conversation would often be heard: 'Keep your arm up, Fred, keep it up'; and it is alleged, though I do not vouch for its accuracy, that, standing at point, he once said to Roberts, who had just hit the batsman on the pads: 'Why don't you appeal, Fred?' and Roberts replied, 'I was waiting for you, sir!'

He was keen to get a batsman out, and on occasions his zeal possibly got the better of him, but his was a lovable character, and he was always very nice and encouraging to young cricketers, and in his old age he was very welcome in any dressing room, for he never 'crabbed' anybody, and had always an excuse for the batsmen who had failed.

He expected bowlers to work very hard, and it is on record that he once kept S. M. J. Woods, the great fast bowler with a beautiful slow ball, on bowling in a Gentlemen v. Players at the Oval from 11.30 to 5.30 without a rest! He was so strong himself that he did not always realise the limitations of the human frame.

He was extraordinarily popular, and two instances of the affection in which he was held may be given here. The first occasion was at a dinner given to A. E. Stoddart in London, after his successful tour in Australia in 1894–5. W.G. was always very fond of Stoddart, and promised that nothing would prevent him from coming to the dinner. At the time Gloucestershire was playing Somerset at Bristol, the famous match in which W.G. made 288 and completed his hundred centuries, a feat which was celebrated by champagne being brought on to the pitch. The game lasted late into the third day, and W.G. could not get to the dinner until about a quarter to nine. As he walked into the room everyone stood up and cheered him for at least two minutes. The old man beamed all over his face and was obviously much touched.

The second occasion was when, on his fiftieth birthday, July 18, 1898, he led the Gentlemen into the field at Lord's in the great annual match between Amateurs and Professionals. As he came down the pavilion steps the pavilion and ground rose at him and gave him a reception such as even he, accustomed as he was to the applause of the multitude, must have appreciated beyond measure.

In his prime wickets were not nearly so good as they are now, but W.G. himself told me that the Oval, Fenner's, Brighton, Canterbury, and the Clifton College ground were perfect for run getting. He was the finest possible player of fast bowling, and literally 'killed' the fast bowlers of the late 'sixties, 'seventies, and early 'eighties.

I remember once asking him whether there was any bowler or any type of bowling which he did not quite fancy, and his reply was: 'I don't mind how or what they bowled if I was in form, but the faster they bowled the better I liked them.' He is said to have remarked that he was glad he didn't have to play the googly, but it is quite certain that he would have mastered that as he did every other type of bowling, had he been called upon to face it.

When I knew him he must have weighed nearly 18 stone, and this naturally made it rather difficult for him to 'get at' a slow bowler, but I should imagine that in his youth what he said was perfectly true, that it didn't matter who bowled to him if he was in form.

He was not what would be called a pretty batsmen. He lacked, for instance, the grace of style of a Woolley or a Hobbs or a Palairet, and he represented sheer force and power rather than style. He was a beautiful late cutter even in his old age, and was exceedingly strong on the on-side, where he placed the ball with great accuracy. He was a very fine on-driver and his defence was extremely good.

It is difficult to compare the cricketers of one generation with those of another. There will be found people who will say that W.G. was better than any other batsman who has ever lived, whilst others will declare that W.G. was not so good as Hobbs or Macartney or Ranji or Trumper. I venture to think, however, that if one maintains a right sense of proportion, a sound opinion would be that a great cricketer in one generation would always be a great cricketer in another.

Conditions at cricket change, and no doubt will continue to change, just as they do in warfare, but I take it that Julius Caesar, or Hannibal, or

Napoleon—not one of whom knew anything of machine guns, heavy artillery, magazine rifles, and gas attacks—would be great generals in the field if they were alive today; just as Nelson, who never dreamt of battle cruisers steaming 30 knots an hour, 16-in. guns, mines, submarines, and torpedoes with a run of 15,000 yards, would be a great admiral in a modern naval action.

It may, I think, be said with certainty that W.G. created modern cricket, that he popularised it, and that he caused thousands to flock to see the game where before there had been but hundreds. So long as cricket is played Grace's name will occupy the first place. He was the champion. No one before or since has ever been styled that, and it is doubtful whether anyone ever will be. He was unique in English cricket, a great figure in the nation's life, and was as well known by sight as even Mr Lloyd George or Mr Winston Churchill.

After his death the Marylebone Committee decided to erect a Memorial Gate at Lord's, and members of the Committee were asked to send in their ideas of a suitable epitaph to be placed on the gates which now stand at the members' entrance. Scores of suggestions were received, some, I am told, in Latin, but none quite satisfied the Committee until Colonel F. S. Jackson (now Sir Stanley Jackson, the Governor of Bengal), a very great cricketer himself, sent in his idea. It was quite short, quite simple, and the words are to be read on the gates at Lord's today: 'W. G. Grace, the great cricketer, 1848–1915.'

Great bowlers, great batsmen, great fielders, or a combination of all three, may arise in the future, but W.G. will ever remain THE Great Cricketer.

Why Leyland had his pads on

Maurice Leyland's last Test was at The Oval, 1938. Everyone recalls Hutton's 364, few Leyland's 187 at No. 3. But then, as Humphrey Brooke recalls, Wally Hammond had a say in the matter

Maurice Leyland, sturdiest of left-handers, put a broad bat to Australian bowling. His first century, 133 not out, was scored in the August 'Roses' match of 1924, before a record Old Trafford crowd of 41,000, when he flayed the thunderbolts of E. A. McDonald, England's main scourge in the series of 1921. He played in 20 Tests against Australia, averaging over 56, and scored seven centuries. For comparison, Woolley, probably the greatest English left-hander, scored only two centuries in his 33 Australian Tests, for an average of 33. Leyland had the ideal temperament for the big occasion, to which he so often rose, even in periods of indifferent form. In his first Test, at Melbourne in 1928, he made 137, but was overlooked by the selectors after the tour of 1936–7, in which he made 126 at Brisbane and 111 not out at Melbourne.

When recalled for his last Test, at The Oval in 1938, he batted as England's No. 3 for the first time and made an impregnable 187 before running himself out. He imparted enormous confidence to the 22-year-old Hutton, set on his way to break Bradman's record with 364.

This rare occurrence of a partnership by two leading Yorkshire bats resulted in a stand of 382, still the highest for any wicket against Australia, and virtually determined the outcome (a total of 903 for seven wickets and victory by an innings and 579).

Yet the odds had appeared heavily weighted against the possibility of Australia having to face such a combination.

At the start of the season Leyland was already out of favour with the selectors and in England's single innings at Nottingham, Barnett, Hutton and Compton all scored centuries and Paynter a double century not out. Naturally he was not picked for the other drawn Tests at Lord's and Old Trafford (where not a ball was bowled). A week before the disastrous fourth Test at Leeds (lost by five wickets), when again not numbered among the team, Leyland's thumb was fractured while batting against Middlesex at Lord's. This was the match in which an alleged 'ridge' first became notorious. In the same innings Hutton suffered a broken finger and Gibb, who had been selected for the abortive Third Test as a wicket-keeping bat to deputise for Ames and had temporarily replaced Wood in the Yorkshire side, ducked into a bumper with injurious effect. Before the selection of a team to level the series at The Oval, Leyland had batted once against Australia, for Yorkshire at Sheffield, and had been l.b.w. to Waite for only 13.

Apart from the apparent risk in the recall of a discard, recently injured, with no exceptional county performances that season behind him and a failure against the current Australian attack. Leyland's expectancy of being told to put his pads on, as soon as Hammond had won the toss, must have been remote.

As he got ready, with Hutton and Edrich on their way, he could contrast this novel responsibility with his other appearances at No. 5 or even No. 6. The batting order had been made out and printed. It offered him the prospect of a day in the pavilion, should the toss be won. Hammond had been England's established No. 3 for a decade, and easily top scorer at Leeds with 76. If the captain feared an early fall of wickets his most obvious deputy was Paynter (28 and 21 not out at Leeds). Yet with Edrich l.b.w. to O'Reilly for 13 Leyland's stocky form was soon emerging. At close of play he was 140 not out and Hutton 160. Coming in, a leading authority commented on his unusually slow scoring rate and got the reply: 'Nay, but I'm playing for m'place in t'team, tha knows.'

Hammond's tactics in promoting Leyland must have been largely due to a wish to confront Australia with the strongest Yorkshire batting at his disposal from the start. Even Hutton was not yet almost infallible. He had made trifling scores in both innings at Lord's and only seven and 18 for Yorkshire at Sheffield. He and Edrich were an untried pair, each exceptionally young—a partnership far different from that of Hobbs and Sutcliffe in Hammond's earlier years. The calculation that Leyland would provide essential stability early on was in line with what appears to have been the selectors' thinking at times that summer, if with an element of hind-sight and without the outcome, in the choice of a side for The Oval, that Hammond probably favoured.

Sir Pelham Warner, in his account of the Leeds Test (*Great Cricket Matches*, ed. Handasyde Buchanan, 1962, p. 234) provides some clues. He deplored the injuries to Hutton, Leyland (who had not been picked) and Gibb, with the result that the side contained no Yorkshire batsman and a tail consisting of Price, Verity, Wright, Farnes and Bowes (contributing 13 runs between them in the fatal second innings). He also wrote: 'I am sure we made a mistake in not playing Wood. . . . he was the sort of man who would have risen to the occasion and *he was a Yorkshireman* [Warner's italics] which means a lot.'

During the series the selectors picked no less than seven members of the Yorkshire team. So their eventual bias in that direction, clear from their calling to The Oval of Hutton, Leyland, Wood, Verity and Bowes, cannot be disputed. Gibb and Smailes, Yorkshire's all-rounder, were also picked for Old Trafford. But it is still not clear why the team for Leeds was so needlessly weak. Sutcliffe could have deputised for the injured Hutton. He was 43 and had not played for England since 1934, but his current form was excellent and a four-day match would not have tested his stamina. Alternatively, Mitchell, specialist fieldsman to Bowes and Verity, had proved himself when called as a late substitute to open at Leeds against South Africa in 1935 (59 and 78, some brilliant catches and a run-out). Smailes would also have strengthened the 'tail'.

The county match at Sheffield, in which Australia escaped through a cloud burst during the lunch interval on the last day, was of particular relevance, taking place between the Leeds Test and the selection of a team for The Oval. The Australian totals, 222 and 132, compared with England's 223 and 123 at Leeds. Smailes took six for 92 and four for 45. The other Yorkshire heroes were Wood with 41 and Sutcliffe, 24 and 36 not out.

This reversal of Australian fortune made a considerable stir and undoubtedly influenced the composition of the team for the final Test. As this was to be played to a finish, the last 'timeless' affair to take place in England, strong hopes were raised that the series might at least be squared. Hammond himself must have had a particular determination to erase the memories of Headingley and of Australia's victories in 1934 and 1936–7. The selection of the side certainly avoided any suggestion of a 'tail'. There were seven batsmen ending in Hardstaff, who was to make 169 not out, and Wood at No. 8, who made an almost superfluous 53, but no experienced opening pair. Verity, Farnes and Bowes were the only specialist bowlers, with Hammond to supply a steady change.

The recall of Sutcliffe as Hutton's partner would have entailed too drastic a change of face among the selectors. After his last tour in 1932–3 his eyesight appeared to dim and then recover. Even in 1939 he scored eight centuries. His average in Australian Tests was 66. The Oval was his favourite ground. J. H. Fingleton in his account of the match at Sheffield refers to his 'unchanged confidence' and enjoyment of the battle. He was still very much No. 1 for Yorkshire and five years younger than Rhodes had been when recalled to take a leading part in winning the Ashes on the same ground in 1926. But this was not to be. Hammond, of course, had the recent image of even Verity being impressed to open for England in 1936–7, and with fair success. It had shielded him from the new ball. In effect, his promotion of Leyland, a gesture of confidence in Yorkshire reliability, was also a gesture of doubt in the selectors' choice, perhaps a sign of an almost nostalgic recognition that had the senior 'Pride of Pudsey' been present, with his polished perfection, no one need have padded up for quite a time.

There is one other ironic twist to Leyland's share in that great partnership. He was the only relief bowler used in the two Australian innings and took the wicket of top-scorer W. A. Brown (69) for six runs. Doubtless he would have been called on for a longer stint if the match had progressed more normally, as part of the overall English plans. So maybe he owed his recall, not so much to his tally of centuries as to his ability to throw up 'chinamen' and googlies, often of a peculiar length. But for that his place, on the precedent of Old Trafford and performance at Sheffield, might well have been filled by his all-rounder colleague, Smailes.

Waterloo

G. D. Martineau looking back 150 years to a 'grand match' at Lord's

On June 18, 1965, many regiments will be celebrating the 150th anniversary of the battle of Waterloo, which began at the time when people in England were attending church on a Sunday morning. This year the date falls on a Friday.

The final phase, completing the defeat of Napoleon, who had sent to Paris an announcement of 'complete victory' in the afternoon, occupied from 7.30 until after dark, and it was on the morning of Monday, June 19, 1815, that the Duke of Wellington, weeping at the terrible losses, received congratulations on his triumph.

Yet, communications being what they were, the truth of the matter was not known in London until late on June 22, Thursday, and the contradictory impressions of what was happening had been reflected in reports that the Prussians were wiped out, the Anglo-Allied Army had ceased to exist, Wellington was dead, and the Emperor had entered Brussels.

How did all this confusion and sinister rumour appear from the green pleasance of Lord's? Could cricket proceed on its peaceful course at such a crisis?

Despite the absence of many cricketers in Belgium, including the Duke of Richmond, who had been playing near Brussels at about the time when Wellington received the first positive information of Napoleon's advance at the head of 74,000 veteran troops, there was a 'grand match' at Lord's, beginning on Tuesday, the 20th (two days after the battle), between teams led by Lord Frederick Beauclerk and William Ward.

Lord Frederick's batsmen fared poorly indeed against the assault of Lambert, the captain's 15 being top score, 'Silver Billy' hitting his wicket without scoring, and the whole side collapsing for 39.

Ward's XI did much better, assisted by George Osbaldeston's undefeated 56, in which he was partnered first by Edward Budd (36) and then by Henry Bentley (42). They ran up 186, and had obtained a winning lead.

It must have been on the 21st, with the fortunes of battle still unknown in England (though Blucher was in hot and punitive pursuit on the road to Paris), that Lord Frederick's side batted again; and now it was his turn to hit his wicket without scoring. J. Slingsby was also out, hit wicket, for 4, and one cannot help wondering whether these were symptoms of nervous tension. Beldham, however, made amends with a score of 55, and, as James Sherman added 41, and a useful stand ensued late in the innings between young George Wells and John Brand, the total rose to the respectable figure of 165.

The initial collapse, however, had given William Ward's side too great an advantage, so that, on the 22nd, they needed no more than 19 runs. These they scored comfortably after Howard had bowled Bentley for 3, and won the match by 9 wickets.

The day concluded with the firing of the Tower guns and the ringing of church bells to salute that narrow and hard-earned victory which was to be the end of practically 22 years of European war.

No cricket match seems to have been arranged by way of celebration, and indeed no more matches are recorded at Lord's that month. Perhaps it was better so. There were so many dead to be remembered, so many shattered lives, going back to the Revolution which had ended by plunging nations into war upon war, till people grew up unable to remember a time when a state of war did not exist.

Three years later, just before the conclusion of the Allied occupation and the Duke of Wellington's return to England, he rode over to see a cricket match at Cambrai. What did he, who could remember representing All-Ireland as an obscure junior officer in 1792, think of the game? That men would be better employed playing cricket than fighting? Or that it provided a good training for the warfare which mankind, despite all peace-loving protestations, was perpetually preparing or inciting in one way or another?

(1965)

Cricket in fiction

Alan Gibson tracks down some outstanding writers whose imagination was fired by the game

The oppressing thing in writing about cricket is that so much has been written about it already: not just because it is so hard to say anything fresh, but because even when you *think* you have said something fresh, the chances are you haven't. In his novel, *A Season in Sinji*, J. L. Carr brings in two cricketers called Wood and Stone. As soon as I saw the names I knew we were going to have the ancient joke about Bishop Heber's hymn,

> The heathen, in his blindness,
> Bows down to wood and stone.

But then it struck me that he had had a Methodist upbringing and might well have thought of it himself. In *Wisden* for 1972, John Arlott mentions 67 items concerning cricket, published in 1971. How many books of any sort do you read? I have kept a list of my reading for many years, and I find it difficult to get much beyond two books a week, properly read: about a hundred books a year, a minuscule proportion. I see that last year I read seventeen cricket books. No doubt it was too many, even for one with a professional interest, but it leaves me a long, long way from being a well-read man even in terms of cricket. So these comments on fictional cricket are far from comprehensive.

I suppose I enjoyed my earliest reading of this kind as much as any since: the 'school stories' which were so popular in the first half of this century. If you can stand the social and moral assumptions, which did not trouble me in my youth, you will find some capital cricket in them. Hylton Cleaver, John Mowbray, Gunby Hadath were all very good. I still find gripping the climactic match in Cleaver's story *The Old Order*, and have kept my copy over many years. I like it better than the classics of the genre, *Tom Brown's Schooldays*, *The Hill*, and *Playing Fields* (I never managed to finish *Playing Fields*). Of course, Hughes, Vachell and Parker were writing, or pretending to write, about real schools: Hughes even makes Tom Brown's last match end in a draw, as historically it did.

At the other extreme was Frank Richards, whose matches nearly always ended in a victory by one run or one wicket for Greyfriars (if he was writing in the *Magnet*) or St Jim's (if he was writing in the *Gem*). I believe that one of Richards' editors tried to make his cricket matches more realistic, but the master was wrathful and the experiment swiftly dropped. Talbot Baines Reed was an excellent writer of school stories, and his cricket matches hold your attention, though I doubt if he was a cricketer himself.

All these writers had one great advantage as writers of cricket fiction: they were writing of a world where cricket was a natural element. In the summer it commanded attention more than anything else in the school. Anyone reading these books would know that, and would expect some knowledge of the game on his part to be assumed. It was thus possible to write a novel (not to argue about the correct use of that word) in which cricket did not have to occupy the whole scene, *or* to be dragged in. It was there already, a familiar part of the setting. You could have as much or as little of it as the author liked.

This ceases to be true when the novelist is writing for adults, many of whom may not be interested in cricket, and is describing situations where cricket is not the main occupation of the summer, but peripheral to life.

Probably the most distinguished writer ever to take cricket as a main theme for a novel was P. G. Wodehouse. He wrote many school stories, and much about cricket in them, when he was young. But after writing *Mike*, a story about public school cricket, he followed Mike Jackson and his friend Psmith ('the P is silent, as in pneumatic') from the cricket fields to their adult pursuits—Wodehouse then allowed his heroes to grow older —and so we followed them to the city, and later to New York, and Psmith became the first great Wodehouse comic character.

Until Psmith took over, Wodehouse was only known as a writer of school stories and sentimental light novels. You could say that Wodehouse's future was won on the playing fields of Wrykyn and Sedleigh: *but*, except in passing, he never returned to writing about cricket. It had served its turn, and he put away childish things.

Cricket fiction intended for adults falls into two categories: (1) books which are dressed-out accounts of cricket matches; (2) books on other subjects than cricket which contain passages about it, put in for colour or atmosphere, usually with humorous intent.

Category 1: I expect Hugh de Selincourt's *The Cricket Match* is still the best. Neither he himself in later efforts, nor his many imitators, equalled the simple beauty of that day in the life of Tillingfold. I would also like to commend (against some influential opinion) *Malleson at Melbourne*. This is an account of the tribulations of an English captain during an Australian tour. I have lost my copy, and cannot even remember the name of the author, and it built up to the last-Test last-over last-wicket finish, just like Frank Richards; but when Malleson at last won I was much moved.

Category 2: there are many examples, of which Dickens is still perhaps the best-known. Writers who bring in a cricket match, as part of the English scene, are liable to be tripped by technicalities. Dickens knew a bit about cricket, but All Muggleton v. Dingley Dell would not read convincingly if you treated it as a serious account. Dorothy L. Sayers often watched cricket, but all the same there are some false notes in the match which occurs near the end of *Murder Must Advertise*. Wimsey would have had a sounder technique if he had really scored a hundred at Lord's for Eton. There is a similar occurrence in *The Berry Scene* (Dornford Yates) when Bertram Pleydell thus describes his efforts against the dreaded fast bowler of a neighbouring village: 'He played clean into my hands. He sent one down dead straight, which kept very low; and I let him have it straight back with every ounce that I'd got. He tried to get out of the way, but he hadn't time.'

The famous match in *England, Their England* rings true because A. G. Macdonell did not need to get the technical details right: he wrote as a young Scotsman playing for an eleven of English *litterateurs* (it was based on Sir John Squire's XI) and the more mysterious the proceedings were, the funnier. Yet this is not the account of an imaginary match which has made me laugh most. That I find in *Fate Cannot Harm Me*, by J. C. Masterman.

From time to time, attempts have been made to establish a third category of cricket fiction: a novel intended for adults, intending to say something serious, but with cricket one of its threads; and yet not *about* cricket. I have never read a satisfying one, if one calls *Mike* a school story. *Pip* (Ian Hay) and even *Raffles* (E. W. Hornung, a good writer) did not amount to much more than an extension of the *ethos* and characters of the public school story.

I doubt if it can be done. I doubt, even, if it is worth trying. J. L. Carr, in the book I mentioned at the beginning, had a good try (*A Season in Sinji*, £1.25, from the author, 27 Mill Dale Road, Kettering). That Mr Carr is a writer of talent was recognised in the success of his second novel, *The Harpole Report. A Season in Sinji*, as he engagingly puts it himself, 'sank almost at once without trace'. I dive after it only to this extent that nothing a good writer publishes is negligible, and that I would have enjoyed it if he had left out the cricket.

He forces his analogies, he strains his language, to show that life is just a game of cricket, which is neither more nor less true than that life is just a bowl of cherries, some of them going bad, or a sack of potatoes, or—well, whatever analogy happens to come to you.

Mr Carr is very strong on breasts and lavatories, which I suppose is mandatory in the modern novel. Just as I was beginning to get interested in the bosoms, there was a piece about cricket; and just as I was beginning to get interested in the cricket, back came the bosoms, and the dirt, and the violence. No doubt life is like that: but since we all have to experience it anyway, I doubt if we have any *obligation* to read about it was well.

But this is a comment on the function of a novel, rather than the possibility of writing a *cricket* novel. I think anyone interested in cricket literature as a species, or in what happened in an RAF station in West Africa during the Second World War, or who does not worry about these learned thoughts but simply lets the story swing him along—I think it would give enjoyment to you, if you are one of these people. But read *Mike*, and *The Cricket Match*, and (I have just remembered it) *Mr Evans* first.

(1973)

Beside the Roses the Ashes paled into insignificance

'The ticket-collector conveyed the terrible news to the driver and the train then proceeded into Leeds more or less by its own volition.' Sir Neville Cardus remembers

As another encounter between Lancashire and Yorkshire looms before us, at Old Trafford on August 3 and subsequent days, the scroll of famous historic county rivalry unrolls in my memory and imagination. The match of the 'Roses' doesn't today arouse the old jealousies or attract the same partisan multitudes. At Old Trafford, in 1926, 78,617 Lancashire and Yorkshire folk paid to watch this annual holiday argument, and consumed almost as many pork pies. Last year not half as many paid at the gates the entire season at Old Trafford.

In those years, dwellers in Lancashire and Yorkshire regarded the 'Roses' match second in importance and family pride to none; England v. Australia came second. In 1905, no fewer than seven players were chosen to represent England v. Australia: MacLaren, J. T. Tyldesley, F. S. Jackson, R. H. Spooner, G. H. Hirst, W. Rhodes, and Walter Brearley. A parson living in the West Riding wrote testily to the Press that the England Selection Committee was jeopardising the best interest of cricket 'at large' by their insistence on representative games, which obliged county cricketers to be drawn from their 'main and primary' duties.

Lancashire and Yorkshire folk, men, women and children, took the 'Roses' yearly disputes greatly to heart. For Yorkshire patriots (and who in Yorkshire isn't a patriot?), the most harrowing of all these games occurred at Leeds, in June 1924, Whitsuntide. On the Bank Holiday, Lancashire were bundled out for 74, leaving Yorkshire with a mere 58 to get for victory next day. If it hadn't been for the traffic on Bank Holiday evening I'd have left the match to return to Manchester, leaving to Holmes and Sutcliffe the formalities of putting Lancashire to death. I went to Headingley on the Tuesday merely to kill time. And Yorkshire were skittled out for 33 by Parkin and 'Dick' Tyldesley, Lancashire's first win, in Yorkshire, over the ancient enemy, since 1899. As the last Yorkshire wicket fell I rushed out of the ground, eager to get back to Manchester to tell the marvellous news by word of mouth. No taxis to be seen, so I boarded a train. The ticket collector came along: 'What 'ave they won by—lose any wickets?' he asked, 'Yorkshire did *not* win,' I replied, 'they've lost by 24.' 'I mean cricket match,' he impatiently snapped, obviously thinking I'd been

referring to some tiddley-winks tournament. 'Yorkshire all out 33,' I said,
firmly. 'Lancashire have won by 24.' He suspended business on the spot;
he didn't give me a train ticket. He at once conveyed the terrible news to
the driver; and the train then proceeded into Leeds more or less by its
own volition. In Leeds itself, gloom was already falling on the city, as the
tidings became known. My train to Manchester would leave Leeds station
at 2.20. I went into the refreshment room. Soon one or two of the small
gathering that had witnessed Yorkshire's evil day came drifting into the
station, on their way back to Laisterdyke, Huddersfield and such places.
One man sat at my table, clearly from Laisterdyke. 'It's a reight do,' he
sighed to me, 'Hey dear, fancy 'Erbert and Percy not bein' up to gettin' 57.
Hey dear, Ah can't understand it.' Then he looked at me sharply, saying,
'Tha doesn't seem to be takin' it very much to 'eart.' I explained that as a
Lancashire man I couldn't quite share his melancholy reactions to the
match. He now looked at me from an entirely different angle. 'So, tha's
Lancashire, art thi? 'As coom all way from Manchester to see match?' I
told him that I had. 'And, tha's goin' back by this 2.20 train?' 'Yes, I am,'
I replied. 'And tha's feelin' pleased with thisself?' he reiterated. 'Naturally,'
I said. 'And tha's goin' back by this 2.20 train?' 'Yes,' I replied, myself
rather getting out of patience. 'Well,' he said, quietly but deliberately, 'Ah
'opes thi drops dead before tha gets there . . .'

I was not much more than an infant when I watched my first Lancashire
and Yorkshire match. On Whit Tuesday, at Old Trafford, Lancashire
collapsed for 44, or thereabouts, George Hirst taking nine wickets. After
the end, my young heart severely wounded, I lingered about the vacant
ground for a while, then got in a carriage on the train at the adjoining railway station, bound for Oxford Road, Manchester. And who should come
into my compartment, even as the train was moving, but my two gods of
cricket, my heroes, my Achilles and Hector—none other than A. C.
MacLaren and Walter Brearley! And as I sat gazing in incredulous wonder
and worship, what did I hear them say? 'You're a nice ruddy slip fielder,
Archie, I must say!' 'Well, why the hell didn't you pitch 'em up and bowl
at the wicket?'

In the late 1920s and early 1930s, the wicket at Old Trafford was a
batsman's dream of heaven. The Lancashire v. Yorkshire match was a
struggle for first innings points; no more decisive result was practicable.
One year Lancashire's first innings total went beyond 500. Leonard Green,
Lancashire's splendid captain, was batting when the score stood at 499.
To himself he said, 'It's not likely that Lancashire ever again will score 500
against Yorkshire, so I'm going to get this single run if it kills me.' He
pushed a ball from Wilfred Rhodes to the off-side, and ran like the wind.

The ball was thrown in vehemently by Emmott Robinson, striking Rhodes on the wrist. Green got home full stretch, by the skin of his teeth. And he heard Rhodes muttering, to nobody in particular, 'There's somebody runnin' up and down this wicket. Ah don't know who it is, but there's somebody runnin' up and down this wicket.' The operative words in that famous lamentation are, 'Ah don't know who it is.'

But Lancashire and Yorkshire matches were not always dour, though personally I preferred to see them contested that way. (I could watch gallantry at, say, Canterbury.) Before the 1914–1918 War, Lancashire and Yorkshire cricket was represented by men such as MacLaren, Spooner, Jackson, David Denton, J. T. Tyldesley, George Hirst, J. T. Brown— stroke-players of brilliance, batsmen of the proud gesture. R. H. Spooner scored 200 in a day (or thereabouts) for Lancashire v. Yorkshire, at Old Trafford. What is more, George Hirst, with left arm fast medium inswingers, employed a close leg-side field; and Spooner repeatedly wristed the ball through the cordon. A sight for all the Immortals of cricket to see —unforgettable. Still, for all these golden (and comic) memories, I am certain that there is skill and character enough in Lancashire and Yorkshire cricket today—if only our cricket writers would look for it, and take their eyes off the seam.

(1968)

Anglo–Australian reflections

Jack Fingleton, in light-hearted mood, crams in golfing-cricketers, the immortal Clem Hill, and Douglas Jardine, a lawyer from Oxford—'possibly a little before his time'

The older we get, the more likely is memory inclined to fool us. Recently, in Canberra, I played an enjoyable game of golf with Leigh Winser who was advised in the mid-twenties to flee England's climate. As Winser is now a hale 83, the advice would seem to have been pretty sound although his medico could well have been ultra-cautious. I remember meeting Winser's elder brother a few years ago in Oxford and he was still putting one foot nimbly after the other.

The younger Winser, who had kept wicket in Staffordshire to the demoniac S. F. Barnes, sadly no more with us—thrived in many ways in Australia. He was secretary for years at Government House, Adelaide, and won the South Australian amateur golf title nine times. He once won the Australian title. In his pristine days he played against the great Gene Sarazen in Adelaide when the squat American disposed of the first nine in 33. Winser, incidentally, also shot 33.

On the day I played with him he was still using an old hickory-shafted mashie-niblick (he thinks ten clubs is enough for any golfer). It had no great wallop of steel on it for easy evacuation out of bunkers yet he emerged neatly and deftly, an art that enabled him to take the odd dollar (even our money here has gone all-American of late) we had wagered on the game.

Winser played many Shield games for South Australia, keeping wickets, and he also hit a first-class century for his adopted state. He played with the immortal Clem Hill and it must have been his latent British patriotism that led Winser to betray Hill to the English. Plum Warner had brought the 1911 team to Australia although illness forced him out of the series and Johnnie Douglas led in all five Tests. Hill was the Australian captain.

To Adelaide, Hill was having only a moderate series. The preceding Test he made four and nought, out both times to Barnes. When the English came to Adelaide, Winser told 'Tiger' Smith, the English 'keeper, that Hill transposed his feet as he made his favourite leg-glance. So Smith and a certain English bowler conspired to trap Hill on his strength and they did.

'Smith stumped Hill for nought off Foster,' Winser told me. We were chewing the regurgitating cud of reminiscence with great gusto but here, I thought, Winser's memory had dunned him. I never saw him but I knew that Foster was pretty fast and a flick stumping on the leg-side as Hill changed feet seemed inconceivable. So I looked up the records and there it was: C. Hill (capt.), stumped Smith, b Foster o. Lightning—and there was surely some of that in Smith's gloves that day—didn't strike twice and Hill made 98 in the second innings.

Just to transgress, in other Tests against England, Hill made 96, 99, 98 and 97 (these two in the 1902 Adelaide Test) so that his five near-centuries was certainly a record. Frank Woolley—still, happily, with us—made 95 and 93 against Australia at Lord's in 1921.

Recently, I was reading some pithy comments in *The Cricketer* by that champion 'keeper, Godfrey Evans, on the tendency of modern 'keepers to flatter even medium-paced bowlers by standing back yards to them. Evans made the salient points that a 'keeper over the stumps (in other words, over his job) raises the spirit of the bowler and the fieldsmen and lets the batsman know that he will stand no nonsense. He argued, too, that even though the retreatant 'keeper has more time to sight and catch, there are many snicks that don't carry. Evens was as good a 'keeper as I saw. I second his notions. Not so long ago here, I saw Ted Dexter stand several yards out of his crease to the slumbrous bowling of 'Slasher' Mackay because the 'keeper was a veritable paddock away. I moan in anguish when such standards are accepted in Test cricket.

In addition to 'keeping for three seasons to Barnes in Staffs., Winser once had the distinction of 'keeping behind Dr Grace. It was at Oundle School in 1900. His most vivid impressions were of how little of the on-side field was visible in front of the Doctor's vast posterior and of how the Doctor whacked the ball on the drive. I wrote of this somewhere once and, lo, there came a letter from New Zealand addressed simply to 'Leigh Winser, Esq., Golfer and Cricketer, Adelaide' which was delivered with no fuss. It was from a fellow-member of the Oundle team who hadn't been in touch with Winser since 1900! And Winser's, shall I say, intimacy with Grace brought him recognition also from England from a band of warriors still loyal to the Doctor's memory.

I was interested recently to see in a certain publication a photograph of several dozen modern players listening to an oration from one on high on what was needed in a certain type of cricket. If I seem recalcitrant in dubbing the scene and those in it, it must be understood that a certain case, —— versus ——, is pending in Australia and a writer these days can't afford to take risks. Why, only recently again, I heard of a commentator who refused to name a player who had missed a ——!

One, therefore, has to scan his offerings and so, to be doubly sure, I plead that it was somebody who told me (although one who repeats a —— is also guilty of a ——, as all editors know) that this bunch of —— looked pretty bored with the whole show. I am not so sure, looking at them again, if some were not just poised waiting for something to be said that would invite action—and that not on the field.

Even a run out could conceivably lead to court. 'Why, you dolt,' will say the aggrieved party when they come together in the pavilion, 'you made a travesty of the truth. You called out "Come on—there's one in it," and any idiot could see there wasn't half a run in it.'

'I have no wish to discuss the matter,' frigidly will say the other. 'It is sub judice. In front of eleven other witnesses and the two umpires you called me a bloody fool. Action lies. You will be hearing from my solicitors.'

'Let us hope they know more about law than you do about a run. I shall plead truth and public interest,' says the other—and the team fields two short because the offended ones have gone off to seek a legal eagle.

Which, for no reason, brings me to Douglas Jardine and a story he told me once of how he went out to bat in Brisbane for M.C.C. against Queensland, which side included an aboriginal fast bowler, Eddie Gilbert.

'I was much amused,' said Douglas, and if he wasn't confronted by an Australian green cap he had a delicious sense of humour, 'to hear some raucous Australian larrikin scream from the outer as I appeared: "Come on, Eddie, give it to this B——. It was his bloody forefathers who took all that land from your bloody forefathers." I doubt if even Gilbert knew what my friend meant but I knew.'

Those who look up Australian history will know of the activities of the Jardine brothers in the early days of northern Queensland. After the tumultuous days of bodyline, Jardine came again to Australia in the 'fifties as a director of a company of absentee Scottish landlords. The landlord's role fitted snugly on the shoulders of Douglas, who didn't permit himself even a sniff as the crowds railed against his tactics in 1932-3. He was Guest of Honour in an Australian broadcast in the 'fifties and when asked about his feelings on returning to Australia he said pertly it was rather like a visit to Hell: a nice place except for two things, the climate and the inhabitants.

Jardine was a lawyer from Oxford who was possibly a little before his time.

Players of any generation would look bored and cynical if preached at and told how to play their game. Like love—if I may rely upon my reading —the playing of cricket should be natural, spontaneous and enjoyable. Only a stuffy oldtimer refuses to see merit in modern players. The material is there. Possibly it is the system—or the mode of modern life—that stultifies it.

On a certain ground in England once—I insist on being cautious to the end—I heard a player say nonchalantly to his fellow as they took the field: 'So I told my broker this morning that if they touched 15/- he was to sell immediately.' What a dilemma to take on to any field! Imagine a player shaping up for a full-blooded hook and the thought crosses his mind that his shares have crumbled to 7/6! No wonder his hook crumbles, also.

Perhaps if the same men could be rushed down from the City, free from the bonds of business for a few hours, they wouldn't half carve the cricket market to bits. But—and I do hope I haven't committed myself to legal scrutiny anywhere—enough of this. I only hope the Editor of *Wisden*'s, for whom I profess a warm and undying regard and who, I solemnly swear, is a man inviolate in character, won't take any other than suitable action when I point out that Winser's name seems to have been slipped out of his famous Births of Cricketers. Mr Winser is still very much alive.

(1968)

The day the record went

Reg Hayter has a few words with Sir Len and Denis Compton. When Hutton had made 40, Ben Barnett missed an easy stumping from Fleetwood-Smith. A very big miss and the bill followed later

On Monday, August 23, 1938, 22-year-old Len Hutton, the Yorkshire opening batsman, signalised the sixth of his 79 Test matches for England by beating Australian Don Bradman's record 334 between the two countries, at Leeds in 1930. He scored 364. As a boy of 14, Hutton had watched Bradman play his mammoth innings. At The Oval, Hutton began batting on Saturday at 11.30 a.m., passed Bradman's record on Tuesday morning and was at the crease for 13 hours 20 minutes, during eight sessions of play. This was to then the longest innings ever played in first-class cricket. He gave only one chance, and that a stumping, hit 35 fours, 15 threes, eighteen twos and 143 singles.

Maurice Leyland scored 187, Joe Hardstaff 169, Wally Hammond 59, Arthur Wood 53, Denis Compton one—and England reached 903 for seven before Hammond declared.

With a gentle prod here and there, the Editor of *The Cricketer* has encouraged Sir Leonard—he was knighted in 1956—and Denis, C.B.E., to delve into their memories about this historic occasion of 40 years ago.

Denis's recollections begin with his own sparse contribution.

'While Len went on and on, seemingly unbeatable, Eddie Paynter, at number five, and I, number six, sat with pads on for a day and three-quarters.

'Suddenly Eddie leaned across to me on the players' balcony and said, "Denis, I bet you a pound you and I don't make ten between us!" Now in those days a pound was worth a bit and, foreseeing some easy money, I promptly accepted.

'You know what happened. While Len watched from the other end, Eddie was out to Bill O'Reilly for nought and a minute or two later I had been bowled by, of all people, Mervyn Waite, for one.

'I purposely say Mervyn Waite of all people. You see this was the only wicket he took in his Test career and he became so proud of his achievement that to this day every time I have arrived in Australia or he in England, he rings me to arrange to buy me a "thank you" drink.'

A year or two earlier Len's fellow-Yorkshireman, Herbert Sutcliffe, had forecast that Len would become an even better player than he had been.

At that time many people thought that the usually cautious Herbert had been momentarily carried away. After all Herbert had retired with a Test average 60·73 in 84 Test innings.

'Len's innings at The Oval,' recalled Denis, 'convinced me that Herbert had not exaggerated. I was struck by his marvellously relaxed stance and the amount of time he had to play the ball. Apart from his endurance, his concentration and dedication were fantastic, he was just never out of tempo. I have never seen anyone who looked less likely to get out.

'I soon realised that Len could play the type of innings that was foreign to my nature. I could not have batted that length of time without having a number of rushes of blood, but he just ground on, unwilling to break his concentration even for one ball.

'When Len was 40, however, he gave his one chance of the innings. This was an easy stumping to Ben Barnett from Fleetwood-Smith's googly. Poor Ben missed it and was never allowed to forget the fact.

'Lunch and tea breaks, Len just sat quietly in the corner of the dressing-room. I think he had fruit salad and a cup of tea—nothing else—each time but, as the innings went on, he showed signs of tiring. Yet Wally Hammond, Hedley Verity and Bill Bowes pressed him to keep going. In the end they were keener on Len attempting to beat Don's record than he was.

'Moreover, Wally seemed determined that England, so often on the receiving end of Don's mighty bat, should turn the tables this time.

'For instance, when Arthur Wood, the Yorkshire wicket-keeper, went out to bat with the score at 770 for six, he was told that many more runs were required before the skipper would think of declaration. To the Surrey member who wished him "good luck" as he ran down the pavilion steps, Arthur solemnly replied! "Ay, I'm just man for crisis."

'At 40 years of age, this was Arthur's first Test for England—Leslie Ames was out through injury—and, thinking it might be his only Test, he celebrated by hiring a taxi to The Oval—from Leeds. Not bad for a professional cricketer then earning some £200 or £300 a year.

'And, but for injuries to Jack Fingleton and Don Bradman—who retired from the match and took no further part in the tour—I believe Wally would not have declared as early as he did.

'Even when it was all over, Len remained his calm, controlled self, I know I would have been over the moon and would have shown my enjoyment to everyone. But, even when the champagne was flowing, Len accepted the mass of congratulations with a quiet "Thank you very much" and little else. Of course, he was tired out, physically and mentally.'

Len Hutton's own recollections are of that very tiredness.

England

L. Hutton c Hassett b O'Reilly 364	D. Compton b Waite.... 1
W. J. Edrich c Hassett b O'Reilly .. 12	J. Hardstaff not out 169
M. Leyland run out 187	A. Wood c and b Barnes.. 53
Mr. W. R. Hammond (Capt.) lbw b	H. Verity not out 8
Fleetwood-Smith 59	B 22, l-b 19, w 1, n-b 8 50
E. Paynter lbw O'Reilly 0	Seven wkts., dec. 903
Mr. K. Farnes and W. E. Bowes did not bat.	

Australia

C. L. Badcock c Hardstaff b Bowes.. 0	— b Bowes............ 9
W. A. Brown c Hammond b Leyland 69	— c Edrich b Farnes.... 15
S. J. McCabe c Edrich b Farnes.... 14	— c Wood b Farnes 2
A. L. Hassett c Compton b Edrich.. 42	— lbw b Bowes........ 10
S. Barnes b Bowes................ 41	— lbw b Verity 33
B. A. Barnett c Wood b Bowes...... 2	— b Farnes 46
M. G. Waite b Bowes 8	— c Edrich b Verity.... 0
W. J. O'Reilly c Wood b Bowes.... 0	— not out 7
L. O'B. Fleetwood-Smith not out.. 16	— c Leyland b Farnes .. 0
D. G. Bradman (Capt.) absent hurt.. 0	— absent hurt 0
J. H. Fingleton absent hurt........ 0	— absent hurt 0
B 4, l-b 2, n-b 3................ 9	B 1
201	123

Australia Bowling

	Overs	Mdns	Runs	Wkts	Overs	Mdns	Runs	Wkts
Waite	72	16	150	1				
McCabe	38	8	85	0				
O'Reilly	85	26	178	3				
Fleetwood-Smith	87	11	298	1				
Barnes	38	3	84	1				
Hassett	13	2	52	0				
Bradman	3	2	6	0				

England Bowling

	Overs	Mdns	Runs	Wkts	Overs	Mdns	Runs	Wkts
Farnes	13	2	54	1	12.1	1	63	4
Bowes..........	19	3	49	5	10	3	25	2
Edrich	10	2	55	1				
Verity..........	5	1	15	0	7	3	15	2
Leyland	3.1	0	11	1	5	0	19	0
Hammond	2	0	8	0				

The memorable scorecard

'Some time during Monday, when I had already batted eight hours or so, I started to relax. I thought I would enjoy myself a bit. I lifted a ball over mid-on's head. Immediately Wally Hammond stood up on the balcony and indicated, in no uncertain way, that he wanted me to keep my head, and my shots down. So I had to go on.

'I don't think the idea of trying for Don's record came into my head until I was around 250. By the Monday night, however, the strain was beginning to tell. In fact Maurice Leyland told me I would probably have difficulty in sleeping and he advised me to drink a port and Guinness.

'I was then a strict teetotaller—not much of a drinker now—and I did as he suggested. It was no good. I should have had five or six. With so many people telling me that I needed another 35 runs to break the record, I tossed and turned most of the night, haunted by one face. That of Bill O'Reilly.

'I could not shut out of my mind the thought of his charging up, ball after ball, as he always did, as though he was going to eat me. My, how that man hated batsmen. What a great competitive bowler. I've never played against a better.

'And, next morning, sure enough Bill asked Don Bradman to field at silly mid-off. With our score at the start of play at 634 for five, you would have thought the Aussies were skittling us out. Every time I looked up there was Don crouching in front of me, other fielders creeping closer and closer, and O'Reilly still breathing fire and brimstone as he galloped in.

'Anyway, in the end Fleetwood-Smith bowled me a long hop outside the off stump. Gratefully, I chopped it through the slips and I had done it.

'Many years later in Australia when Fleetwood-Smith was down on his luck, he came up to me and asked if I could help him a bit financially. I remembered the long hop in 1938—and I reckoned that had been worth a fiver of anybody's money.

'On the way from The Oval at the end of the game, I stopped at traffic lights. A woman in an adjoining car pulled down her window and said! "Well done, Len, but why ever didn't you score one more—one for every day of the year?"

'As I said to Denis later: "Denis, tell me, can you ever satisfy a woman?"'

(1978)

'Oh, my relics and my Barlow . . .'

Brian Bearshaw looks at a stained-glass window in Southport

In a large house in Southport, close to the cricket ground where Lancashire play each year, is a stained-glass window portraying three of the county's most famous players of the last century, R. G. Barlow, A. N. Hornby and Richard Pilling. For years the window was in the vestibule door of Barlow's own home in Blackpool, presented to him by M.C.C. for achievements in Australia, where he toured three times in the 1880s. It was just one of hundreds of items Barlow collected through the years, and on his death in 1919 most of his valuable cricket souvenirs faded away with him.

Barlow was buried in Layton Cemetery, Blackpool, his resting place topped by one of cricket's most famous headstones, one Barlow designed himself. I first came across it six years ago when I lived in Blackpool and was wandering through the cemetery close to my home. Near the main entrance stood the large white stone showing a set of stumps with the ball passing through middle and leg and at the bottom, three little words . . . 'Bowled at Last'!

Barlow had made sure the stone would do him justice, choosing the words himself: 'Here lie the remains of Richard Gorton Barlow, Died 31 July 1919, aged 68 years. For 21 seasons a playing member of the Lancashire County XI, and for 21 seasons an umpire in county matches. He also made three journeys to Australia with English teams. This is a consecutive record in first-class cricket which no other cricketer has yet achieved.'

Barlow would have liked to have added much more, but unfortunately there wasn't room.

He was born at Barrow Bridge, Bolton, in 1850. By the time he was 21 he was professional at Farsley near Leeds and in that same season, 1871, he played his first game for Lancashire. He became a solid, stubborn opening batsman and no doubt would have liked to have told on his tombstone of his feat of carrying his bat through the innings more than 50 times. The term 'stonewaller' arose through Barlow batting two and a half hours for five not out against Notts 'on an extremely bad wicket' at Trent Bridge in 1882, a feat recorded in the *Guinness Book of Records*.

'Bowling at thee were like bowling at a stone wall,' said Barnes, one of the Notts bowlers, who toured with Barlow on two of his visits to Australia.

Barlow played his cricket in an uncompromising fashion, a hardened Northerner who did not believe in walking and who had no hesitation in running out a batsman backing up too far. He claimed more than 12,000 runs and 1,000 wickets, but for all his fine reputation as an opening partner with his captain, 'Monkey' Hornby, he scored only two centuries for Lancashire.

When I tried to trace descendants of Barlow some years ago, a letter in the Blackpool evening newspaper produced a reply from Barlow's grandson, Leslie Barlow Wilson, initials purposely contrived by the cricket-loving family. He recalled the walls of his grandfather's home being so full of photographs and mementoes you could not get a pin between them. I had been told that Barlow had had only one child, Alice, but her son, 'L.B.W.', put me on to a son that few people knew about.

This was R.G.'s illegitimate son, Reginald Gorton Barlow Thompson, who lives in Southport, a sporting man whose major interests have been motor cycle and motor car racing.

'My father was very unhappily married,' Mr Thompson told me. 'It was on one of his regular morning walks along the cliffs at Blackpool's North Shore that he met my mother, the bookkeeper at the Imperial Hotel, Blackpool, and a very beautiful woman. They fell deeply in love and I was the result.'

Young Reginald was brought up by his mother. But R. G. Barlow's wife died six years after the boy was born, and Reginald lived with his father and mother until Barlow's death in 1919. Reginald was then eight, but the vivid impressions his renowned father made have lived and grown with him through the years.

'He was an autocrat,' he recalled, 'And a man very proud of his many achievements, and whose whole life was cricket.'

Barlow's devotion to the game was shown in the house he built in Raikes Parade in Blackpool for £1,500. His initials were carved in stone over the door, his stained-glass window greeted the visitor at the vestibule, and a gas lamp in the hall showed the names of famous Lancashire players, plus W. G. Grace himself, who was dismissed by Barlow 31 times.

The walls of the hall were covered with historic team pictures. Lord Sheffield's ground was depicted in tiles in the dining room, and by the fireplace, also in tiles, were portraits of Hornby, Barlow and Pilling.

'I had several items and some of his gold medals left to me in his will,' said Mr Thompson. 'But I had to wait until I was 21 to collect them and I have treasured them since.' He had to wait until 1948 for his prized possession, the stained-glass window that now stands on the landing of his house in Weld Road, Southport.

'My half-sister, who was 40 years my senior, refused to let me have anything while she was living, and when father died the vestibule window was built into a summer house at her home. After she died I went along to the house and offered the new owners stained-glass windows throughout the house in exchange for the old vestibule window.'

He also has three bats, one of which travelled around the world with Barlow in 1881–2, and was 'carried' in six innings and made 4,000 runs. He also has cups, tankards, and a delightful silver, mounted gong presented to Barlow by W. G. Grace 'for his fine cricket against the Australians in 1886'.

An unusual item is a cap which belonged to the Australian captain W. L. Murdoch in the 1880s. 'He took off his cap and gave it to my father in admiration for him after England had won the Ashes,' said Mr Thompson, 'and that led to the saying "I take my cap off to you".'

Mr Thompson has several prized possessions, yet they are but a fraction of the souvenirs that once adorned Barlow's home in Blackpool.   (1976)

To John Berry Hobbs
on his seventieth birthday
(December 16, 1952)

There falls across this one December day
The light remembered from those suns of June
That you reflected in the summer play
Of perfect strokes across the afternoon.

No yeoman ever walked his household land
More sure of step, or more secure of lease,
Than you, accustomed and unhurried, trod
Your small yet mighty manor of the crease.

The game the Wealden rustics handed down
Through growing skill, became, in you, a part
Of sense; and ripened to a style that showed
Their country sport matured to balanced art.
There was a wisdom so informed your bat
To understanding of the bowler's trade
That each resource of strength or skill he used
Seemed but the context of the stroke you played.

The Master: records prove the title good:
Yet figures fail you, for they cannot say
How many men whose names you never knew
Are proud to tell their sons they saw you play.

They share the sunlight of your summer day
Of thirty years; and they, with you, recall
How, through those well-wrought centuries, your hand
Reshaped the history of bat and ball.

JOHN ARLOTT

Has the game changed all that much?

Gordon Ross on the laws, the spirit and the history. 'Overall, very little has changed'

Historians will always differ on the precise origins of cricket, citing monks in the fourteenth century, and plots of land in Guildford in 1598. Oliver Cromwell was described by Sir William Dugdale as having, in his young days, thrown himself 'into a dissolute and disorderly course', as becoming famous for football, cricket, cudgelling and wrestling. This would, in all probability, have been about the year 1613.

Perhaps the most surprising aspect of the game is that in its basic structure it has changed very little. Admittedly, the lawmakers have been as busy as bees, year in year out, tampering with legislation in some way or another frequently rather more for worse than for better, which once prompted a frustrated captain to exclaim: 'Can't we forget the laws altogether and just get on with the game!' Billy Griffith was supposed to be gathering together all the amendments, errata, codicils, riders and other appurtenances in the laws to shape them into a thoroughly readable document, but whether this can be the work of one man in one lifetime can only be answered some time hence. Yet, overall, very little has changed. Wides were first recognised in the Laws of 1816 when one run was included in the byes. In 1827 wides were differentiated from byes. Leg-byes began to be recorded separately in 1948, but words such as 'bowled', 'catch' and 'running . . . out' were incorporated in the Laws as far back as 1774. The first recorded dismissal for leg-before-wicket is said to have been made in 1795. In 1823 (Burnham v. Docking) a man was out for striking the ball twice. In 1829 (the year of the first University boat race) there appeared an entry in a scoresheet which cricketers the world over will think should have been recorded hundreds and thousands of times since, in most cases, concerning themselves: 'Cheated out.' There was another ominous entry in the scoresheet for a Stamford player against Grantham in 1832—'Absent without leave.' I always think that so little attention is paid in cricketing folklore to the men without whom the game would not be possible at all— the umpires. If you care to take down your 1977 *Wisden* from its shelf and begin reading on page 1058—The Laws of Cricket (1947 code, 5th edition) —and continue to page 1080, you will surely be impressed by the sheer volume of an umpire's duties. The umpires are responsible for any rolling that is permitted; the umpires shall allow such intervals as have been agreed; the umpires shall not award a match under this law etcetera; the umpires shall call 'Time' and at the same time remove the bails; an umpire should revoke the call if the striker hits a ball which has been called 'Wide'; the umpire must decide whether the obstruction was 'wilful'; before the toss for innings the umpires should acquaint themselves with any special regulations; the umpires must not allow the attitude of the players or spectators to influence their decision under the laws . . . *ad infinitum.*

It may not be universally known that it used to be common practice for there to be four umpires per game and not two. The reason given was to allow them to get adequate rest and refreshment, and not, as might be suspected, that the more compliant one should officiate when his side was in the field! . . . though by the same token it must be admitted that umpires of bygone days were not always the men of honour and high principles that befit the profession today. It seems that neutral umpires were not used until about 1836 and, hitherto, provided the umpire was a gentleman of good repute, no objection would be taken to his having placed a bet on his team. It would be a point of honour with him to carry out his duties impartially. In this respect times have changed; eyebrows would certainly be raised now, even though Messrs Bird and Constant are gentlemen of good repute, if it became known that they had each placed £1,000 with Ladbrokes on England to win the first Test next summer against Pakistan in which they were both to officiate!

But there are, of course, umpires and umpires. One wretched man who was officiating in a match in which the prize was a cricket ball disappeared, and it was subsequently learned that he had sold the ball for two shillings and a quart of ale! On the other hand, in a match between Yarm and Stockton for a stake of £100, played halfway between the two, the Yarm players were extremely sorry they had not a favourable opportunity of returning thanks to two of the umpires who had to go some distance after the game, and had their carriage waiting in the lane. It might be added, just as an afterthought, that Yarm won!

The spirit of the game was as much in evidence in 1819 as in 1919 and later. At the close of a game on September 13 and 14, 1819, the Radcliffe players, on learning that their competitors were for the most part poor workmen out of employ, very generously returned them ten shillings each man out of the stake. The competitive element was clearly apparent, too. A dispute at a game of cricket at Maldon led to a duel between Ensign P. Mahon and Assistant Surgeon Lewis O'Hara, both of the 11th Regiment of Foot, which resulted in the death of the latter. At Derby Assizes in 1775 William Waterfall was charged with unlawfully killing George Twigg in a cricket match at Bakewell Common. He was found guilty of manslaughter, burnt in the hand, and to be imprisoned nine months.

What about ladies at cricket? Well 1978 is 1978 and of course they play an important part in the structure of the game . . . but this has not always been the case. At Sileby feast in 1833 the women so far forgot themselves as to enter upon a game of cricket, and by their deportment as well as frequent applications to the tankard, they rendered themselves objects such as no husband, brother, parent or lover could contemplate with any degree of satisfaction. Today, one imagines, the frequent applications would be to pink gin, though still with a certain amount of decorum, and rather less frequently than more. One day, surely, the name Packer will be a piece of cricket history, just as 'Lumpy' Stevens is now. It was suggested that 'Lumpy' got his nickname because he once did eat a whole apple-pie; come to think of it, Mr Packer may well have done so, too, in his time, but the game will still go on in much the same way, give or take a little either way.

(1978)

READERS' LETTERS

1922

Sir,—I notice that M.C.C. state in their annual report that they are making a grant of £500 to Eton and to Harrow. By all means let the boys have good wickets and keen and competent coaching, but it may be doubted whether the excessive publicity given to public school boys, and the tendency to run the cricket on the lines of a professional nursery, are in the best interests of the boys themselves or of the game. Cricket is the best of all games, but it should be treated as a game, and not a vocation. If, however, the M.C.C. have made this grant on the ground of assisting young cricketers, surely the two schools selected are the last and not the first that really need assistance, for the parents of boys at these schools can obviously afford to pay for their sons' reasonable amusements.

If, however, the M.C.C. have money to spend, may I suggest that the general cricket public who support them have a prior claim upon their considerations. The arrangements at the last Test Match were, to put it mildly, inadequate. Thousands could not get in, and hundreds each day paid 2*s*. to stand about the ground without the chance of seeing a single ball bowled. If it is urged that money cannot be found simply for the sake of one Test Match, I would offer two other suggestions for the encouragement of cricketers and past cricketers of small means: (1) Schoolboys half-price, provided they don't bring autograph books, and half-price at the tea interval, so that the keen city clerk may occasionally snatch an hour to watch first-class play; (2) Erection of a covered stand, with a sandwich bar attached, for which a season ticket would be issued at a moderate price, admission to be confined to members of recognised cricket clubs. There are hundreds of keen cricketers who can never hope to become members of the M.C.C. Give them a stand where they can foregather, and I think you will do a great deal in maintaining and strengthening the best traditions of the game, which it is the pride of Lord's to foster, and preserve.—Yours faithfully,

ONE OF THE CROWD

[M.C.C. have made considerable alterations and improvements at Lord's during the winter in the way of additional luncheon, cloak-room, and other accommodation, a sum of nearly £9,000 having been expended. The question of increasing the stand accommodation is also engaging the attention of the Committee.—Editor, *The Cricketer*.]

1921

Sir,—I hope you will be able to find room to insert this short letter with reference to a proposal I have seen lately advocating two divisions for the present first-class counties.

I cannot help thinking that such a division would be injurious to the best interests of the game, in that it would tend to make it even more a matter of £ *s. d.* than it has already become.

Generally speaking, I suppose it can be said that the five strongest counties in England are Middlesex, Surrey, Kent, Yorkshire, and Lancashire, and most of these are to be found there or thereabouts in the running for the Championship.

Now these are the richest clubs, because they can command enormous gates, being the most thickly populated centres in the country. They can command the services of the best professionals, because they can afford 'nurseries' for the same, have the money to employ them, and can give them substantial benefit matches. With the exception of Middlesex, which has but five regular professionals—Hendren, Hearne, Lee, Murrell, and Durston—they all play an overwhelming number of professionals.

Looking at the paper today, Lancashire have only two amateurs in their side, Kent three, Yorkshire one, and Surrey three. And these figures represent about the normal number played. Hobbs is actually a Cambridge-shire and not a Surrey man, and I daresay there are others playing for the above-named counties who are not men of those counties.

On the other hand, take the five counties that may generally be said to be the weakest—Somerset, Derbyshire, Northants, Worcestershire, and Gloucestershire. These all must necessarily play an overwhelming preponderance of amateurs, many of whom cannot give their whole time to the game. Somerset, for example, have for some years played what is practically an amateur side.

Now all these have hard work to keep their clubs going owing to lack of funds. With the exception of Gloucestershire, they are among the more sparsely populated portions of the country, and therefore cannot get 'gates' to compare with those of the Home Counties, or of Yorkshire or Lancashire.

One is driven to the conclusion that money does mean better cricket, as it means better polo, and surely this is not to be encouraged. There is no intention to detract from the splendid and sporting services professionals have rendered, and are rendering, to the game, but surely everything should be done to spread and popularise the game, and not to confine it within narrower limits than at present.

The glorious uncertainty of cricket has caused the Championship to be upset again and again by a victory of one of the weaker counties in a match of all importance, and thus keeps alive the interest and excitement of the competition.

Again, no one can accuse the weaker counties of not playing the most sporting, if it is less scientific, cricket than their stronger rivals. It is now only too difficult for a really great cricketer, who happens to play for a weak side, to get recognition in the representative games—Dipper, J. C. White, and Morton (of Derbyshire) are all examples.

Do not make it still harder by following the example of professional football, which has become a sort of gladiatorial contest of picked professional athletes.—Yours truly,

R. H. B.

A. P. F. Chapman: a reader's letter of a very special brew

Sir,—It was very interesting to read, in the November issue, E. W. Swanton's note on Percy Chapman's extraordinary innings in 1925 for Hythe Brewery, and, in a day when great personalities have virtually disappeared from cricket, and are only invested in 'pop' singers, the actual score of the match gives much the best picture of what happened. Incidentally, if there is a legend that Chapman went in at number nine 'in order to make a match of it', this is incorrect, for he was on the century mark when the eighth wicket fell. In all, he made 183 out of 190 from the bat, or no less than 96 per cent, and was last out.

ELHAM DIVISION, KENT COUNTY POLICE
v. HYTHE BREWERY

At Hythe, Tuesday, September 8, 1925

ELHAM DIVISION

P.C. Rowe, c Dray, b Moore 27
P.C. Stokes, run out 2
P.C. Goodall, b Gubbins 28
P.C. Green, b Moore... 24
Sgt. Burren, c Dale, b Moore 22

P.C. Holman, c and b Chapman 4
Sgt. Waters, st Middleton, b Chapman .... o
P.C. Sheepwash, b Moore....................................... 10
Sgt. Marsh, not out 9
P.C. Green, b Moore... 6
P.C. Avery, b Chapman... 11
P.C. Pay, c and b Chapman 4
Extras 4
                                                            ——
Total 151

HYTHE BREWERY

R. Down, lbw, b Holman .... o
C. Tugwell, b Holman .... o
B. Middleton, b Holman .... o
A. P. F. Chapman, c Green, b Burren 183
J. Davidson, c Marsh, b Holman................................ o
W. Gubbins, b Holman.. o
C. Dray, b Holman .... o
S. Dale, run out 1
A. Moore, run out .... o
F. Wright, run out.. o
H. Wood, c and b Green 2
H. Rose, not out.. 4
Extras 11
                                                            ——
Total 201

Probably unique in the annals of the game. Mr Swanton gives a 'next best' to Chapman of 5, but my record shows the odd 7 he did not make were distributed as above.

ERNEST K. GROSS, 'Keturah', 87 Ramsey Road, St Ives, Huntingdon
(1965)

Dress sense

Sir,—Mr Alistair Cooke once said in a broadcast that, having studied the sartorial awfulness of Soviet delegates to the United Nations for many years, he assumed they received their clothing by air drop. Rumpled and dowdy as they are, those Russians must surely rate as dandies compared to our cricket umpires. The general performances of these men in white (or off-white) may be impeccable—they are rated as the best in the world —but their garb is something else. Frankly, they look messy. Just how messy was revealed at The Oval against Pakistan this year. Hatless and pink-cheeked, W. E. Alley looked as spruce as that unfortunate three-quarter jacket would allow. However, H. D. Bird was hardly resplendent: white cap jammed low on his head; over-long black trousers drooping into unsightly rolls around his ankles; his sleeves either peculiarly bunched or rolled halfway up his forearms. Mr Bird would have looked infra dig officiating at a social match between works teams, let alone in a Test match.

Some years ago, English umpires were mercifully released from the shroud-like folds of those Edwardian dustcoats they used to wear. The three-quarter-length coat that superseded those horrors drapes more neatly; theoretically it should look smart. It doesn't. The fault seems to be that it seems to be made of an inferior synthetic material that is semi-transparent; it looks cheap; braces can be seen all-too-clearly through it.

Down the years, visiting players might have grumbled at the decisions of Australian umpires, but there is little cause for complaint about their dress; they are worth emulating. Since the English cricket authorities are habitually obsessed by appearance rather than performance, could they not consider making compulsory:

*standard headgear for umpires;

*a breast-pocket emblem. Australian umpires wear them; they give a crisp look of authority;

*high-quality white jackets of natural fibres; away with the cheesy-looking synthetic ones. Cost is surely no problem; jackets must be tax-deductible. Umpires to conform; jackets either short-sleeved or long-sleeved; no hideous sleeve rolling;

*standard footwear, either old-fashioned white boots (still the best) or both men in identical makes of lighter shoes. This last feature would deprive us of the sight of C. E. Pepper's two-tone golf shoes but I'm sure he would make a sacrifice; he did so without qualms as a player.

Cricket needs umpires who grace the general scene with sartorial sharpness, instead of resembling a pair of Balkan refugees clad by Oxfam.

JOHN SHEPPARD (1974)

Ladies in the Pavilion

Sir,—On looking at the picture of King George V watching England v. The Dominions at Lord's in 1918, I was amazed to see ladies sitting in the pavilion enclosure! Was this as unusual an occurrence in those days as it would be today?

JULIA F. WHITE, Port Lion, Llangwm, Haverfordwest, Pembrokeshire

(1966)

Why wicket-keepers should stand up

Godfrey Evans' pertinent letter on a great art

Sir,—I'll tell Tony Lewis why it is better for the wicket-keeper to stand up to the medium-pacers. It helps the fielding side to keep on top of the batsman and it helps the fielding side to keep on top of its job.

Psychologically, I am certain that the batsman feels more restricted if the wicket-keeper is standing up. He knows he cannot take guard outside the crease. He cannot go for a walk, and he knows he must always be thinking about the position of his feet, otherwise he might get stumped.

I also doubt whether the wicket-keeper standing back *does* hold more catches. He misses plenty that don't carry to him and these compensate for the difficult ones he might miss if he is standing up. He never stumps anybody, either.

Not only that, I am certain that if the wicket-keeper is standing up, the whole effort of the fielding side gets a lift. They have got someone to throw at. They know where he is, they can relate their position to him at all times and their work is nothing like as sloppy as it is when the wicket-keeper is running backwards and forwards all the time.

I always wore ordinary gloves and my hands are unmarked, except for my little fingers. I broke those in diving for low catches and stubbing my hands into the ground, *not* through taking the ball.

(1966)

Bishops for Lord's ground

Sir,—One of the joys of cricket is that from time to time something new happens. I confine myself to the ecclesiastical angle. In December 1963 at the St Andrew's School ground, Bloemfontein, South Africa, a match took place between the Anglican Clergy and the Rest. I played for the Anglicans and our opponents batted first. My lot was to keep wicket and as the game was about to begin I noted that the batsman at the bowler's end was the Salvation Army Captain but it was some time before I discovered that his partner was none other than the Jewish Rabbi. I recall that the present Archbishop of Capetown, then Bishop of Bloemfontein, bowled well, keeping a good line and length. And now I am overjoyed to learn that the Anglican Bishops when they were assembled at Canterbury had paused from their deliberations to pay attention to the next best religion to Christianity. I have only heard the bare facts, viz. that a Bishop's Eleven played a local side and I should be grateful to know who these cricketing prelates were. Incidentally, should not the game have been played on the LORD's ground?

ALBAN PERKINS (REVD)

Modderport, OFS, South Africa (1978)

MORE ARTICLES

Vivian Richards

Superlatives wither when he's on song; Alan Gibson gets him right enough

Many West Indian parents like to name their children with a flourish, and when Mr and Mrs Richards, of St John's, Antigua, called the son born to them in 1952 Isaac Vivian Alexander, they gave him plenty to live up to. He calls himself Vivian—'the lively one'—but this season he has really been more of an Alexander, a conquering hero; and I dare say the Isaac may come in useful yet, for many conquering heroes have ended up as patriarchs.

He first dawned upon the public in this country when he joined Somerset in 1974, though he had already had some successes playing for the Combined Islands in the Shell Shield, and against Denness's touring team in the preceding winter, in his home town, he had scored 42 and 52 not out. *Wisden* wrote of the 'immense gusto' of his batting in this match. His first match for Somerset was in the Benson & Hedges Cup, at Swansea. He reached 50 out of 89, was 81 not out when the match ended, and won the Gold Award. In his third Championship match, at Bristol, he made a century. He went in at 28 for 2 (soon to be 37 for 4) and scored 102, 70 of them in boundaries, out of 132. At the end of the season he had scored 1,223 runs at an average of 33. Eric Hill, never a man to throw superlatives around, described him in *Wisden* as 'a wonderful phenomenon', who 'made the biggest impact of any player [for Somerset] since Gimblett in 1935'.

Yet there were those in Somerset who felt that, with all the talent he possessed, Richards ought to have scored many more (something which was, I remember, also said of Gimblett). They loved the hard hitting, the daring strokes, the general demeanour of laughing exuberance: but, they said, he sometimes takes risks when there is no need to, and gets out, and a match is lost which might have been won, or at least saved. Why, sometimes he had even been known to laugh when he got out. A drive which might have broken a window in St James's Church (as one of Clive Lloyd's once so nearly did) rises vertically and is caught by the wicket-keeper, after they have run one-and-a-half, and he laughs. *Tain't nothin' to laugh about.* But Somerset supporters have become a little bitter in the last few years. They will become their cheerful selves again once they have won something, even if it is only the Sunday League. With all these competitions, it becomes a slur if you do not win something, instead of a natural state of affairs, as previous generations of Somerset supporters had taken for granted.

Richards went that winter with the West Indians to India and Pakistan. He did not seem likely, at the beginning of the tour, to get in the Test side, but Rowe had to withdraw at an early stage with eye trouble, and this gave Richards his chance. After failing in the first Test, he scored 192 not out in the second. D. J. Rutnagur has said how, even in the course of this innings, it was noticeable that Richards matured in temperament and improved in technique against the spin bowlers. At the end of the tour he was second in the West Indian averages in all matches, 1,267 runs at 60.

The 1975 season was, of course, an exciting season, but perhaps no special help to a young cricketer striving to develop, who was caught up in both its international and its county aspects. Richards did not, as it happened, do very well in the Prudential World Cup. For Somerset, he did better than the year before—1,096 runs, average 41—but not so dramatically better as they had hoped in Norton Fitzwarren and Nether Stowey. Then he went to Australia with West Indies, and into his year of glory.

Since January 1, 1976 he has scored, in Test matches, against Australia, against India, and most recently against England, 1,710 runs, which breaks the record for a calendar year (I do not much approve of these 'calendar year' records, a device by statisticians to provide themselves with more work, but there it is, not a figure to be passed off with a shrug). In the series against England, as you hardly need reminding, he scored 829 runs, missing one Test, with an average of 118. Bradman scored 974 for Australia in England in 1930, with an average of 139, the only really comparable performance. Nineteen-thirty was a good, dry summer, but not quite such a batsman's festival as this one. Bradman scored his runs against better bowlers (Larwood, Tate, Peebles) than England has had this season. I am not suggesting that Richards is another Bradman. But it says much for him that such a thought should cross our minds.

What has happened to him? It is not, I think, that he has taken fewer risks, become a little more cautious. No, it is that wider experience has enabled him to develop his technique, so that he can still take as many, if not more, risks—but has the ability to cope with them. He is as 'exuberant' a batsman today as when he first played for Somerset; but he plays better.

No doubt later in life he will have to take fewer risks—even Bradman did. But he is only 24: he can cause much more havoc yet.

My colleague John Woodcock, the Sage, who has watched all the great innings of Richards this season, compared him to the famous 'three Ws'. 'Worrell was more elegant, Walcott more powerful, Weekes was the most like Richards of the three, though I doubt whether he hit the ball as hard.' The best West Indies batsman of all, I suppose, was Headley, if only because he had so much more burden to carry in the early days of their Test cricket. I was once discussing a World XI with Sir Learie Constantine. 'We must choose Headley first,' he said, 'and then we must choose Bradman, for he is the white Headley.' One day we shall be discussing the great batsmen of the 1970s, and someone will say, 'We must choose Vivian first; and then we must choose Barry, because he is the white Richards.'

(1976)

S. C. Griffith

Michael Melford on an eminent soldier who built a house in Sussex but had to sell it because he was never there

To the cricketer, Billy Griffith was a wicketkeeper of Test class who played for Cambridge University and Sussex. To the statistician, he is a collector's piece, scorer of his first hundred in first-class cricket in his first Test innings.

To the general public he is the harassed-looking man pictured leaving the Home Office one gloomy day in May under the headline, 'Jim reads the Riot Act.' Much good it did Jim.

To those who for one reason or another in the last few years have attacked him, almost, it seemed sometimes, to the point of persecution, he is the personification of those pillars of reaction and perennial Aunt Sallys, the Cricket Council, the Test and County Cricket Board, M.C.C. and the International Cricket Conference. He is secretary to them all and, for good measure, president of the Quidnuncs, a recently retired president of the Sussex Martlets and vice-president of umpteen other clubs.

At a time when many of his assailants were at school or not yet born, he was also a notable soldier, rising in the Glider Pilot Regiment until towards the end of the war he was the acting commander. It was he who flew General Gale, commander of the 6th Airborne Division, into Normandy early on D Day, after which operation he received the D.F.C.

At that time Griffith was 30 and had behind him a year in the Cambridge XI, a tour of New Zealand and Australia in 1935-6 and, after a match for Surrey, a few matches each season for Sussex. The Fates have not spared him from difficult confrontations—nor has he tried to evade them —and it was very much in the pattern of later years that his first first-class innings, as a freshman from Dulwich, should have been played against the turbulent Notts of 1934 captained by A. W. Carr and including Larwood and Voce.

In those pre-war years after leaving Cambridge he was a schoolmaster and entirely happy. 'I wasn't a great academic,' he says, 'but I kept one page ahead of the boys and I loved taking part in all the school activities, especially the cricket and rugby.' As a centre three-quarter he had played for Cambridge without winning a blue.

After the war his teaching career foundered on a familiar snag—the descent from the pay of a senior officer to that of a schoolmaster, but in any case his love of cricket would doubtless have prevailed. He became secretary of Sussex—captain as well in 1946 until Hugh Bartlett took over —and this allowed him not only to play in the summer but to spend much of the winter resuscitating the game in the towns and villages of Sussex. In two of the winters he went on tours—to West Indies in 1947-8 when he was also assistant manager to G. O. Allen and in 1948-9 to South Africa where he was vice-captain to F. G. Mann.

In Trinidad he made his historic 140 in nearly six hours, opening the innings because of injuries to others and showing unparalleled self-restraint for one whose basic inclination has always been to hit the ball as hard and as far as possible without much thought to the risk involved. In South Africa he kept wicket well enough to displace Godfrey Evans in two Test matches.

By 1950 he was playing only occasional matches for Sussex—though as late as August 1953 he was called back when a stern challenge was being made for the Championship—and had become cricket and rugby correspondent of the *Sunday Times*.

But in 1952 he was asked to apply for the assistant secretaryship of M.C.C. It meant leaving his beloved Middleton in Sussex and going to live in London. It meant leaving a job at which he was doing very well. But, as it also meant a more intimate and important service to cricket, he went.

In 1961 it was announced that in the following year he would succeed Mr Ronald Aird as secretary, but at about the same time he met the biggest crisis of his life, more daunting than any created by bishops or politicians later. His doctor showed him the picture of his lung. With typical forthrightness the patient asked what it meant. It was explained that there were two or three possibilities. 'Would you say I had a 50-50 chance?' he asked. He was told that it could be that but probably was not as good. He was told that an immediate operation was necessary and he was asked where he wanted to go. He asked to be taken to Midhurst and so back to Sussex he went, as he thought for the last time. He was operated on at once.

Four days later on my way home from a match at Hove I took a message of good wishes from the Sussex and Glamorgan teams to the King Edward VII Sanatorium and to my consternation was shown into the patient's room, I suspect through the error of a young nurse.

We had a somewhat disjointed conversation, he being scarcely able to speak and I wanting only to get out again before I exhausted him or was discovered by matron. But though tired, thin and pale, he had all the gaiety of someone starting out on a new life. On Tuesday morning the surgeon had come in 'smiling all over his face as if he'd made a hundred'. The growth was non-malignant.

After months of convalescence Billy Griffith returned to Lord's and next year became only the tenth secretary in the history of M.C.C. It was to be a tenure of office carrying burdens inconceivable to any of his predecessors and to a sensitive man used to dealing with people as honest and straight-forward as himself, it must at times have seemed a nightmare. He built a house in Sussex but had to sell it because he was never there. He rarely finished a holiday uninterrupted. He had one break of five months away from the office as manager of M.C.C. in Australia and New Zealand in 1965–6 and made a great success of the job. But I doubt if he would recommend it for his successor, as he found himself with two men's work. When the normal manager might have been able to relax, he was often called on to make speeches or attend meetings in his capacity as secretary of M.C.C.

In 1969 after a particularly taxing period which included a whole day in the witness box at the Law Courts, he was persuaded to go on a cruise but immediately on his return was plunged into another political crisis after which he considered resigning in the 'best interests of cricket'.

The full M.C.C. committee promptly passed a unanimous vote of confidence in him and told him, in the words of *Wisden*, 'to give the matter no further thought'. To the committee, no doubt, as to many other people concerned with cricket, his integrity, sense of fair play, lack of pomposity, conscientiousness and devotion to cricket were too important to be lost.

(1970)

[Griffith's services to the game were far from over. He completely re-drafted the laws, and M.C.C. honoured him with its presidency, 1979–80.]

Botham

A bit of a perfectionist
'All gifts and all the talents'
Ian Botham, as seen by Eric Hill in 1978

Ian Botham is the schoolboy dream sort of player. Hitter of straight sixes, a fine fast bowler, fine fielder anywhere, there is an air of incipient drama about his cricket. He has a habit of exploding on to a scene.

Since his days of returning from the Lord's ground staff to play for Somerset Second XI that has been the way of it. He burst on the Second XI scene with a memorable 90 against Cornwall. His performance to win the Gold Award against Hampshire in an unforgettable Benson and Hedges match in early 1974, described by *Wisden* as an epic, was an amazing effort of skill and courage. His first two Tests brought him five wickets in the first innings of each against Australia. Now his resounding performances against New Zealand and Pakistan have created new items for the record books.

I asked him what his ambitions were. 'Just to play for England all over the world and break a few cricket records' he said, in a matter-of-fact sort of way. He is firmly for cricket's Establishment—'I don't see how you can serve two masters'—and not surprisingly reacts sharply and negatively to any suggestions of joining Kerry Packer.

Even so, he admires the involvement and commitment displayed by Tony Greig on the field, and likes to emulate it. He says of Brian Close, his first county captain, 'He gave me the killer instinct', which is an interesting comment when, in the early days, there were some vivid differences of opinion between the fiery, enthusiastic, gifted teenager and one who had been much the same 20 years before. They have been family friends for a long time now.

Botham freely admits the great help he has had from all sorts of people in the cricket world. The list covers nearly every corner of cricket knowledge from the hardly known to the well-established. One, Bill Jones of the Lord's ground staff, is remembered especially warmly as 'the best late outswinger I ever saw. He was a great help. He is a very refreshing person to talk to, and I still see him. If he sees anything going wrong on the box, he still tells me about it.' Last winter, Mike Hendrick and Chris Old, two touring team mates, spent a lot of time with Ian at the nets ironing out a run-up problem. Ian is still slightly amazed at the help he gets from rival players. Youthful exuberance and fierce competitiveness sometimes reduces the quality of his performance, and he seems to be aware of this. There are people in the cricket world who tend to pencil in the wretched epithet 'big-headed' alongside his name. However, he is, after all, entitled, in the best old-fashioned phrase, to a 'good conceit' of himself and the critics would do well to answer one question. What would they have been like if they had his gifts, stamina, build, courage and record when 22 years old?

Recently at Taunton there was something of a bumper war against Zaheer, which did not make edifying watching, but which got results. Botham and his captain Brian Rose had worked it all out. They knew Zaheer always hooks, and usually upwards. Somerset had made plenty of runs, and 'it didn't really matter if he made 150, as long as we got him out'. Botham dismissed him with bouncers twice in the match for 20 and 141, besides seeing him missed off short balls earlier in both innings. Somerset won by ten wickets. This was a strange juxtaposition with the studious, quiet Pakistan Test player who joined the Kerry Packer Circus, being worked over by the fiery young anti-Packer enthusiast.

Sport runs richly in the family. Botham's mother and father were both useful cricketers, and Ian's golden 1977 brought the birth of his first son. Since his Test debut against Australia—the day, whimsically enough, when Brian Close announced his retirement—all sorts of rewards, sponsorship, money and adulation have descended on him. He already appreciates how transient all this could be. 'Nothing is more up and down than cricket,' he observes, 'but I like to think I'm a bit of a perfectionist, and I want to keep improving to do everything as well as I possibly can.'

His courage shone through that 1974 performance, just six weeks after coming regularly into county cricket. After a notable bowling and fielding effort, he won the match for Somerset with some dazzling batting, having been hit full in the mouth by West Indies paceman Andy Roberts soon after arriving at the crease.

Botham is tremendously competitive but extremely receptive. 'I don't change any things that come naturally,' he says. 'But I try to watch and learn, and make use of it. When someone says he can't learn anything about cricket, it's time for him to pack up.' He noticed Eddie Barlow the shrewd Derbyshire captain get Somerset colleague Viv Richards, one of the world's best batsmen, out with a slow off spinner one day. He practised this, got it wrong a few times, began to get it right, and has taken a few good wickets with it this year.

Originally a medium-paced outswinger, he has learned to use the in-swinger, which is often a telling yorker, and spice it all with the odd bouncer.

The Boycott I knew

A personal view (1978) by Richard Hutton

At the risk of being accused of keeping it boiling, it is reprehensible that such emotional nonsense as is being purveyed by certain commentators can go unchallenged without retort from someone who watched from close quarters the development of the character and career of G. Boycott. The sentiments uttered there will be echoed by a vast number of cricketers, past and present, throughout the world who have had neither the opportunity nor the inclination to express their feelings publicly.

Neither party to the present dispute warrants sympathy although one's feelings incline towards the Committee for having decided finally to take the action which they have been contemplating for years. [In September 1978, Yorkshire C.C.C. relieved Boycott of the captaincy. They expressed their thanks for his services over many years and as captain for eight years. He was replaced by John Hampshire.] By appointing Boycott to the captaincy in 1971, the Committee committed the county to what some might consider to be the most damaging position in its history.

In terms of cold statistical facts, it is unusual for Yorkshire to prolong a captain's reign for as long as eight years without winning a title, other than that of Lord Hawke, who had to wait eleven years before he embarked on his eight championships. But things were different in those days. Furthermore, although Boycott can lay claim to the Fenner Trophy, his predecessors did not have the opportunity of four major competitions to choose from for their titles.

In the years of the modern championship, beginning in 1878, to 1970, Yorkshire have won the county championship 30 times, and in those 63 years when the championship was not won the county failed only 15 times to feature in the first four. In six of Boycott's eight years, the county has failed to make the first four. In the old days and in my early days as a player, it was the pursuit of performances such as the former that gripped the imagination of a great Yorkshire public and gave expression in its support, not the building up of a personality cult.

Much can be said in defence of the county's reversal of fortune. The past eight years have been made more difficult by the higher standards of opposition from other counties associated with the influx of overseas Test players, and the introduction of a large complement of young and inexperienced players into the county side. But youth and inexperience do not last for ever, and four years ago Yorkshire was said to have the best clutch of youngsters it has had for a long time. With a similar calibre of man to J. R. Burnet, who led a young and relatively unknown side to victory in 1959 following an unhappy period of major personality clashes within the club, achievements might have been possible.

My first encounter with Boycott was as a young, impressionable, free-striking (never to be the same again) public schoolboy batsman opening the innings in a Yorkshire 2nd XI match at Bridlington. Against a team of friendly and enthusiastic amateurs from Cumberland, Boycott and I made 60 for the first wicket in just under an hour when I was out for 49. In mid-morning of the following day our innings was declared closed with Boycott 155 not out. I remember as little of that innings as of many others of similar length which Boycott played in subsequent years. The momentum of his batting has remained remarkably constant although his repertoire of stroke was to widen considerably.

There was never any doubting Boycott's exceptional playing ability but, after the normal settling-in period allowed to newcomers in the Yorkshire team, it became apparent that he was tending to play a different game from everyone else. In those days of the early mid-sixties, Yorkshire was an aggressive, vigorous side, looking to turn every situation into a winning one. The quest for the county championship was paramount, and individual ambitions were not supposed to obscure the main objective. Wickets were sacrificed in an effort to force the pace and provide the bowlers with the maximum possible time to get the opposition out twice. As the match winners, the bowlers had to be accommodated, and all the batsmen, in their turn, suffered as they put team before self. Boycott has never found it easy to conform to this community policy.

By 1964 Boycott had had his first taste of international cricket, and his drive to become No. 1 for England and the best player in the world super-seded all else.

Nevertheless, his appointment as captain for 1971 came as a shock to most players in the side. One can only speculate at the logic behind the committee's appointment. Seemingly it was based on the premise that Boycott was the best player in the team, and appeared to have a greater grasp of the 'tacticalities' of cricket than anyone else.

Regarding the events of Boycott's first and subsequent years of captaincy, I would not want to run the risk of being thought disloyal but it is no secret that this was not the happiest or most settled period in the history of York-shire cricket.

By the end of the 1971 season, there was sufficient discontent within the team for the committee to be aware of it, and they called a meeting between players and captain to thrash out these domestic troubles. Most critics were strangely silent. Nothing was resolved and the personality problem remained.

In particular it could be argued that Boycott's batting tactics were not always suited to the cricket that we then were playing in profusion nor did they take into account the importance of batting bonus points. My personal objection to Boycott as a batsman in comparison with other 'greats' that he was hoping to emulate and surpass was that, by and large, he was a one-pace player.

On the slow and wet pitches which abounded in Yorkshire, he displayed a technique which none of us possessed, in that at times he seemed to insist on making batting look horribly difficult. At times he could get bogged down to such an extent that his only way out was to call for and run desperate singles without reasonable regard for his partner's safety. Furthermore, the temptation to concentrate the strike on himself in favourable conditions was not always resisted. All this created pressure on other batsmen.

Apart from the possession of a sound tactical approach to the game, it is my view that Boycott has not shown the same qualities of good leadership as Brian Close, whose captaincy many of us had enjoyed and who, despite his faults, was a fine forward-pulling leader for Yorkshire, offering encouragement, sympathy and reprimand as required by the situation. He stimulated others to revel in the heat of the battle and was at his best himself when under heavy bombardment on the field. Above all, he protected the players under his control and tried hard to get the best out of them. His approach earned him the support and loyalty of his team, and made his verbal ear-bashings the more tolerable.

By mid-season 1974 the team's morale was low and matters were not helped by the captain's run of injuries. A small group of us made submissions to the committee, but further action was suspended when rumours of Boycott's impending retirement became current. In the event before the season was over, three of us departed under a variety of circumstances and Tony Nicholson faded from the scene during the following season.

The broad impression to be had of events since that time is the firm concentration of the Yorkshire power-base in Boycott's hands. Several factors appear to have contributed to this. But Boycott has always had his own particular forceful arguments, supported by his unchallenged position as England and Yorkshire's leading run-scorer.

The approach adopted by the committee played straight into Boycott's hands and by 1977 they appeared to have lost control of him. In my opinion, the appointment of Ray Illingworth as a member of the county staff to overlord selection and other team matters from 1979 onwards was the final relinquishment of responsibility by the Yorkshire committee. The conclusion to be drawn was that Illingworth, still retaining some sympathy with the Yorkshire public, would counter-balance Boycott. Such an intriguing contest is now no longer in prospect.

Another factor in the matter has been Boycott's gathering around him of a youthful and inexperienced team, most of whom stood in awe of his prowess as a run-maker and this has tended to show itself in the approach which some Yorkshire professional batsmen have now developed in their batting.

Finally and, in my view most damagingly, there has been a switch of the focus of public attention from the team as a unit to an individual, created by a press, commercial sponsors, and other motivators for a public which has tired of waiting for Yorkshire to win titles, and needs something or someone with which to identify itself. It has been an exceptional marketing effort, but for its success depends on Boycott's consistent amassing of runs, and smashing of records. It requires Boycott to be supreme and unchallenged in any team. As long as he scores runs, in whatever fashion is irrelevant, even if detrimental to the team effort, nothing else seems to matter.

It could be years before what, in my view is a damaging trend, is reversed and Yorkshire become a county worth playing for once again.

Yorkshire captains and their records since 1878

Year	Official captains	No. of seasons	Championships won	Other pos'ns when Championship not won
1878–1882	T. Emmett	5	—	6th, 6th, 5th, 3rd, 3rd
1883–1910	Lord Hawke	28	8	2nd, 3rd, 2nd, 4th, 3rd, 2nd, 7th, 3rd, 8th, 6th, 2nd, 3rd, 4th, 3rd, 3rd, 2nd, 2nd, 2nd, 3rd, 8th
1911	E. J. Radcliffe	1	—	7th

1912–1914	Sir A. W. White	3	1	2nd, 4th
1919–1921	D. C. F. Burton	3	1	4th, 3rd
1922–1924	Geoff Wilson	3	3	
1925–1927	Maj.A.W.Lupton	3	1	2nd, 3rd
1928–1929	Sir W. A. Worsley	2	—	4th, 2nd
1930	A. T. Barber	1	—	3rd
1931–1932	F. E. Greenwood	2	2	
1933–1947	A. B. Sellers	9 (excluding war years)	6	5th, 3rd, 7th
1948–1955	N. W. D. Yardley	8	1 (joint)	4th, 3rd, 2nd, 2nd, 12th, 2nd, 2nd,
1956–1957	W. H. H. Sutcliffe	2	—	7th, 3rd
1958–1959	J. R. Burnet	2	1	11th
1960–1962	J. V. Wilson	3	2	2nd
1963–1970	D. B. Close	8	4 (plus 2 Gillette Cups)	5th, 4th, 12th, 4th
1971–1978	G. Boycott	8	—	13th, 10th, 14th, 11th, 2nd, 8th, 12th, 4th (equal)

Floodlights, waiters and a white ball

Reg Hayter: the day the foreman went to France

Cricket was not in my immediate thoughts on that freezing February day 13 years ago. True, I had just counted the weeks till the start of the next season, but the bat and ball seemed very far away as I watched snow settling on the window-sill of my office.

The fascination of a journalist's life is that the next 'phone call may be about anything from a Cabinet crisis to a weather report. Nothing so dramatic as the first came when I answered the tinkling bell on my office desk. Instead, the voice of a friend from Agence France Presse.

'Can you raise a cricket team for me by next Monday?' I looked out at the snow, asked him to repeat the request and finally spluttered: 'What the devil are you talking about?'

'No, I haven't been drinking,' came the reply. He had received a request from his head office in Paris enquiring whether an English side could be got together within the next three days to play an exhibition match there.

It was all rather obscure but I was told that a M. Maurice Gardet, an impresario with ambitions of getting into Parliament, had a novel idea of 'selling' cricket to the French people as part of his election platform. The story was that he had undertaken to pay the whole cost of an exhibition game between the Supreme Headquarters Allied Powers in Europe cricket side in France and a team specially brought over from England. The game was to be played under floodlights on the Parc des Princes stadium, Paris, on Monday evening. It was now after 5 p.m. on Thursday. Although suspicious that it was a gigantic leg-pull, I promised I would go ahead.

At eleven o'clock the following morning a short, bearded figure bounded into my office. Breathlessly he announced, 'I am Maurice Gardet, I have just arrived from Paris. Can I have the names of your team?'

Almost before I had time to tell him that I had not contacted any prospective players, the telephone bell rang. He was wanted by Paris. SHAPE were caught up in something vitally important and couldn't raise a side. That did not worry Gardet.

'In that case, you must bring *two* teams,' he decided.

As patiently as I could, I explained that a cricket match required more than twenty-two players.

'It doesn't matter, bring whatever are necessary,' said Gardet. 'I will ring you from Paris tomorrow morning (Saturday) and give you your travel arrangements. How many will there be?'

The opportunity was too good to miss. 'Twenty-two players, two umpires, two scorers and'—my greatest ploy—'two baggage men.' I would be one up on M.C.C. They only took one baggage man for a six-months' tour —and he did the scoring as well.

Nothing perturbed Gardet. Everything was easy, for him. Not quite so easy for me. Between midday on Friday and that evening I had to find a party of 28 who could stage a cricket match, had—or could get—passports, and could escape from business for the best part of two days.

There was only one way to tackle this—an all-out assault by telephone. So to the first call.

'Roger, can you get Monday off?'

'Why?'

'I want you to play for me.'

'Play for you? What at?'

'Cricket.'

'Cricket? You're barmy! Have you been on the bottle?'

'No. I'm serious.'

'Look, stop wasting my time—I'm busy. What's this all about? Where is it?'

'In Paris.'

Hilarious laughter greeted this statement.

One by one, I persuaded cricketing friends to meet at the Café Royal on Monday evening at 6.30, complete with cricket-bags and up-to-date passports. These included the then England captain, Ted Dexter, and the wicket-keeper, Godfrey Evans, a number of other county cricketers, one or two cricketing journalists and players from my own club.

On Saturday morning, the Passport Office in Petty France was raided by a variety of disbelievers. On Saturday morning, too, M. Gardet telephoned me at home to say that twenty-eight seats had been booked on a plane leaving London Airport at midnight on Monday.

'You'll have to make us a special tie of course,' I told him. 'Cricketers always expect a tie to signalise an outstanding occasion.'

'That will be no trouble, my friend,' countered the buoyant Gardet.

On Sunday, three French newspapers rang me for information about the English cricketers and Gardet himself was also back on the 'phone. The ties had been designed and were already in the process of manufacture; full arrangements had been made for our entertainment and he himself would head the reception committee at Orly Airport.

Snow was falling outside the following night when we gathered at the Café Royal. In the warmth of the bar, 28 widely-assorted characters quickly caught the escapist feeling of the evening. All the time I parried the question: 'When do we leave?'

By 10 p.m., however, most had decided it was a gigantic hoax. Never mind, they'd had a laugh together but they ought to be on their way home.

'All right,' said I. 'Follow me.' Down the carpeted stairs of the Café Royal we tumbled. At the foot, I fulfilled an ambition by asking an astonished commissionaire to get me eight taxi-cabs.

Into these we piled. 'London Airport the next stop.'

Some *still* wouldn't believe me. They only did so when they were on the plane—some making their first air-trip. Those who had discreetly placed liquid refreshment in their cases helped to maintain the spirit of the occasion during the hour's flight to Paris. There, true to his word, was the organiser.

'What have you lined up for us?' we clamoured to Gardet—after telephone, radio and television interviews had been concluded.

'Everything is organised. Don't worry: follow me,' announced Gardet. It *was* organised, too. We were taken to a night club. The only drink offered us there was champagne, lots of it. Not surprising that the floor-show went on in a noise not dissimilar to that of a Rugby club bar.

All good things come to an end. Our good things finished at 4 a.m. But, suddenly, everyone was overwhelmed by the same craving—hunger.

'Leave it to me,' said Gardet.

Taxis again down to Les Halles. Over some abattoir where the restaurant lights glittered invitingly piled the party. Menu cards were thrust into our faces and at once the ordering began—no one had forgotten it was 'all on the house'.

Oysters, smoked salmon, river trout, steak, mushrooms and tomatoes, chips—the orders were being given and taken with great relish.

'Stop, I have already ordered for you,' beamed Gardet. 'I have ordered the speciality of France.' Mouths watering, we waited, ten, fifteen minutes. Then out came the waiters . . . bearing twenty-eight bowls of thick, onion soup, covered in cheese—or was it blotting paper? Never mind, we hadn't the heart to register our disappointment. Instead we made that the hors-d'oeuvre. Afterwards, we scattered our various ways and in various groups. Ted Dexter, Godfrey Evans, John Warr and myself were eating escalope of veal at 6.30 a.m. Others dined even later. Some did not dine. But none arrived at the hotel allocated until 7.30 a.m. In the next hour, all checked in and fell into bed, either fully clothed or fully stripped.

At a quarter to nine my telephone rang. It was Gardet. 'The coach will be there for you at nine o'clock,' he announced. 'What coach?' I demanded.

'We have arranged a sight-seeing tour of Paris for you, starting off with wine-tasting in the vaults near the Eiffel Tower.'

Ten minutes later a waiter arrived, complete with breakfast and a further instruction from Gardet that we must not keep the coach driver waiting.

Sleepy-eyed, we crept aboard the coach and were soon deposited at the vaults, where we were taken underground for a long mazy walk before being invited to taste the wine of the country. Once again, the brew was Freeman's. Next came a trip up the River Seine followed by lunch in the restaurant of the Eiffel Tower several hundred feet above ground.

We were invited to make a tour of the shops to buy presents, but Ted Dexter and Godfrey Evans had a conscience about inspecting the playing conditions for the evening match. While the rest explored the Paris arcades, the two England cricketers visited the ground where, we had been told, a magnificent cricket pitch awaited our delectation. To their horror, they found it was a rough football ground on which any attempt at cricket would have been a hazardous adventure for batsmen, bowlers and fielders alike. In an instant, they were off to the SHAPE headquarters, where they borrowed a coconut mat the length of a cricket pitch, went back to the ground and laid it themselves.

Meanwhile, with shopping over, the remainder of the party gathered at the meeting place, clambered aboard the coach and set off for the ground. What was all that noise outside? The *important* visitors had been provided with an escort of motor cyclists playing fiercely on their klaxons.

Through the streets of Paris we proceeded to the ground, which was encircled by police and armed soldiers. Then into the dressing-rooms to change for 'Le Cricket', as it was widely advertised on the hoardings. The weather was decently mild and we decided only one sweater each would be necessary—that is, apart from two sets of underclothes. As we changed six waiters, resplendent in morning dress, marched sedately in line and in step, bearing huge silver tea-trays, complete with silver urns, jugs, the lot. Yes, the Englishman had to have his cup of tea.

Finally came the call to cricket. Gardet explained the procedure. 'You will proceed to the entrance to the pitch, line up in your two teams and run on to the field, where you will form up in one line.' Leeds and Liverpool at the previous year's Cup Final had nothing on us.

We did as we were told. As the two national anthems were played a beautiful girl appeared, acknowledged the wolf-whistles and threw us the ball for the match to begin. She was a French film actress—we never learned her name.

A ball? Yes—but a white hockey ball. We played for an hour each. Photographers crouched all over the field. They swarmed into action when one man was struck a blow over the eye and led off, bleeding profusely. For most of the spectators, this made the evening. They had seen that 'Le Cricket' was, after all, a man's game.

But many had fears for their own safety as, time after time, Dexter or Evans or another big hitter sent the ball flying into the stand, out of vision of the floodlights. 'Stop it! Stop it! Someone will get killed', were the cries. But, for us, it was all good fun, especially when we were being interviewed for the radio between overs on the field.

We did play fairly seriously as we had considerable regard for M. Gardet, especially as he had told us that, apart from using cricket as an election appeal, he had decided to buy a village and to rename it 'Cricketville'. Especially, too, seeing that on our short coach journey from the vaults to the River Seine he had proved his unflappability when, in answer to his query, 'Is there anything you want?' we had told him 'Alka Seltzers'. He had stopped the coach within seconds and came back immediately with six dozen bottles of the stuff.

After the match, the inevitable party. A party . . . It was held in a huge pavilion under the stand. After three hours of abundant hospitality I committed the one *faux pas* of the tour for which I have still not been forgiven. We were invited to stay another night instead of returning, as arranged, by plane that night. Regard for reputations, moral cowardice, fear of retribution, I don't know what it was, but I decided we must go back. As it turned out, it was probably for the best as, an hour after we had left Orly airport, the fog closed in and not one plane left there for another three days. Some were speechless at my insistence on going home. Some were just speechless. It is on record that one—who had to be carried through the customs and whose name we signed as Malinovski—did not murmur again until three o'clock the following afternoon.

The ties? Each was presented with a green cloth tie on which the Eiffel tower and a set of cricket stumps had been blazoned. We were also given two huge silver cups, specially struck, half a dozen flags and presents for the ladies.

Four days later my club, Stanmore, held their annual dinner at Lord's. Halfway through the meal a little Frenchman marched in. M. Gardet had flown over specially to reiterate his thanks.

The sequel? I just don't know. If M. Gardet is still around. I am one of 28 people hoping to hear from him again. . . .

(1979)

The Dexter enigma

by Clifford Makins, former sports editor of the Observer

I hired him, fired him, and now we are partners in crime—in the fictional sense. After I left the paper we met, by chance, at Lord's and revived an old idea—to write a thriller about a cricket match. This was *Testkill*, a minor feat of invention about a Test match at Lord's between England and Australia. I wanted to call the book 'High Noon at Lord's' but this was shot down by the publisher. A second book, based on golf, will be published in July. We have narrowed the angle; the scene is The President's Putter at Rye where golf blues from Oxford and Cambridge compete in the first week of January. The provisional title is 'Putter' but the publisher doesn't like that one either.

Dexter, as captain of England, entered journalism in 1963 with the blessing of the splendid Billy Griffith, then secretary of M.C.C. I gave him a weekly column in *The Observer* with the encouragement of Michael

Davie and the late John Gale. We called it 'Dexter Talking', then 'Dexter Writing' and finally, admitting defeat, 'Dexter'. He was, and still is, a dilemma; cricketer, golfer, aviator, gambler, devoted husband, generous host and aloof companion. I should say at once that, apart from a habit of switching off when he doesn't want to listen, I have never had a moment's bother with him. But others think different. I may be The College of One.

See *Wisden 1961*, 'Five Cricketers of the Year': 'Few batsmen, or writers, announce themselves as Dexter did when batting for Sussex against Surrey at The Oval last summer. His first ball, from the pavilion end, was slightly over-pitched on middle and leg. Feet moved fractionally, head hardly at all, but the bat swung the ball for six over long leg and they fetched it back from the seats under the gasholder.' This observation by Robin Marlar was a hint of things to come. Again from the same source: 'No English cricketer bred since the war has so captured the imagination of those inside, outside and far from the boundary ropes of our big cricket grounds . . . "Lord Edward" indeed. But how apt! A handsome figure, at the wicket he stands stock still. One can sense the latent power. The stance is all-important.'

But there were complications. Take this school report written when Dexter was seven years old. 'He shows promise at cricket, but he must remember he has still much—in fact almost everything—to learn and is not yet in a position to control and give instructions to his fellows, who quite rightly resent it.' Just so. Self-confidence, arrogance, bossiness, indifference, innate athleticism—the blend was there from the start.

I met a dancer and choreographer the other day who was at Radley when Dexter, getting into his stride, was head of school. 'We were terrified of him and, what's more, were rounded up to watch him play cricket.' A dreadful thought, but then Dexter had been playing for the first eleven since the age of 14. Before then he had been a very good wicket-keeper. To add to the damage he was sprinting, playing rackets, rugby and golf and already had an eye on the horses. The fillies came later.

A confusing pattern begins to emerge. But there is also singleness of mind. And not only on the cricket field. 'At Cambridge,' Dexter recalls, 'in spite of sport, which had really taken hold of me by now, the most important decision of this time was choosing my wife. I walked into a room and saw one person, one person only, and moved straight in. It was Susan Longfield, who is now my wife.' She still is, a former model and still radiantly attractive. There's a touch of the Scott Fitzgeralds about the Dexters but only in the sense of 'the beautiful people'—the agony, alcoholism and insanity that plagued the lives of Scott and Zelda is conspicuously absent from the Dexter family.

They live very quietly with their two children, a dog—and a vintage Bentley, a Lancia, a Moto-Guzzi bike and a modest little moped. The latest addition is a greyhound which Dexter bought in Ireland. We went to see it run the other night, in awful weather. It came second. And once upon a time there was a racehorse. . . .

In the cricketing context 'the Dexter enigma' (if we may call it that) has, always, been shrewdly observed by Alan Ross. On Dexter's character Ross is very sharp indeed. Take this from *Australia 63* when Dexter was the surprise choice to captain England when, to most people, it seemed a choice between Sheppard and Cowdrey. 'On the surface there was little against him; what remained to be seen was whether he could thaw out sufficiently as a human being and make taking an interest in other people seem less of an obvious effort. . . . As a captain, Dexter had proved, mainly at county level, enterprising, wayward, but under pressure or when bored by adversity or lack of success, inclined to dissociate himself from the whole proceedings. He is a temperamental cricketer, and temperamental cricketers depend on the stars being right for them.'

It was to prove a tough, grinding series. Afterwards, Crawford White wrote, 'If Ted Dexter survives the latest broadsides to captain England against West Indies this summer he will be a very lucky man.' Survive he did and the stage was set for the Lord's Test which shook the game, the country and even turned away the public from its devouring interest in Christine Keeler, John Profumo and Stephen Ward.

Ross again: 'What nobody could suspect was . . . that they would be present at one of the greatest innings seen at Lord's since anyone could remember. . . . Dexter, all told, batted for only 80 minutes, receiving some 70 balls . . . off these he scored 70 runs.' It was an astonishing spectacle. I was there to see it. England were 20 for two when Dexter came in to face Hall and Griffith. Ross moves in without any fuss: 'Suddenly Dexter was 50, the innings not in ruins, but classically erect, like pillars soaring with eagles'.

Dexter's plunge into politics was mind-boggling. This was one thing no one had considered, not even Dexter I suspect. But suddenly there he was, the Conservative candidate to contest Cardiff South-East, a seat held by the then Shadow Chancellor, Mr James Callaghan. I remember giving this news to Mr David Astor, then editor of *The Observer*. He looked astounded. So did I, I think. There was some laughter and derision but Dexter was as accustomed to this sort of thing as he was to face bowlers slinging down a cricket ball at 80 miles an hour. He recalls: 'Someone knocked on my door and here it was again, this new experience, this challenge, this opportunity.'

Mr Callaghan, sensibly, kept quiet, but for a short time was known as 'the demon bowler of Cardiff South-East'. Then another eminent man wrote an article in the *Daily Express*, the latest to have a crack at solving the Dexter dilemma. Here is the late Sir Neville Cardus: 'Apparently he is undecided at the age of twenty-eight whether he is (a) a great batsman, (b) an unpredictable bowler, (c) a journalist, (d) a television star (in Australia), (e) a potential golfer or (f) a future leader of the Tory Party. . . . It is beyond me that Dexter, a young man with his talents as a great cricketer, should think for a moment of giving up any of his days or nights to Westminster and politics.'

Then on June 24, 1965, Dexter, in true character, was driving home in his Jaguar after a day at the races. He ran out of petrol, pushed and steered the car off the road, lost control and the vehicle ran down a short slope to smash into locked doors. It also smashed his leg. That was the end of his career as a first-class cricketer—at least he chose to make it so. Since then, this eminently fit man has managed to contract housemaid's knee, tennis elbow and a touch of arthritis in the hip. But he goes on jogging along, round the common most mornings with wife and dog as company. He keeps up the golf (and a mighty striker of the ball he is) and still wants to win The President's Putter, a prize that has so often slipped from his grasp with victory in sight.

It's difficult to pin him down, but he certainly has style (though in my view his *prose* style has slipped a bit since he left *The Observer* for the *Sunday Mirror*. But that's journalism; books is a different matter). Dexter's off-handedness—one of his charms—still persists but in the two works of sporting crime/fiction we have written together he has caught on very quickly to the tricks of this highly specialised trade. It's a strange relationship when you come to think of it, and there are some people who believe that it doesn't exist But it does. If we live long enough (and who knows Dexter may be the first to go) we hope to complete the triology with a thriller about horse racing. Call it *Fontwell Park*. Dick Francis, beware!

Finally, two brief conversations I had with cricketing knights. 'What do you think of Dexter?' I asked the late Sir Jack Hobbs. He replied: 'Whenever he's batting at The Oval I always find time to go and watch him.' Then he shut up. I asked the same question of Sir Leonard Hutton. There was a classical Hutton response. He bent forward and whispered (I strained my ears to catch the words): 'Well, you see, Clifford, he's a great player but he lacks . . . he lacks . . .'—a dramatic pause seeking for the right word while I stood on fire—'he lacks what I call . . . concentration.'

(1979)

The long black telegraph pole

Peter Roebuck, a Somerset colleague of Joel Garner, talks about the great Big Bird

A couple of nights before our Gillette Cup semi-final the Somerset players were entertained by one of our most devoted supporters, John Cleese. During the brief interludes when the players managed to escape the attentions of dead parrots, John Cleese was to be seen in deep and profound conversation with Joel Garner. This provoked a most diverting thought— could this be a new comedy team developing? Certainly both men have remarkable limbs, including several arms and legs each acting independently of all others. Perhaps they might start with a guest appearance on Come Dancing, offering a fresh approach to the Tango. Anyhow, let the Muppets beware.

John Cleese's comic abilities are well known (and at least partly unconscious; Denis Breakwell could scarcely control himself when Cleese attempted to pour him some wine. Perhaps the cork should first have been removed!). That Joel Garner is a figure of similar hilarity is less well known. Indeed, most opposing batsmen seem quite unable to appreciate his talents —the somewhat improbable cohesion of Big Bird's arms and legs as he flaps in to bowl provokes not one whit of joy in these dour opponents. Not that they ignore him entirely. The more-long-in-the-chewing gum among them will greet Joel with a cheerful 'Good morning' and will add a sympathetic, if trifle optimistic, 'a bit chilly for fast bowling, isn't it?' But, apart from such pleasantries, few appreciate the range of Garner's talents.

Of course, there are good reasons for this widespread ignorance. For a start, it is almost impossible to understand anything Joel says. He talks in a strange lingo, presumably a broad Barbadian banter, which shares no words (so far as one can tell) with the mother tongue as she is spoken from Chewton Mendip to Nether Stowey. Consequently, conversation with Joel tends to be a hazardous business. Ask him for the time and his reply might vary from the earthy 'in the car park' to the wholly mystical 'well, I haven't been there for a while'.

Naturally, being a fast bowler, Big Bird can afford to be a little elusive. He need only say a few words and follow with a great laugh for the whole dressing-room to be in uproar. And when he pops in to the visitors' room for a little social chit-chat, he enjoys a marvellously attentive audience. The room practically falls apart at the slightest hint of a witticism. Fast bowlers are treated with the most touching affection.

Big Bird rather likes being so very black, so very large and so very difficult to decipher. He feels no obligation to hide his considerable light under a nearby bushel (not that they make bushels like that nowadays, at any rate) like some reluctant debutante (and where have they all gone?). He fairly relishes using his long reach to best advantage in a darts game, placing rather than propelling his darts into the board. After a particularly success-ful day he will stroll around the main streets of Taunton with the whites of his eyes and gleaming teeth visible for miles around, thoroughly pleased with the glances of astonished children and terrified babies.

Or, if there's a bit of a crowd in, Joel will charge around the boundary with kangaroo strides, pick up the ball in one gigantic hand and hurl it as far as possible in the general direction of the stumps. If, perchance, wicket-keeper Derek Taylor is the correct distance away, the ball will land with a thud in his gloves. If not, well at least the crowd will appreciate the spectacle of the throw and the sight of fielders diving around (some trying to stop the ball, others desperate to avoid its perilous path).

This slightly mischievous use of his powers sometimes extends to Joel's batting. As with most fast bowlers, Big Bird is immensely impressed by his own style. Often he talks of his desire to 'flick' the ball here and to 'lick' it there. Occasionally, the most ambitious strokes succeed gloriously, for instance when Les Taylor was despatched for a powerful straight six at Leicester as Joel tried to coax victory from defeat. Even if success eludes him, Joel is well worth watching at the crease, particularly when in tandem with Derek Taylor. Derek runs in very short, scampered steps which contrast dramatically with Big Bird's massive strides and frequently leave him in danger of being lapped in most entertaining fashion.

Not that Joel Garner is content to be the happy-go-lucky West Indian fast bowler all the time. The cheerful days are interspersed with periods of reflective silence during which Joel retires behind one of the thrillers he reads so voraciously (or, if the mood is really black, *The Gulag Archipelago* —not perhaps the most jolly book ever written). If these dark thoughts do surface, it is usually to express resentment at some administrative decision that has particularly annoyed him

Joel is sensitive to the treatment of players, and determined that cricket should concern itself more with the well-being of its cricketers. One suspects that this 'irreverant bump' grew as a result of experiences within the intense turmoil of West Indian cricket, a turmoil in which, by all reports, Big Bird thrives with a mind as lively as any Rumpole.

In some ways the strength of Joel's feelings as regards the running of cricket is surprising. For he is far from being a passionate person. To the contrary, he has repeatedly shown himself to possess a cool, detached temperament, which is rarely roused to anger or mistrust. Possibly Joel is a person more offended by insults to his intelligence than by affronts to his emotions. He responds with neither words nor gestures to the most provocative attack by opponent or spectator. Should a fast bowler be so sadly misled as to whistle a bouncer past Joel's ears (no mean feat in itself), Big Bird will merely smile benevolently down the pitch as if to say (as might the frog to the tadpole), 'Your turn will come.' Another Somerset bowler has been known, in similar circumstances, to inform the ill-advised bowler that 'if you had another brain cell, you'd be a plant'—but that's not Joel's style.

Nor does Joel permit himself the luxury of being upset by crowds. At Harrogate a supporter addressed some unpleasant remarks to Big Bird as he lolloped out to bat (just when, as chance would have it, the groundsman was warming up the heavy roller). Rather than give any indication that he had so much as heard these remarks, let alone been hurt or angered by them, Joel proceeded to bat with aplomb, contributing a flamboyant 53 before bowling some distinctly hasty overs to Boycott and Lumb.

So, despite his keen intelligence, Joel is far too full of fun to be irritated for long. He enjoys life far too much to let the cheap inadequacies of the world upset him. He is not to resort to petty deeds himself; his quiet self-confidence prevents him envying the abilities or personalities of rivals. Big Bird is a calm professional who loves to do well and who does not need the artificial motivations of hate or ambitions to stimulate his performance.

It is as easy to underestimate Joel's bowling as it is to undervalue his other wide-ranging abilities (which, incidentally, include a delicate touch on the typewriter, despite long fingers). His run-up is short and his delivery deceptively effortless. But no colleague or opponent of Joel will deny that he is one of the very fastest bowlers in the world. Certainly, he is one of the most awkward, hammering the ball into the grass from a height far above sightscreens which were built with less prodigious mortals in mind. Joel generates remarkable bounce from apparently docile pitches and has the ability to change pace without any noticeable change of action. With these abilities it is not easy to decide whether Joel most resembles Jeff Thomson or Tom Cartwright.

Like Thomson, he is capable of bouncing the ball from a good length into the batsman's ribs and of maintaining a menacing hostility on slow pitches. And, like Cartwright, he can produce controlled movement in either direction (not at the same time, unless bemused victims are to be believed, but often in the same delivery) without sacrificing line and length.

Perhaps the truth is that Big Bird will bowl like Cartwright when the mood so takes him and like Thomson if he feels sharp and aggressive. In the West Indies team, Joel is usually used as a stock bowler to hold the fort while Roberts, Holding, Daniel, Marshall et al are resting. And it may be that this use of Joel is founded upon a shrewd appreciation of his nature, with his relatively mild temperament and whole-hearted dislike of conceding runs.

As a defensive bowler Joel is well-nigh supreme. Few others could bowl at the end of a thriving Sunday league innings to Allan Lamb and Peter Willey with only seven men in front of the bat. Nor are many bowlers of his pace as willing to bowl long spells for their team—not many fast bowlers would have volunteered to bowl all afternoon and evening one hot Harrogate day to save their side from defeat. It is never difficult to persuade Big B to bowl but sometimes it can be hard to stop him.

No doubt Joel will play cricket for only a few years more. He enjoys life at Somerset but longs for a more tranquil and leisurely existence on the beaches of Barbados. Until he retires all Somerset hopes he will continue to entertain friend and foe alike. Somerset's batsmen ask only one favour of the 'long, black telegraph pole': Please keep away from the nets.

If all this seems a little flattering, remember that Somerset plays the West Indians next season and down here we are a shade longer in-the-chewing gum than we look.

(1979)

'George'—the bowler they all admired

Eric Todd writes on the ideal cricketer's cricketer—Brian Statham

On a hot day in August 1953 at Swansea, Lancashire had Glamorgan's first innings in ruins at 34 for six. Between telephoning the glad tidings to Manchester, I strolled round the ground and came across Willie Jones, that admirable little Welshman, who was watching the play with an expression compounded of admiration and awe.

Seeking to console him, I suggested that the wicket might be difficult. 'Wicket? Wicket?' replied Willie. 'No, there's nothing wrong with the wicket, man. It's that Brian Statham. He's bowling so bloody fast.'

Two years later, against Lancashire on that same ground, Glamorgan lost eight wickets while adding 16 runs. Again I sought out Willie. 'Hello, there,' said he. 'He's still bloody fast.' In those two innings, Statham took eleven wickets for 31 runs in 27 overs, 15 of them maidens.

John Brian Statham—he preferred to answer to 'George'—was neither the fastest nor the most aggressive among his species. Nevertheless, few who played alongside him or against him denied that he was the most consistently accurate. In an impeccable career extending from 1950 to 1968, he took 252 wickets in Test cricket, 1,816 for Lancashire, and nearly 200 in extraneous matches. Those figures, however impressive, take no account of near misses, dropped catches, or unsympathetic umpires.

He never lodged an appeal unless convinced that his cause was just. Only once, in fact, did I see him register emotion in the face of apparent injustice. It happened at Edgbaston where he appealed for l.b.w. against Hitchcock of Warwickshire, but umpire Arthur Fagg would have none of it. Mention of Fagg is a reminder that he was Statham's first victory in county cricket—l.b.w. at that—but that is by the way.

Statham arrived at Old Trafford in 1949, backed by a strong recommendation from the R.A.F. with whom he did his National Service, and from Denton St Lawrence for whom he played occasionally. He was welcomed with open arms because Eddie Phillipson had retired, and Dick Pollard, 'th'owd chain horse', was about to follow suit.

He had a season with the second eleven and the Manchester Club and Ground side, and made his bow in county cricket in June 1950—his 20th birthday—at Old Trafford against Kent.

The first intimation of what lay in store for the world's leading batsmen was delivered against Somerset at Bath in July that year. At that time, I worked for a Manchester evening newspaper, and my first despatch for the early editions consisted of team news, and the state of the wicket and weather.

My telephone was sited some distance across the ground and I was absent for half-an-hour or so. By the time I returned to the Press tent, Statham had dismissed Gimblett, Angell, Buse, Irish, and Tremlett—four of them bowled—for only five runs in seven overs.

Later that season, Statham had his baptism of a 'Roses' match, and twice fell flat on his back at the end of his run. Not until Dodds of Essex pulled his first ball for six at Brentwood did Statham suffer any comparable blow to his pride and dignity. At least on the field.

In 1964, when Ken Grieves surrendered the captaincy, Lancashire astonished us by advertising for a successor. Only when they failed to get a suitable response did they go, cap in hand, to Statham who, to his everlasting credit, accepted the post. Having received a testimonial of £13,000 three years previously, Statham welcomed this opportunity of endorsing his appreciation. Which cannot be said of every beneficiary.

The Lancashire yearbook for 1969 devoted 18 pages to the departing champion's career in statistics which could not convey adequately the resignation to the inevitable with which some counties awaited their dates with Lancashire and Statham. Glamorgan, as we have noted, suffered enough in the early 1950s, but Statham had not done with them. In 1958 at Cardiff they were dismissed for 26, Statham's figures reading 16-9-12-6.

Leicestershire, too, had more than their fair share of demolition. In 1955 at Hinckley, they were dismissed for 42, Statham taking six for 20 in 14 overs. Three years later at Old Trafford, where Roy Tattersall and 'Ranji' Wilson put on 105 for Lancashire's last wicket, Leicestershire were beaten in two days, Statham having match figures of 13 for 64.

In 1960, Leicestershire again were on the receiving end, Statham's aggregate for the match at Grace Road being 29-9-58-14, seven wickets in each innings, and all bowled second time round.

In that same season—in which he captained the Players against the Gentlemen—he took his 1,000th wicket for Lancashire, and had the best Lancashire bowling average in 80 years (Statham appealed six times for l.b.w. against Yorkshire in the Old Trafford match and was successful every time. He scarcely could believe it).

With such a vast selection from which to choose, I imagine that Statham's outstanding memory would be of a game in May 1957 at Coventry where he scored 53 in under half-an-hour, and took eight wickets for 34 and seven for 55.

He performed the hat trick twice for Lancashire, and might have achieved another one at Hove. Robin Marlar, the third man so to say, was not expected to deny Statham, but he batted in a pink cap which so distracted the bowler that he lost his direction and Marlar survived.

Over the years, Statham had all sorts and conditions of men as his opening bowling partner at county and international levels—and his collaboration with Ken Higgs, which began in 1958, certainly was the most impressive for Lancashire.

For England, of course, it just had to be Statham and Freddie Trueman, the rapier and the broadsword. Or Raffles and Bill Sykes as someone put it—out of Trueman's hearing.

In August 1968, Statham called it a day in Higgs' testimonial game at Old Trafford against Yorkshire. Yorkshire, 12 for five at one stage in their first innings, were dismissed for 61, Statham six for 34. Like Bradman before him, Statham did not score in his last innings, and when Yorkshire batted again, Statham's only victim was Phil Sharpe . . . l.b.w. When it was all over, Statham trudged off the field to an ovation granted only to the truly great.

Statham was an unobtrusive yet always amiable travelling companion. He enjoyed a good film and, although he rarely took a hand at cards, he

Sir Pelham ('Plum') Warner, founder and first editor of *The Cricketer*.

Left: 'Hobbs was the bridge over which classical cricket marches to the more complex epoch of the present,' wrote Cardus.

Opposite: Don Bradman as a 21-year-old in 1930, during the first of four tours to England. He received the first knighthood ever bestowed upon a *playing* cricketer.

Top: as memory still pictures him (1924), and (bottom), on his 80th birthday in 1962.

Walter Hammond—his stroke play was an adornment to the game.

Opposite: Youthful days for the Huttons: (top), Len, with an even younger admirer, and (bottom), many years later, in 1971, his son Richard, who also played for Yorkshire and England.

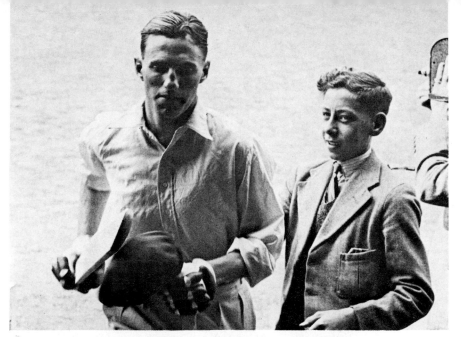

Left: Denis Compton. He made his debut for Middlesex in 1936, and retired in 1957 having played 78 Tests.

Below: The subtlety of the game's Peter Pan—Freddie Titmus, who has played County Championship matches in five decades, from the 1940s to the 1980s.

Ted Dexter, who made his name as a batsman of daring, often high-class, stroke play, in June, 1963.

Left: Sir Frank Worrell,
one of the West Indies'
greatest cricketers. Sadly,
he died of leukaemia in
1967, aged 42.

Below: Moments of high
elation as Brian Statham
takes his 250th test wicket
for England at the Oval in
1965.

was a regular kibitzer among those who did, often with astonishing results. He was an outstanding and chivalrous performer the world over and, in my opinion, he was to cricket what Tom Finney and Bobby Charlton were to football.

Today, Statham is a respected and successful representative for a firm of brewers. He serves on the Lancashire committee and, not least of all perhaps, a large block of offices has been named after him.

W. G. Grace himself had to be satisfied with a pair of iron gates.

(1980)

'Ian Chappell and Lillee—theirs is the example which young people follow'

Tony Lewis talks about acquiring the right habits for life. Where cricket is concerned there is a growing anxiety about the on-the-field antics of some players

My history master used to award penalty kicks for dull play on the rugby field. If a boy ever risked a punch or a tantrum, he would expect to be sent to 'the cooler', which really meant standing still on the touchline until recalled to play.

The schoolmaster's name is worth recalling because it came to my mind in Australia a short while ago as I sat watching first Ian Chappell's bat-throwing argument with the umpire at Brisbane, then Dennis Lillee's aluminium equivalent at Perth. Sam Evans would have had them both on the sidelines.

Schoolboys will accept a discipline which adults will not, but should they both not hold to the same standards of behaviour? In a recent article written for *Radio Times*, the headmaster of Radley School near Oxford revealed a sentence or two of the speech with which he greets each fresh intake of boarders: 'You come to school for one thing really—to acquire the right habits for life.'

That headmaster, the warden of Radley, is Dennis Silk, a marvellous sportsman in his day who played cricket for Somerset and rugby for Bath. Anyone seeing these credentials merely as the pleasant pastimes of the erstwhile amateur may also like to know that in his double Blue career at Cambridge he first played centre-three-quarter in the University match.

Then, one year when the team's need arose, he transferred to prop-forward. Mr Silk therefore understands the hard grind of face-to-face competition.

Although Ian Chappell and Dennis Lillee are a long way out of school jurisdiction, a million schoolmasters are still desperately interested in them. Theirs is the example which young people follow, even more so now that billions of viewers are watching cricket on television.

The post-war generation did their pads up with buckles on the outside because Denis Compton was said to do it that way. I have seen a schoolboy off-spinner kiss his cap because Tayfield used to do it; young West Indies fast bowlers wear their shirts open and carry a medallion of sorts on a neck-chain because Wes Hall blasted them out that way. What Lillee and Chappell demonstrated was an example which might make schoolmasters tear out their hair and youths throw beer cans on the Sydney Hill.

Someone wrote to me shortly after Lillee had thrown his bat, and accused me of bias. Why was I suggesting a ban on Lillee but not on Geoff Boycott who, the year before in Perth, was said to have tossed his bat to the ground and had called umpire Don Weser a cheat? I must plead, first that I did not see the Boycott incident and, if that is not an acceptable get-out, I must confess my own confusion.

Are fines and suspensions meant to be part of professional cricket? The worry is not the matter of an extra onus being thrown on the Boards of Control; it is of the cricketers themselves abandoning personal pride. This is just one of several happenings during the Australian winter's experiment which has thrown responsibility on to the top players. In Australia, West Indies and in England, the Cricketers' Associations will no doubt place them on an agenda.

It is obvious that the Packer Revolt was all about cricketers fighting for the status of their profession and for money which was a fair compensation for being among the best players in the world. Finally, Mr Justice Slade undid the cage which had trapped their aspirations.

The Australian Board gave them wings by setting up the triangular commercial experiment, and many sponsors came up with the hard cash.

Most players, I know, understand that with their new incomes from commerce comes a widening of their responsibilities. No longer does their involvement begin and end on the field. There are receptions to honour, prize-givings to attend, and many miles of video-taped promotion to act out.

At the reception which launched the Australian winter back in November, England turned up smartly in their uniforms, the West Indies took the trouble to don suits, even waistcoats, but there were those Australians who looked dog-eared in sweat shirts and thongs.

On another occasion, Clive Lloyd, so disgusted with the closing actions of one match, did not even appear for the presentation. Deryck Murray deputised. David Hookes threw his bat, causing about £25 worth of damage to a dressing room. Viv Richards' bat bounced off a seat through a window.

I am certainly not the judge of any of these reported happenings, but it is worth the new regime of international cricketers standing back, while the guns are cooling, to consider the style, indeed the image, of their profession as a whole. Surely the right sponsors will only stay with a game of honourable behaviour?

No one likes to see the schoolmaster-little-boy attitude adopted by administrators in cricket, though clearly, if you choose to earn a living in the game as run by the various Boards of Control, you must abide by the laws and playing conditions. But perhaps golf is a good example of how individuals, for slow play, bad sportsmanship and other blights on their game, are fined, suspended or banned by their fellow professionals.

Would a formally elected Cricketers Disciplinary court work best? It would mean that the restraint comes from within the profession.

Yet everyone knows that the discipline we are looking for must come from within the player himself. There is nothing like the trials of Test cricket to examine the habits you have acquired for life.

(1980)

Oxbridge must seek talent

Robin Marlar, an old and literate hand at the game, considers Schools and Universities cricket in 1980

He sat in the corner of the new pavilion at one of our academic institutions, this very influential person. The pavilion may have moved but his corner seat still has a 'park-here-if-you-dare' sign on it, unwritten, unseen, but violated only by the unfamiliar.

Very influential person alleges, and no doubt his birth certificate confirms, that he is almost 70. But his voice is that of a strong man of 25 in the prime of life, an unhesitating, confident voice. If it looks to be an effort for this entitled pensioner to move about the cricket field, then that has been the case for nigh on half-a-century, since a leg was horribly broken on the football field and worse set in hospital.

Cyril Coote, Lord of the Manor of Fenners, training ground extraordinary for cricketers for well over a century, still producing the hardest pitches in the country in the month of May, is fit and well although talking of retirement.

The man had a good winter. One of his captains, Mike Brearley, took England to Australia and succeeded in making a little slam where other Cambridge men had gone down, sometimes when doubled and redoubled, in bridge parlance.

A fierce spirit of possession concerning his old boys rules the man still. It is that which makes this very influential person such an enduring joy to those who have passed through his academy. Here is one post to which a boat can continue to tie up for the rest of its life.

Yet these cricketers who win and wear the light blue are not all cast in the same mould. Cyril Coote, master groundsman and so much more besides, is not the proprietor of some cricketing foundry. Whatever books there are in the pavilion, and there are many fewer now than 25 years ago (will borrowers please return, thank you), there is no coaching manual to be seen. Nor is there now or ever any hint that those who pass through Fenners must have the rough edges of their personality chiselled off by the local carpenter. Not that he does not grieve, out loud but with understanding, when a batsman as close to Test potential as Matthew Fosh, late of Essex, gives up cricket in favour of the guitar.

What is taught at Fenners is basic first-class cricket: application, effort, the significance of everything—yes, everything—that happens on the cricket field in a particular game. The facilities for practice are perfect and are there to be used even if they may be spoiled in the wet. What more can any aspirant hope for in a season so short that it is over before the horse-chestnut lanterns have changed into conkers?

Cyril Coote can say with pride that Cambridge men still have a contribution to make to cricket. The names still speak for him, but he needs to reassure himself against change by recalling the roll of honour. Long may the stream of talent flow. It will not do so if someone stops up the source. It is common knowledge that Paul Downton was refused admission. Overseas players are sometimes rejected by one of the Universities playing first-class cricket and picked up by the other, as Imran Khan was by Oxford. That was one talent saved from wasting.

Imran and his cousin Majid demonstrate one feature of University cricket which is important above all others. If you are able to become outstanding as a University cricketer, and there are 22 possibilities for that and not just a mere handful, then the surge of confidence is such that it is possible to leap the gap between County and Test cricket as if it was no wider than one of the minor streams which divide and adorn the Cambridge backs. Many, indeed most, players who do not enjoy the benefit of University entry into cricket find that particular chasm as wide as the Ganges. Every England tour drowns its quota. To be fair, some blues have also been seen to be non-swimmers.

However, every cricketer will know that this surge of confidence is more likely to come when a side is uniformly good than when its diamonds are embedded few and far between in less valuable rock. Look at Kent today. Or Yorkshire yesterday. The England team of last winter displayed the most consistently high standard of fielding of any team sent to win or hold the Ashes in Australia—at least when it was winning.

It always used to be said of University teams that, if they could not bat or bowl, at least they ought to be able to run round the boundary, pick up and throw. It is a fact that throwing arms are ruined by the Siberian cold drifting across the Fens to threaten keen undergraduate shoulders but the point has merit, as does the insistence at Grange Road and Iffley Road that University rugby fifteens should be fit enough to beat strong club sides in the last ten minutes if they have survived the first hour.

In the final analysis it is not fielding or fitness which makes for success. Only talent can breed that. It is a hoary old chestnut, but one that can never be brought out often enough, that the Universities which have first-class fixture lists, Oxford and Cambridge, have a duty, yes a duty, not only not to reject sporting talent but to go out positively and find it in the schools.

Just as the Colleges, their gardens so glorious in the spring, the teaching faculties, the libraries and the laboratories are assets, so, too, are the playing fields and the skilled men who look after them and help to prepare their young men for a future in sport. How many admission tutors at Cambridge or Oxford would regard themselves as sporting as well as academic scouts? How many turn up to the significant matches in the under-19 calendar?

The cost of a good University cricket team need not be high, the development and maintenance of adequate communication with schools and County Cricket Associations. The price ought not to be too high either: a few failures in Tripos are a small loss compared with the production of a Brearley once a decade—not that he gave Dons any trouble with pen and ink. They say that some undergraduates simply cannot face the examiners and pull out altogether.

At least that Cambridge giant of long ago, Sammy Woods, the Sammy Woodcock beloved of contemporary cartoonists, stepped up in cap and gown with the same fearlessness with which he bowled at W. G. Grace. His problem was that he did not know whether it was Plato or Socrates who wrote the beastly book.

Some years ago, when I was writing for the *Sunday Times*, permission was given for an article on schools cricket, more or less on the theme that the old grey mare ain't what she used to be. Among the brickbats and bottles was one treasured letter from a headmaster of a school which made me most relieved that I had not kicked his writing hand off his wrist when he used to hold the ball while I tried to kick goals at rugby.

(There's that *rara avis*, an increase in productivity for you: 30 years ago two men were needed to complete the two points of a conversion, now only one.)

The point of his letter was that my timing was wrong, that cricket *had* almost died at the turn of the decade in the schools but was by then much healthier. How this trend can be monitored would be as important a discovery to administrators in cricket as the philosopher's stone to old scientists, for that, too, could turn base metals into gold.

Certainly the connection between the umbilical cord, the public schools and cricket, which you can read about in any history of the game, has perished. In Edwardian days batsmen all came from such schools, or so it seemed, and all bowlers from the by then scattered descendants of the Hambledon men. One of the differences between the world of cricket after the war of 1914–18, and that which existed before it, was that no such certainty existed any more. Society, including cricketing society, was no longer regulated in such ways.

It was, however, still possible to hear people say, even after the war of 1939–45, that you could tell a Malvernian by his cover-drive. After seeing how short the cover point boundary was on that ground near the bottom of the hill it was easy to understand why.

By the end of that second war no one much cared at what school a cricketer had been taught. What then mattered was how well he could play. Not many Malvernians, not even E. R. T. Holmes, could play the cover-drive against the in-swing of the one new Malvernian to make a mark on the first-class game in the late 40s and 50s, George Chesterton, the master of inswing. You could put money on the fact that the Tolchards, the latest from that academy to tread the county grounds, have never heard of the old adage about the cover-drive.

What school life is about now is an individual's ability to make something of the facilities provided for him. If the academic route is closed because the mysteries of algebra and French grammar remain as impenetrable as the school walls, then wise heads stop beating brain on brick and seek out a life dependent on hand or eye. Others get incurably bitten by the sporting bug merely because the opportunities are there.

Almost every county now has its quota of players from schools with traditions as proud as that of Malvern. No longer do they come into the side in school holidays or for a week or two before the grouse moors open in August wearing their fancy caps and old-fashioned gear.

Judgments are made not on where a player has been taught his cricket but on what he can do. Like all harsh rules there does seem to be one factor capable of tempering its starkness. Members of the cricketing family still get most favoured treatment. In cricket, still a sentimental game, the family includes more than sons of fathers like Hutton, Cowdrey, Graveney and Herman playing for father's county.

It has been widened through relaxation of the system so that the young Tremlett is being given a show by Hampshire and the young Shackleton by Gloucestershire, just as Bob Herman was originally tried by Middlesex. Admission to county trial is now at the point where coaches, both here and in, for example, South Africa, are quick to spot and recommend genuine talent. Because that evaluation from a known member of the enlarged family is immediately acceptable. The flow from South Africa is a welcome release of the talent bottled up in South African schools with English coaches.

Nevertheless it remains the case that the facilities for cricket in the schools which were the traditional English nurseries are, in most cases, still ahead of those provided in the average modern comprehensive. Governing bodies of public schools may be encouraged by the knowledge that there are 46 first-class cricketers whose schools are members of the Head-masters' Conference. Out of a full complement of registered players between 310 and 320 that represents a significant 15% contribution.

Lest I be accused of assumed bias, an argument of some passion last winter in Australia should be cited between a county committeeman who left school at 14 and myself over the qualifications of a former public school-boy to captain a county: the argument hinged on his ability to keep a place in the side and, doubtless, we were both sad that the place was lost after the season was only a month old, as I had regretfully predicted.

There is now neither the habit nor the excuse for most favoured treatment for public schoolboys.

The amateur tradition, that of the dashing, flashing extrovert, his place guaranteed by his office as captain, is over. Commercial competitiveness is now the key to the dressing-room. We may mourn the absence of the modern Colin Ingleby-Mackenzie. Today's colourful, popular players are the big men who can sustain their performances. The Procters and Rices and others from South Africa show how well the products of fee-paying schools there can respond to that challenge.

Talent with contribution is the only measurement. Nevertheless it is a source of pride for any school when one of its cricketers visibly makes the grade. At the moment King's, Canterbury, are making a show with Gower and Rowe among the most promising newcomers: Sevenoaks, too, Tavarè and Downton.

What this argues is the strength and interest in the game at all levels in the county of Kent.

The various levels adhere much more than ever before. Gone are the days when a county hired a former public school coach who did his best to ensure that any boy from that school never had precedence over the young apprentices in his charge. This was the understandable post-war reaction to the pre-war order of privilege and preference.

With all that ullage out of the way, cricket is stronger. The rise of the national competitions to which all schools can look is one of the major organisation changes for the better in the 1970s. No county wants to lose a young player who had made his mark at under-19 level.

For years now the principal factor limiting the supply of cricketers to counties has been the freedom of recreational choice which has become another welcome feature of school life. Only by dedication on the part of concerned masters, coaches *and* senior boys can those schools which have a long cricketing tradition hope to sustain it. The evidence of the moment is that their case is being well served.

(1980)

Clive Lloyd

M. H. Stevenson on the cricketer with the uninhibited characteristics of 'The Keystone Cops'

Whoever it was that described Clive Lloyd as '. . . a great, gangling, be-goggled supercat' must (temporarily at least) have been inspired; nevertheless, he has been in county cricket just long enough to invite our taking him for granted.

Equally readily can be forgotten the immense impact of overseas cricketers from 1968 onwards, after the strict laws governing their inclusion were relaxed. A seasoned professional of the school of 'ritual cricket', writing home thereafter, might have couched his epistle in the following terms:

Old Trafford
Friday, 13th.

Dear Mum,
    Tell Dad it's a b . . . . . .
    We're playing Lancashire first go off and I'm wheeling away on a nice

length when this great, bloody bespectacled bully starts belting me over the top as if we was in club cricket. I bowls it a bit shorter and 'e 'ooks me. Then to cap it all, he digs me best yorker out and that goes for 4 an' all.

When we bat, I push to cover, to get off the mark and blow me if the flaming idiot doesn't throw down the bowler's wicket before I've got half-way.

Eeh! I do wish I'd gone into the shop, like you said.

Love, Joe.

To his admirers, Lloyd must appear unique; yet he belongs to the West Indian tradition as clearly as Sobers, whose influence is clearly written on the younger man (as Sobers, when bowling, transfers the ball from right to left hand before delivery, acknowledging an early debt to Sir Frank Worrell). Surely much of the West Indies' success results from this tendency for the heroes of one generation to be copied by their aspiring juniors.

By contrast, English batting is so cerebrally over-theoretical: 'Open up,' says the coach, 'and take the inswinger on the thigh-pad or let it pass down the leg-side.'

'Rubbish!' says a Sobers or a Lloyd, 'I believe in the old-fashioned leg-hit. I may get a top edge every now and again but please note what has happened to a number of reputable bowlers in the meantime.' Clive Lloyd believes (sing Hallelujah!) that attack is almost always the best form of defence.

Should the batsman, subscribing to the Pauline theory that '. . . all things be done decently and in order', play each ball on its merits? Surely the length ball played with decorum breeds confidence and efficiency in the bowler, whereas the length ball hit on the rise leaves him wondering just where to bowl the next one.

Any bowler confronted with Clive Lloyd must know the terrifying fascination of Russian Roulette. 'Will it be this one . . . or this one . . . or . . .? That one nearly killed me and it's broken the sight-screen!'

One former England player described Lloyd as a 'mere slogger'. Apart from taking exception to the 'mere' (sad that there are so few 'sloggers' among our 9s, 10s and 11s these days), it is palpably absurd to describe anyone possessing the variety and precision of stroke-play at Lloyd's disposal in such disparaging terms.

A more valid criticism is that (like virtually all players) he is not relatively as good a batsman when the ball is moving as on a plumb 'un. When facing Tom Cartwright on a seamer's wicket at Southport, his batting suggested desperation, if not death-wish; but, to his credit he got runs.

Certainly he is less vulnerable to the bouncer than he once was and one only has to consider the methods employed by several of the present Australian batsmen, when facing the England attack, to realise that there is a vast difference between periodic uncertainty and impotent capitulation.

Whatever attack he faces, Clive Lloyd tends to get runs or get out; last season he found himself confronted by a couple of medium-pacers clearly intent upon demonstrating his much-publicised Achilles heel. The first time a ball was bounced at him, its next bounce occurred around 40 yards over the long-leg boundary. You can't kill tigers with a tooth pick.

However exciting Lloyd's batting, it is his fielding that has already earned him a place among the immortals. With the strings of the puppet slack, he slouches like a double-jointed gangster. (It amazes me that so fine a mover can sometimes look so unathletic.) But seconds, it seems, before an average cover would have moved, the elastic, hunter's stride carries his huge frame to impossibly distant regions, where the telescopic arm will click out and the slick pick-up and shy, nudge the poor David of a batsman into belief that Goliath has beaten him to the draw.

Perhaps Lloyd's salient cricketing quality is his unpredictability, something which appears to have spread from his cover-driving to his car-driving, which shares many of the more uninhibited characteristics of 'The Keystone Cops'.

He has enjoyed his time in Lancashire and Lancashire has enjoyed him. His two years at Haslingden in the League made him many friends, among whom is John Ingham. 'We were batting together against Enfield on a freezing day just after Clive had landed. There was a gale too and we'd both been pushing up the line automatically. I thought Clive was in a stupor, when there was an explosion the other end. I'd just time to turn my back before the ball took me on the backside and felled me like an ox.'

A friend of mine said of him: 'I've never known anyone laugh longer or more helplessly': a different view of the man who has so often played the Demon King to Harry Pilling's inimitable Fairy Queen.

But the last word on Clive Lloyd, twenty-six years old, of Guyana, Lancashire and the West Indies, demolition expert, Chan Canasta of covers, consistently under-rated bowler and shy but friendly individual, should be allowed to his county captain. Jack Bond said of him: 'We don't tolerate "stars" in the Lancashire team. Clive has fitted in excellently and he's a great team man.'

Lancashire must be delighted to have acquired a star of Clive Lloyd's brilliance; they must be equally relieved that he resolutely refuses to behave like one.

(1971)

Jewel of the East

Sunil Gavaskar, one of the world's supreme batsmen, has been savouring the unique atmosphere of county cricket with Somerset. Now he is returning to his home in Bombay to prepare for India's winter tour of Australia. Peter Roebuck gives his impressions of the player they dubbed 'Swoop' in the dressing room at Taunton

Forewarned is forearmed, as the sages have it. So visitors to Somerset are kindly introduced to the horrors of scrumpy. Sometimes, though, it is more fun to let the unsuspecting guest slip on the rural banana-skins. Soon after he arrived from Barbados, Hallam Moseley approached a host of green stinging nettles at speed in pursuit of a cricket ball. If any kind soul thought to warn him as to the hazards of his course he held his peace. The effect was spectacular, akin to Fred Astaire with St Vitus Dance. Our newest recruit to the cider-county has been too worldly wise to rush in where Denning and Dredge fear to tread. Sunil Gavaskar has avoided nettles, scrumpy, the Wurzels and skittles with the ease born of experience. Eating curry and sleeping on beds of nails encourage a healthy suspicion of the strange habits of the Occident.

Mind you, Sunil has made one slight mistake. Out of the kindness of his heart he fed a poor, stray, lonely pigeon that appeared on his window sill. Alas, wisdom and generosity oft suggest different paths. The pigeon knew when he (or she?) was on to a good thing. 'Free grub at the Gavaskar's' he called to his mates who arrived with manic optimism, chirping at the window like a barbershop quartet in the depression. Sunny's flat began to resemble Nelson's column.

One wondered whether the SAS would need to be called in. Or, if things got really bad, would Botham turn up with his air-gun?

Sunny arrived at Taunton with the aura of the great batsman. Everyone was a little nervous. But, after the pigeon incident (sounds like one of the 'causes of the first World War'), Somerset players realised that Gavaskar has a touch of Harry Worth and need not be taken too seriously. Apparently simple operations are beyond him. He is never quite able to release the hand-brake on his car. It is Hyde Park corner in the rush hour when he remembers he has left his wallet at The Oval. He is appalled at the thought of driving in London. And neither he nor his wife has the slightest notion of how to cook and wash without their retinue of servants.

Oh yes, and Sunny is terrified of dogs. Petrified in fact. If one appears on the field during a Gavaskar innings his composure is shattered. Needless to say Ian Botham misses no opportunity to invite dogs into our dressing-room; or if he can't find a dog Ian will offer a few hidden woofs of his own. In either case Sunil beats a faster retreat than any Italian army yet recorded.

This vagueness ensured that Sunny merged easily into the Somerset team. Suspicions of Oriental mysticism raised by Derek Taylor (who says he once played for Leyton Orient) vanished. Someone who is defeated by a hand-brake does not for long remain on a pedestal.

So the gloves are off, and Sunil is teased and cajoled with the rest. His nickname is 'Swoop', a loose description of his fielding at mid-on. Where most fieldsmen hurry towards the ball in order to intercept it more easily, 'Swoop' ambles along, leaving it until the last possible moment to dart out a hand to effect the stop. Naturally this produces tremendous applause from the crowd, accompanied by an outrageously innocent smile from Gavaskar.

In the field Sunny does retain a little of the majesty of the Raj. He never dives. Apparently it is dangerous to dive in India, for fear of the tetanus injections that follow. And 'Swoop' is too old a dog to learn new tricks, or so he says.

Sunil Gavaskar is well able to cope with the company of other cricketers. Though he does not smoke, drink or swear (Botham says he once exclaimed 'Oh, my goodness', but Botham's been watching 'It Ain't 'Arf 'Ot Mum' too often!) 'Swoop' soon captures the atmosphere of a dressing-room and thrives in it.

For, in a mellow, gentle way, Gavaskar gives as good as he gets. It did not take him long to remark upon the stark resemblance between the Taunton dressing-room and the Black Hole of Calcutta. More often his humour is the humour of understatement. After several severe maulings he suggested that 'our bowling seems more friendly than theirs'. And with Ian Botham on 198 one tea-time he produced a calculator and informed Ian that he was on course for 418 not out—more if he accelerated once his eye was in!

No doubt had 'Swoop' served in the court of Henry VIII he would not have ranted and raved about the iniquities of the Pope. He would have slipped up to Henry and speculated as to whether 'Popes aren't getting a bit big for their mitres nowadays?' The seeds sown, he would then have been withdrawn.

This quiet underplaying of personality may be an Indian trait, a product of a humble philosophy. Certainly Sunil is a remarkably balanced individual. He does hold some extraordinary views, though. He regards cricket as 'only a game', defeat as 'not the end of the world'. He even has a regular job. Nor is he especially impressed by his own achievements, regarding success and failure as the playthings of the fates.

Were he English, of course, one would assume he had had an unfortunate accident as a youth. *Cricket only a game?* There are limits to man's credulity. And Sunil has brought his family with him. Not many international cricketers take their parents, wife and son with them on their travels. Some travel specifically to escape from their entourage!

But the Gavaskars are enjoying Taunton immensely. Little Rohan (4), whose hero is Viv Richards, fairly revels in playing with the children of 'Swoop's' colleagues. He joins in fielding practices with gusto, bats left-handed (preferably with a Jumbo—Viv uses one) and pops into the dressing-room when he's lonely—braving even the dark threats of fierce Uncle Ian to seek 'Papa's' solace.

Maybe it is not surprising that the Family Gavaskar came to Somerset. Taunton must be an oasis of calm after the strain of life in Bombay. Sunil receives 85 fan letters a day at home (Rohan gets 5!). He dare not venture into the streets for fear of being mobbed by admirers. A Sunday League game, the most exacting cricket he will play this season, must be like a hit in the park after India v. Pakistan at Madras.

Small wonder that Sunil relishes a few months of relaxed cricket as part of a modest county team playing in a mild provincial town.

Meeting this gentle man it is easy to forget his marvellous Test record. That ready smile must conceal nerves of steel, for Gavaskar has scored well-nigh 6,000 Test runs, including 23 centuries. He has formed the backbone of Indian batting for a decade. This in a country where cricket is followed with fanatical zeal, where success can bring the hazards of worship and failure the pain of ignominy.

No wonder that he is happier when someone else is carrying the burdens of leadership. He has enough curry on his plate already. Much more relaxing to be an ordinary member of the team, able to release tension once the day's deeds are done. And no wonder that 'Swoop' is a little impractical. The atmosphere of calm chaos that pervades his life must help restore his powers. As the fates blow in the wind it is fortunate that Gavaskar has that self-deprecating humour, too. If he, for too long, took things to heart his burden might seem profoundly heavy.

In any event, for all his foibles in everyday life, as a batsman Gavaskar is superbly professional. His method has survived the most rigorous examination. Runs have been scored against Roberts and Holding in West Indies, Snow and Botham in England, Thomson in Australia and Underwood in India. Sunil is a craftsman, master of the techniques of his profession. And, as a craftsman, he continually re-examines his methods and

makes minor adjustments. To improve his performance on English pitches
Sunny decided to use a larger, heavier bat. This helps him to stand upright.
And he plays the ball a little later in England, lest he be defeated by un-
predictable movement.

These are the changes made to counter particular threats. They are the
product of careful thought by a batsman who knows he must attend to the
details of his science.

With a performance as excellent as his there is no doubt that Gavaskar
is extraordinarily gifted. Yet defining his peculiar talent is not easy. His
personality is too self-effacing for his batting to be too dramatic. Nor does
Sunil adopt an idiosyncratic stroke as his hallmark (as with Richards' on-
drive, Boycott's square-cut and Zaheer's off-drive). He scores without fuss
and at his own pace. His excellence lies in his mastery of the simple principles of batting as they have been handed down the generations. His head
is always still. He watches the ball with the utmost care. He bats with
devoted concentration, rejecting any laziness of the mind. If he chooses
to take a risk it is calculated, not an undisciplined reaction to a tense
situation.

Somerset folk are enjoying Gavaskar's visit. His batting is discussed from
Charlton Adam to Farrington Gurney. Peter Robinson, our coach, is
pleased too. Until Sunny arrived most youngsters seemed either to smash
good length balls through mid-wicket (à la Richards), or despatch them
over extra-cover (à la Botham) or play and miss at them (à la modesty
forbids). Discriminating between the good ball and the bad is creeping
back into favour this season, and Peter is sleeping a lot better!

And this season has settled one longstanding argument between Vic
Marks and myself. Vic, a little on the short side, argues that big men have
an advantage at the crease in that their reach is so much greater. I, on the
other hand, as a man of some stature, hold that the small batsman has a
tremendous, almost overwhelming advantage in that it is so much easier
for him to hook, cut and use his feet.

Watching Gavaskar, I think I'll win the day. Indeed, the only confusion
now felt at Taunton is why our reserve wicket-keeper Trevor Gard, a man
of similar size to Sunil, cannot bat as well or hit as powerfully!

Everyone at Taunton will be sad when 'Swoop' returns to Bombay. It's
been fun studying him, and fun trying to detect the tough, determined
core that lurks behind those humorous, faintly mischievous eyes.

(1980)

Hammond used to take a breather: you should too

Colin Cowdrey on the art of relaxing at the wicket—by courtesy of Wally Hammond

Eighty-five Test matches brought him more than 7,000 runs. 'The greatest off-side player the game has ever seen,' Sir Donald Bradman assured me. 'There never could be a finer slip fielder,' said Denis Compton. 'He could be a more than useful fast-medium bowler in the Maurice Tate vein, but he never really put his mind to it,' said Leslie Ames.

I saw very little of him but I shall always treasure the memory of him striding through the Long Room, down the pavilion steps, gliding to the middle to the acclaim of the throng, cap slightly to one side, a very cream shirt and his own particular characteristic, his alone, a corner of blue handkerchief sticking out of his right pocket.

If Hobbs was the master craftsman, Bradman the greatest run maker, Walter Reginald Hammond was for me, as a schoolboy, everything that a cricketer should be.

When I toured South Africa in 1957 I spent several days with him in Durban. He was quiet, self-effacing, ready to praise the present-day cricketer and full of understanding of the batsman's difficulties as he has to cope with more and more leg-side bowling accruing from the change in the l.b.w. law.

I was startled by a question he put to me concerning the day that I scored my first Test hundred at Melbourne. A strange thing occurred when I had reached 64 in the middle of the afternoon, with the ball getting old and the conditions all in favour of the batsman. I failed to score for 40 minutes which to me, of course, seemed an eternity. At long last I plucked up courage and lofted Ian Johnson over mid-on's head for four. Mid-on got his fingers to it but the luck was with me. It was a narrow escape and I cannot bear to think what my captain would have said for getting out with such a suicidal stroke.

Apparently, Wally Hammond had listened to this on the radio. Out of the blue, looking me straight in the eye, he said, 'Tell me how you came to get stuck on 64 for 40 minutes?' My heart sank a little. Here was a rocket, I thought, from the great man. Whilst I was preparing to answer, his face softened into a smile and he added, 'I know exactly how you felt. I lived every minute with you and I could not help shouting into my radio, "Take a single."'

He went on to enlighten me further about building an innings. He recalled how he used to be prepared to take a breather every now and again throughout a long innings. It was not just a matter of relaxation after a bout of running between the wickets for, obviously, he was just about the fittest man ever to play cricket. But, he maintained, to play exciting strokes against good bowling, in a tense match in front of a big crowd, set the heart racing a bit. This was human nature. After a spell of quick scoring he had disciplined himself, to quieten down for a few moments so as to be in full control. Then, with a smile, he turned to me and said, 'Mind you, I used not to let my breather go on for 40 minutes, like you at Melbourne.' This is always the danger of course, he went on, that having taken the bowler by the scruff of the neck, it was not necessarily the best policy to relax the grip. But in my early days I got myself out so many times just when I had reduced the bowlers to their knees, that I trained myself to pause, every now and again, for a breather. If by doing so the bowlers seemed to find their feet again and started to bowl a length, I would then seek to re-establish myself with a single.

'I was very pleased,' he continued, 'to see you stop for five or ten minutes on 64, for I felt that this would set you into the right frame of mind for a hundred, but when fifteen minutes became twenty, the situation cried out for you to take a single.'

I have never forgotten this conversation. In my earlier Test matches I was very inclined to get stuck when in full flight. Nowadays, when I look like being bogged down, I say to myself, 'Where would W.R. push his single now?'

Whenever I watch Bob Barber in full flow resembling C. J. Barnett (but for being left-handed) I cannot help feeling that he could benefit from the Hammond advice. I saw Kent's Michael Denness in brilliant form in both innings against New Zealand at Maidstone. Both times he got himself out in the eighties. Did he, I wonder, get just a little too excited?

Most school teams have a gifted stroke-maker, even if they have not a great player. I am sure he will admit to getting himself out more times than he is got out. He gets himself out by being a little too ambitious, maybe, as a result of over confidence. He has allowed his own excitement to run riot.

Wally Hammond never inferred that you should stop playing strokes. He meant, rather, that after the thrill of producing a series of good strokes you should pause and relax for a few moments to calm down and then restart the flow with a single. For stroke-makers this is the best way to build an innings.

Women at play

Netta Rheinberg on women cricketers—'they cannot be grown at will like a field of wheat'

It is intriguing to look back over the playing of cricket by women during the two and a quarter centuries of its existence and some interesting facts emerge from its evolution. At the start the game was played by women, as distinct from ladies. The sponsors of the matches played by the women provided prizes for the victors, a regale of tea, a barrel of ale, a plum cake, or sometimes all three. Many of the games were riotous and the spectators of whom there were usually upwards of a thousand, were inclined to be bawdy. They gambled, swore, fought and even on occasion broke up the game. The sponsoring of these events, fashionable then in the eighteenth century, and becoming more and more sought after today in the twentieth century, indicates that the wheel has turned full circle and not only in this way. In olden times the social amenities following these functions played a distinct part. After the game the company of both sexes, bosomy beldames and roistering males, gathered together, drank tea and ale, and danced. Today a cricket match played by women is not deemed complete without its gathering of mixed company afterwards and the imbibing which goes with it.

In between these two eras a century apart, there is a different scene. Ladies, not women, played the game and many blue-blooded clashes took place on the grounds of the stately homes of England. These ladies, no less than the original women of Hambledon or Bramley, had watched their menfolk play and knew a good deal about cricket. However, in contrast to their earlier sisters they took the arranging of such events into their own feminine hands. They pioneered the first women's cricket club and behind the scenes, influenced, cricketwise, their fathers, brothers and sons quite considerably. The cricket, too, was of a different nature. No more a spectacle put on for the amusement of onlookers, it was played with an enthusiasm and a genuine liking for the game, mostly inherited. Prizes and rewards for the victors vanished and there is no record of social gatherings being an added incentive.

These ladies of the stately homes and their friends were the forerunners of the women who play in this country today and who started to organise and administer the game for women officially 40 years ago. During this time the pioneering lady players have slowly but perceptibly changed into efficiently administered and organised women cricketers, still exclusively running their own show but again willing to accept outside help and sponsorship.

It must be realised that women who wish to play cricket, and there are today still plenty, have first of all to make a considerable sacrifice in terms of time and expense. No other team game in which women take part lasts a minimum of three and a half hours, to which must be added travelling time. In these days of mini skirt and maxi opportunity a girl will not devote precious time to cricket, even though she may love the game, unless there is a prospect of social comforts and friendship at the end. For these and other reasons connected with the complex life of today the membership of the Women's Cricket Association is decreasing. This decrease of women cricket players is no new manifestation. It has happened before and will happen again. In early Victorian and in Edwardian times very little cricket was played by women. The pendulum will undoubtedly swing forwards again when the time is ripe. Meanwhile, any overdose of administration or interference aimed at correction may do more harm than good.

Women cricketers cannot be grown at will like a field of wheat. With good leadership, encouragement, and the building up of confidence they seed themselves and thereafter have to be tended as carefully as any hothouse plants until they are well established. Gone are the confident, smiling ladies who strode briskly with determined air to the wicket and clouted the ball to all quarters of the ground, or bowled a ball which literally whistled through the air. In her place there strolls today, bat or ball in hand, an attractive athlete, technically far better qualified, more knowledgeable, but far less sure of herself. Her bowling is much the same in pace and variety as practically all her foes' or friends'; her batting style is pleasant but shows no individuality. She has the will to win, but not at any cost. None will deny that she needs very badly encouragement, confidence, and leadership. Without transfusions of these, her cricket is bound to remain somewhat anaemic.

The difficulties which beset women's cricket are much the same as those which beset men's cricket. Fortunately there are as yet no professional women cricketers and, praise be, it is unlikely there ever will be. Women players have always been true amateurs, even though today this term is liberally interpreted. The administration of the game from club level upwards is short of recruits. Secretaries, treasurers, team secretaries and the like do not come forward readily for these honorary posts and many have to be talked into them. Nevertheless those who do shoulder these responsibilities do a fine job of work behind the scenes, and it is surprising what is achieved in the way of efficient organisation, a great deal of it remaining unrecognised.

Women cricketers suffer, as do our men colleagues, from a veritable sea of official words and paper. By the time we have extricated ourselves we are unable to see the ball clearly. Many of our younger members complain that they do not understand all this paper output and it seems all the more ironic that it is for them that the legislations and schemes are devised. A committee of junior players working alongside the main executive committee and chaired by an experienced older person might well help to clear away a deal of clutter which older committee members seem to create around themselves.

The Women's Cricket Association no longer has a majority of contemporary players on its executive committee, those who have first-hand experience of all the problems. This is a pity. When all is said and done, the Association was founded 'for the furtherance of cricket among women and girls,' in other words simply to enable those who wish to play to do so. In the desperate, competitive, high-speed profit-seeking sportswoman's world today, we should do well to remember this quite simple fact.

(1968)

Bill Hudson lost 100 schooners of beer when Walters made his hundred against the Poms

The Dungog Dasher? 'I doubt if it will stick', writes Ian Wooldridge

The frustrated poets who write newspaper headlines sweated blood to have him neatly and alliteratively labelled for life by the morning-after, but the best they could do was the Dungog Dasher and I doubt if it will stick.

For one thing Kevin Douglas Walters does not come from Dungog. For another, while 'dashing' vividly describes his first blistering scoring stroke in Test cricket, it evokes an image of a latter-day Miller destroying an attack between games of poker. Walters will never play his cricket like that.

The first physical feature that strikes one about him is a quite un-Australian paleness. The second is a baffling agelessness of face. You might guess at 25 or even 30 but at Brisbane you would have questioned or even suspected, as some actually did, his 19 years 11 months and 23 days. The effect, then, is less of a supreme athlete with a glowing Olympian presence than of an old head on young shoulders. If you glanced twice as he passed you in Regent Street you might take him for a youngish family man recently promoted to head office from Portsmouth.

You could certainly complete a long conversation with him without knowing that he had recently been promoted to the exclusive brethren of ten Australian batsmen in 100 years who have made centuries against England on their first appearance.

His speaking voice is an octave lower than Sir Donald Bradman's but he wastes about as few words. He talks in neatly rounded sentences. The same economy applies to his cricket. He stands motionless in the crease, bowls medium pace off the shortest effective run.

His apparent slightness is deceptive. He is 5 ft. 9½ in. and slender. But he weighs 11½ stone and has great physical strength. At 19 and 2 months he scored 253 for New South Wales in Adelaide and went straight back to take 7 for 63. He enjoys bowling as much as batting which perhaps, after all, is an admission of innocent youth. Otherwise, at Brisbane, there were only 48 minutes in which he looked anything less than totally calm, totally mature, totally in command of his destiny.

Those 48 minutes came as he edged his way along the precipice of the 90s. It was an unforgettable passage of cricket, played out in the rich, stained-glass hues of a lowering sub-tropical sun. Few writers of even the most lurid schoolboy fiction would have dared manufacture such an implausible climax. The interruption for drinks, the distraction of the runaway mongrel, the remorselessly tight bowling of Titmus and Allen stretching his nerve to snapping point, the near run-out at 98. . . .

It was rightly recorded in some of the most colourful writing of the tour, but it would have been less colourful had one known what was passing through his mind. 'It never occurred to me at that stage,' he said later, 'that I wouldn't get the 100. I was careful because they were bowling so well.'

He took the ovation and the acclaim of a nation as calmly as he had advanced to 90. He has made 100 on his first appearance at each new level of cricket except for the New South Wales state side. This, quite amazingly, was only his twentieth first-class match yet failure seemed barely to have occurred to him.

He knows precisely where he is going. There was, for example, no press of businessmen at his door the following morning, out-bidding one another for the exclusive rights to endorse their bats with the Douglas Walters autograph. Those arrangements had been completed a year before. It is a strangely sophisticated picture for a boy whose background is authentically provincial and unprivileged. The Dungog of the headlines is merely the nearest railhead, some 130 miles north-west of Sydney. Walters' home is

at Marshdale, still deeper in the sticks. It is claimed that the entire population of 112 listened to every ball of his innings.

He is the third of four children born to Ted and Fay Walters on their
13,000 acre property. By Australian, let alone Texan standards it was
prosperous enough to have supported a son at Timbertop. But Walters
read the three r's at a rural school, left at 15 and milked the cows. It is
perhaps this parallel, more than any other, that will burden him with comparison with Bradman. Yet the lines veer sharply apart when you probe
his cricketing education.

By 16 he was a prodigy, being slipped into the New South Wales Country
Districts side to make 0 and 17 against Ted Dexter's team at Tamworth.
But he cannot recall when he first held a bat and denies any compulsive
urge to play cricket at all. 'I was probably about nine,' he said. 'I remember
we rolled out a pitch on the farm and some of the lads used to come in. It's
as vague as that, I'm afraid.'

Even while his name was spreading through school and junior cricket
there were few privileges. His first visit to a Test match was to watch
Goddard's South Africans for a single day in Sydney. His second visit was
to score 155 in Brisbane. By then, however, the talent net had caught him.
He landed in safe and experienced hands, moved to Sydney to work in a
sports store and play grade cricket with Cumberland and Richie Benaud.

Despite eye-catching feats in his first full Sheffield Shield season he was
left home when Simpson led Australia's 1965 side to West Indies. His next
chance came against M.C.C. for New South Wales. He took it with a
century and a fortnight later was opening 93 telegrams on the occasion of
his maiden Test 100. The one he valued most came from Norman O'Neill
who, having made 31 runs in four innings at the start of the season, was
home in Sydney. Another came from a Canberra opportunist who had
rushed from the maternity home to wire: 'It's a boy and we're naming
him Douglas.'

Back home in Marshdale, Bill Hudson lost 100 schooners of beer when
he bet that Kevin Douglas Walters could not make 100 first time out
against the Poms. Only when you have seen him bat and tested his self-
possession do you realise how rash that wager really was.

(1966).

On watching cricket

'One of life's major pleasures', by Norman Birkett

There must be many who read these works to whom watching cricket is one of life's major pleasures. For all such, it matters little whether the ground is Lord's or Old Trafford, Canterbury or the village green; the mere watching of cricket is enough. The emotions may vary, but the underlying sense of complete felicity is the same. Why this should be so, nobody has ever been able to explain. Just as the elusive charm of cricket is scarcely to be captured in words, so the joy of watching cricket is quite incommunicable. In his latest book of essays, Mr A. A. Milne, who has himself given so much pleasure to cricket lovers everywhere, is content to say in all simplicity:

'Watching cricket has given me more happiness than any other inactivity in which I have engaged. Lord's on a warm day, with a bottle, a mixed bag of sandwiches and a couple of spare pipes in a despatch case, and I don't care who is playing whom. Cricket is the only game I can enjoy without taking sides.'

It may be said with some confidence, that for all sorts and conditions of men, there is no game that gives the same deep and abiding satisfaction to the watcher as does the game of cricket; and the rich and glowing literature of the game bears eloquent and impressive witness to the fact. For cricket rarely disappoints its devotees wherever the scene be set. Even in distant lands, when cricket is far, far away, and the blissful sound of ball on bat is never heard, however ardently and passionately it may be wished for, the Englishman may be found searching with loyal and desperate haste for the air-mail edition of *The Times* in order to set his mind at rest about the scores in the county championship, to 'see how Hutton's gone on', or whether Surrey has fallen from its high estate. And when the cricket disdains the English winter and journeys south to the Indies or the Antipodes, the memory of days in the sun is kept alive with almost keener zest than when cricket is to be seen for the asking. For some of the greatest pleasures of cricket are in retrospect, when the dark days of December are lit up with the memories of high summer and the great moments of seasons long past. To recall Hobbs as he once was, in all the pride of his majestic supremacy; to remember Bradman, emerging from the Pavilion at Lord's on a June evening to enthrall the mighty crowd with an innings of supreme beauty; to live again those moments of sheer ecstasy when the last pair smote the bowling to all parts of the field; to see an English captain return-

ing to the pavilion with the cheers of an adoring multitude sounding in his
ears for a display of skill and courage that saved the day; all these things
have an added savour and thrill, and they are the rewards of the watcher
of cricket that nothing can ever take away. How well the Rev. John Milford
knew this experience:

'Peep through the shutter of my snug parlour, and behold me and envy.
There is the small oak table (it is now mine), with the pint of Geneva and
the jug of hot water, and the snuff-box smiling on it. One cricket bat . . .
for occasional exemplifications, and Harry Bentley's volume of the matches
is open beside it. . . . We fill the tumblers anew: and for the hundredth
time I ask: "What was young Small's favourite hit? How did John Wells
get his runs?" '

But though the devotion of the watcher of cricket has its exceeding great
reward, the active participation of the watcher means much to the essential
life of cricket. There is a spark between the player and the watcher, that
must be touched off, if the great and unforgettable moments are to be
achieved, and the full thrill is to be gained and enjoyed.

This is not to condone, of course, the vulgarian playing to the gallery;
but nobody who has once been present at Lord's on a warm Test match
Saturday will deny the crowd its most important part in the atmosphere.
For the crowd is the best barometer of the play; it is often more sensitive
to the gravity or humour of a situation than the players themselves. Many
a captain must have caught a warning of disaster or success from the
attitude of the crowd. In two matters only is the crowd infallibly and most
magnificently deceived: one is the bump ball, which, if caught, never fails
to make the watchers cheer as for the fall of a wicket, particularly when
the batsman is a humorist like Hassett who begins a sad and dejected walk
to the pavilion, and then turns back to the crease: the other is the over-
throw, which to most watchers means a certain extra run whatever the
circumstances, and the batsmen are urged to take it with the impatience
and exuberance that more properly belongs to the last thrilling moments
of the Derby.

The response of the crowd to the thrilling moments of a match or to the
memorable occasion can be moving in a way that sometimes escapes the
event itself. The thunder of applause that greets a great batsman as he
comes down the pavilion steps has power to transform and transmute into
something dramatic and memorable an innings whose significance in the
match may be quite small. And was there ever such an occasion when a
batsman stood at 99 when the crowd did not strain for the extra single with
much greater intensity than the batsman himself? But the watchers can
be rebellious too. Happily the days are gone when the crowd invaded the

field as they did at Sydney in 1879, and not only assaulted Lord Harris, but so threatened the English players that they had 'difficulty in reaching the safety of the pavilion'. The modern psychological weapon of the slow clap is no doubt much more effective than any number of bottles thrown on to the pitch. But it is rare that the crowd misjudges the batsman. Usually it finds out with amazing accuracy whether the cricket might or might not be brighter. Occasionally, of course, the stupid and ill-mannered parade their stupidity and ill-manners by clapping an anxious batsman scoring slowly on a treacherous wicket. But the crowd is after all composed of human beings, and is as remarkable for the variety of its component parts as for anything else. Indeed, Lord's on a fine day in summer is a sight indescribable even by John Arlott, our most persistent and attractive observer of eccentricities and human foibles.

It is usual to speak of the crowd as a whole, but the enjoyment of individuals is a joy to behold as they watch the progress of the game. There are those whose eyes are permanently glued to their binoculars, and those who sit in a kind of happy trance enjoying the sun and the clouds and the moving players. There are the small boys with score books finding some new and exciting record with every ball, as Herbert Farjeon once so amusingly described; and there are ageing men with sun hats made from the morning newspaper. There are even those who live in a kind of fearful expectation, half horror, half ecstasy, that they might yet catch one of the fashionable hitter's mighty sixes as it climbs the sky and comes to rest in one of the stands. The enjoyment of a cricket crowd is never to be defined or limited; it takes every conceivable form. Even amongst those who never watch a match there may often be an inexplicable affection for cricket. There are few Englishmen who come suddenly upon a game of cricket deep in the green summer fields without experiencing a certain illogical catching of the throat, that betokens an affection for cricket, deeper than mere enthusiasm for the game and respect for its players, but which appears to be one of the happiest of our native instincts. Sir James Barrie was conscious of this deepseated feeling when he said in a famous speech:

'It has been said of the unseen army of the dead, on their everlasting march, that when they are passing a rural cricket ground, the Englishman falls out of the ranks for a moment to look over the gate and smile.'

(1952)

[William Norman, 1st Baron Birkett, was one of the world's foremost lawyers. He played cricket for Emmanuel College, Cambridge, and retained a lifelong affection for the game.]

Fred Titmus

*Gordon Ross asked the man why on earth he had been chosen to tour at the
age of forty-two. He replied, 'Well, I suppose it is because I have just kept on
bowling'*

At a time when the principal subject of discussion among cricketers was
the game's most complicated player, and his withdrawal from the party to
tour Australasia this winter, it was a breath of fresh air to be talking to
the most uncomplicated cricketer of them all, Fred Titmus, who, when
asked why it was he thought he had been chosen to tour at the age of 42
(he was 42 on November 24) replied simply and succinctly, 'Well, I suppose
it is because I have just kept on bowling.'

Those few words are not the first that came into his head; they are a
philosophy; they are, in essence, the way he plays his cricket, simply but
effectively. Spin bowling is a subtle art of flight and turn, and variation of
pace, but to a great extent dependent for its success upon the state of the
pitch, and Titmus believes that the greatest single factor in the decline of
the craft of spin is the pitches, which, largely because of the excess of top-
dressing, have become slower and slower. 'I find I spend half my life
bowling uphill these days,' he says; 'the pitches have been built up so
much, and when you do get one that suits you, you need to be Derek
Underwood's pace to take advantage of it, as the ball rarely flies, it dollies
up instead.'

It is widely thought that one-day cricket has been the villain of the piece
in the spin bowler's life. Titmus does not share this view. There was a
phobia, he admits, among captains to rule out spin bowlers altogether when
the Gillette Cup began; they were simply dropped from the side; time
proved the error of these ways, and, except in the Sunday slog, the spin
bowler can often be the most economical proposition; bowlers like Norman
Gifford, Derek Underwood, David Hughes and Jack Simmons have, at
times, proved worth their weight in gold.

How much does Fred Titmus study the strengths and weaknesses of
batsmen? Not as much as many might imagine. 'It matters more what I
am doing than what the batsman is doing. If I am bowling well, he can
only hit me in certain directions, and I set a field accordingly. I like to feel
that I am dictating what is happening, more than the batsman.'

Titmus is an interesting cricketer because in his early days he had
precious little coaching. His idol was Denis Compton, but as a footballer,
and it was only the fact that Denis played cricket as well that served to

stimulate a passionate interest in cricket. When watching Middlesex, Titmus was fascinated by Jack Young, and likes to think that he is a right-handed version of him. In fact there was a time when he had that little hop in his run-up that Jack's did, though somewhere along the line Titmus lost it. Jack Young became his mentor, and what he said was canon law. He rarely told you how to bowl, he told you what to bowl.

Titmus feels that the players of his early days were more willing pupils of experience than they are, perhaps, today, though this is just a passing comment and not a condemnation. The discipline was more rigid, of course, especially if you happened to have Walter Robins as captain! . . . but you were all the better for it.

His selection for this tour was no surprise to the connoisseur; whatever his age may be, he just happens to be the best off-spin bowler in the country. Tours in the past have been crucial turning-points in his career. On the 1962–3 tour of Australia and New Zealand he was one of the three off-spinners chosen, a selection pretty strongly criticised on the grounds of bad balance. The three were Allen, Illingworth and Titmus, with Titmus not expected to be the front-runner, but as events turned out, he was. He took 21 wickets in the Tests, one more than Trueman, achieved a batting average of 36·40, and was bracketed with Ken Barrington as the outstanding success of the tour. This established him as an England player and he has now played in forty-nine Test matches with the strongest possibility of more to come, when it had seemed in tragic circumstances that his Test career was at an end.

Having played in the first two Tests in West Indies in 1967–8, Fred Titmus was involved in a boating accident in Barbados which caused the loss of four of his toes on his left foot, which had become caught in the screw of a small boat, placed in the middle of the craft and, contrary to regulations, without a guard. He returned home with his future as a cricketer considerably in doubt, let alone as a Test cricketer. Ray Illingworth moved into the England side, was successful, and despite a remarkable recovery by Titmus, the place was never there for him again, but as he says himself, he 'just carried on bowling', and now with this fairy-tale ending.

E. M. Wellings wrote at the time: 'So, injury almost certainly ended the Test career of Titmus. A total of 1,311 runs and 146 wickets are witness of the value to England of his gritty cricket. He scaled the heights during the 1962–3 tour of Australia and that of India a year later. Though suffering from nagging shoulder trouble, he still held his own in big cricket and was Cowdrey's vice-captain in West Indies.'

At school at the William Ellis School, Highgate, Fred Titmus made his debut for Middlesex in 1949 at the age of sixteen; his promotion from the ground staff to the Middlesex XI had a story-book touch about it. It happened in June, 1949, when Middlesex, with Robertson, Compton, Edrich, Mann and Young engaged in the first Test match against New Zealand at Lord's, found themselves short for their game against Somerset at Bath. Walter Robins and 'Gubby' Allen went out to the nets to have a look at the aspiring talent being coached by Fowler and Watkins, and collected Titmus.

So instead of selling scorecards at the Test, he was in the Middlesex side, aged 16 years and 6 months. His career was subsequently interrupted by National Service in the Royal Air Force, but he got plenty of cricket for the R.A.F. and Combined Services, and his first trip in an aeroplane piloted by Bob Wilson, now secretary of Nottinghamshire, was en route to play cricket for Combined Services.

The summer of 1955 saw Titmus, at the age of 22, establish himself among the leading all-rounders by recording his first 'double' in remarkable fashion. His total of wickets bounded to 191, average 16·31, and he nearly doubled his runs by scoring 1,235, with a highest of 104. His tally of 158 wickets in all matches for Middlesex beat the previous county record set up by A. E. Trott, with 154, as far back as 1900.

Now he has done the 'double' eight times. He has taken more wickets for Middlesex than any other bowler; he did the hat-trick against Somerset at Weston-super-Mare in 1966, he took four wickets in six balls for England against New Zealand at Leeds in 1965, and in the same summer shared in a sixth-wicket record partnership for Middlesex of 227 with Clive Radley against the South Africans at Lord's. He has taken over 450 catches.

There is hardly room on his record card to mention that he also played soccer for Hendon and Watford, but it is as a cricketer of supreme qualities that he will long be remembered by the habitués of Lord's; when Titmus is gone, a piece of Lord's will be gone, but at the moment we are not thinking of the sunset of his illustrious career, but of new brave deeds he might perform this winter. We all wish him well.

(1974)

Australia v. England: 1974
A tornado named Thomson

John Woodcock on the bowler who became a face, a threat, and finally a destroyer

England's batsmen endured their worst battering for a long time in losing the first Test match in Brisbane by 166 runs. The reason for this was a treacherous pitch on which Australia's new fast bowler Jeff Thomson took 9 for 105, besides breaking Amiss's thumb and inflicting more bruises upon the England team than their masseur can have cared to count.

The pitch had been prepared, or underprepared, by Brisbane's Lord Mayor, more a benevolent dictator than a professional curator. In the match against Queensland and the Test match, on Alderman Jones's pitches, 36 out of 75 wickets fell to catches in the gully, at slip, or behind the wicket. It was not unlike Lord's in the days of the ridge, when the ball used to fly unpredictably.

Against most sides England would have fancied their chance; but not against Thomson. What he and to a lesser extent Lillee achieved in the way of lift, Lever and Willis were unable to match. Although nasty, England's two never endangered life and limb in the same way as Thomson and Lillee. There was as much short bowling from both sides as there can have been in an Anglo-Australian Test match since the Bodyline series of 1932–3. It was a bad start to the rubber, and for England a disconcerting one.

England did well enough on the first day which Australia finished at 219 for 6. On the second, Australia reached 309 after being 229 for 8, and England had their first taste of Thomson. On the third, Greig kept England in the game with a defiant hundred in which he did his best to provoke the Australian bowlers to get cross with him. On the fourth, England contained Australia effectively in their second innings, with some good, tight bowling and unflagging fielding, until Walters and Marsh added a fast 98 together as a prelude to Chappell's declaration. With bad light stopping play before Thomson and Lillee could get up steam on that fourth evening, England began the last day needing to score 323 to win or to bat for six hours to draw, which, on that pitch as it was, was their main objective.

It was never going to be easy, especially with Edrich, who had lasted longer than most in the first innings, able to bat only after a pain-killing injection for a badly bruised hand.

Quote from The Times :

The day began to the echo of some unedifying remarks made by Lillee on television last night. The idea of the bouncer, as he uses it, is to hit the batsman 'somewhere between the rib cage and the stomach'. That is what he said, and he had written it previously in a book. Thomson is already on record as saying that he enjoys felling a batsman with a bouncer. This is the talk of the underworld, not of Test cricketers.

In the event England only twice, and then fleetingly, looked as though they might survive: first during a partnership of 48 between Fletcher and Denness, and then when Underwood stayed with Knott for seventy minutes. There was less than two hours left when Underwood was eighth out, and when Hendrick was bowled by Thomson Australia had won with eighty minutes to spare. It seemed reasonable at the time to hope that if England, without batting well and on a pitch which turned Thomson into a killer, could get to within eighty minutes of a draw, they would do a lot better when they came upon a better pitch.

Australia's victory was only their third in seventeen Test matches against England in Australia since 1959. It was England's fifth defeat since the war in Brisbane, where they last won in 1936-7.

Thomson burst upon the scene with a suddenness that can seldom have been equalled by a fast bowler in Test cricket. Within a fortnight he became first a face, then a threat (in the Queensland match) and finally a destroyer.

We had hardly heard of him when we arrived in Australia, except as a young man who liked the taste of blood—or was said to—but who had failed to get a place in the New South Wales side for most of the previous season. By the time we left Brisbane for Perth he was the talk of Australia. On the day following the first Test match he said he still had a lot up his sleeve, which remained to be seen. Lillee was nothing like as fast as Thomson, except for the occasional ball in England's first innings; but he was still fast enough to make a formidable partner for Thomson, and it is in pairs that fast bowlers hunt most successfully. It was therefore a side under siege that Cowdrey flew out to join between the first Test and the second.

The Brisbane Test was watched by larger crowds than in 1970-1 (the aggregate attendance was 62,079 as against 42,376). The ground had been transformed, under the auspices of the State government (prompted by the Lord Mayor) and with some help from the greyhounds which now run there once a week. It has grown into a fine sporting 'complex', unrecognisable from the corrugated roofs and low sheds and grass banks of not twenty years ago.

In another way the first Test match was different from others recently played at the Gabba. It never rained, from first to last, and it was seldom humid. Even when the temperature reached the nineties it was not unbearably hot. All this aside, though, England were pleased when the time came to leave Brisbane. What with the Lord Mayor's pitch and the advent of Thomson and the loss of a Test match with heavy casualties it had not provided them with the best start to the series.

(1975)

Alec Bedser

Ted Dexter—not the world's most outstanding extrovert—takes on one who is thrifty with his views

Getting to know Alec Bedser is not the hardest task in the world if you are able to spend a modicum of time with him. He is ready enough to voice his opinions and, in common with most successful men, has firmly set ideas on what should be done for the best in any given circumstances.

If you want him to react quickly and hotly then you need only mention loafers, prima donnas, and barrack-room lawyers—in something like that order—to draw his full firepower. If such people have the temerity to wander into first-class cricket and, furthermore, expect to play for England, then they inevitably become that much more disagreeable to him.

Another pet subject that raises his blood pressure is the politician or civil servant who interferes with the normal process of running his office equipment business; but, all in all, he is stern rather than harsh in his judgments.

Incidentally, anyone who happened to see and hear Bill Shankly deliver his televised New Year message to us all, prescribing 'work, hard work' as the panacea for 1975, will unwittingly have had a further insight into the mind of 'Big Al'. It might have been the chairman of selectors himself talking!

As I write, he is away managing the M.C.C. team in Australia, so it is difficult to provide an up-to-date sample of his views (his comments on the bikini-clad girls tangling with Tony Greig on the Melbourne pitch are the sort I had in mind) but since Alec rarely changes his position I feel fairly safe in relying on past material as still dependable.

As a schoolboy I watched him bowl to Bradman. As a new boy to county cricket I had the nerve to hit him for six at Hove when he was on the point of retirement. We met again when he became a Test selector in 1962 and travelled as assistant manager to Australia of the M.C.C. team which I had the luck to captain.

Alec has always been proud of his arduous apprenticeship as a bowler with Surrey. He believes in learning the hard way, and this attitude explains his quiet, almost diffident approach to his new roles.

As an ex-professional cricketer under successive ex-amateur chairmen such as Gubby Allen, Walter Robins, and Doug Insole, it was probably some time before anyone thought of him as likely material for the senior position. The factor that contributed most to his assuming the chair was probably the success of his business and its merging into a bigger group, which left him more free at a time when fewer and fewer nominations for the selection committee were being put forward. It was the old story, for better or worse, of being in the right place at the right time.

Like all those who held the office before him, he has had his share of successes and his failures too. For instance, the inspired choice of Ray Illingworth to captain England must be set against the problems raised by the presence in the team of Mike Denness.

But more so than any chairman in my time he seems increasingly to hold sole power and sole responsibility. The fact that his colleagues on the committee of recent years have had little or no experience of Test cricket may well account for the growth of this image.

He has also simply been around for a long time, which adds weight to his position. And to cap it all he has agreed to manage the team to Australia after choosing it. If I doubt that this heaping of responsibility on to one man is for the best, it is only because no one individual can claim to possess every quality—and Alec Bedser is surely no exception.

J. J. Warr, his biographer in *The World of Cricket* (general editor E. W. Swanton; Michael Joseph, 1966), writes of 'an endearing aura of pessimism' which permeated his cricket. It is a trait which persists today and is not necessarily ideal when it comes to encouraging men, young or old, to play above themselves in a Test match. Perspiration always did come a long way ahead of inspiration in the Bedser vocabulary, which is why, no doubt, he became the great bowler he was without ever threatening to develop as a batsman.

To be blunt, I think the whole business of batting constitutes a fair-sized blind spot to our present chairman. Perhaps Freud could explain it as the natural result of spending so many years at the opposite end of the pitch. Perhaps he simply envied the likes of me our comparatively easy life, if that's the way he saw it. All I know is that with the exception of Dennis Amiss his record as a discoverer of batting talent is lamentable. Someone sitting at home reading the county averages could have picked

England's batsmen equally accurately for the past few years. He and his co-selectors may stress the importance of actually watching county matches, but they never seem to see anything that the scorebook can't tell them. All this despite the recorded view of a more successful chairman in this respect, Gubby Allen (*Wisden*, 1962), that 'it is sound policy to put faith in character and class if it is within reach rather than in a successful record in county cricket'.

It is cold comfort to know that the first selectorial venture into the non-specifics of character and class reintroduced Colin Cowdrey on to the stage at least ten years past his prime.

All this and Boycott to boot. Something must be wrong somewhere.

There is also the chilling fact that England teams have been growing progressively older during the Bedser regime, but I am hoping that we really are seeing the apogee of that curve right now in Australia.

If you draw the conclusion from the foregoing remarks that I am really calling for Bedser's resignation, you are, I'm afraid, wrong. Not until there is a ready replacement of at least equal calibre would it make any sense at all and I see no such figure on or below the horizon at present.

If he doesn't take on too many extra roles and takes off the batting blindfold, then he can extend his enormous services to English cricket indefinitely—with my blessing!

(1975)

Fifty years—batsman and umpire

Arthur Dumbrell on the Langridges

During the tea interval of the John Player League match, Sussex v. Glamorgan, at Hastings, on July 23, 1978, Doug Insole, as Chairman of the Tests and County Cricket Board, presented John Langridge with a silver coffee-pot and a cheque to mark his fifty years in first-class cricket.

John played for Sussex from 1928 to 1955 and has been a first-class umpire to date. His story is of unusual interest.

On September 1, 1928, John Langridge of Newick, at the age of 18, made his way to the wicket with beating heart in his maiden first-class cricket match for his county of Sussex against Essex at Leyton. John, the younger brother of James Langridge, who had played in his first match four years previously, had appeared in a number of matches for Sussex Club and Ground, but first-class cricket was different, and, although this was the last Sussex match of the season, and the result would make no difference to either Essex or Sussex in the County Championship, to young John, going in at the eighth wicket down, his contribution to the score was all-important; the Sussex score was a good one, just over the 500 mark, Ted Bowley had scored 188, brother James 70 odd and 'Tich' Cornford and Duleepsinhji had each scored over 60.

John took guard as composed as possible and scored six runs before he was caught. Shortly afterwards the Sussex score closed at 538. Essex, endeavouring to pass the Sussex score, mustered 476; John's contribution to the excellent Sussex fielding was one caught, and he bowled one over from which six runs were taken but he did not get a wicket. On the last afternoon of the three-day match Sussex batted again and scored 302 for 3 wickets, Jim Parks (Sen.) making 148 and John Langridge 39. John was more than pleased with his effort and returned to Newick with a happy heart.

The next two seasons were frustrating for the young cricketer, getting few first-class matches and scoring few runs. But 1931 was far brighter. He played in more matches than his first three seasons together and scored his first century—161—against Glamorgan at Cardiff. His total runs for 1931 were 874 and his average 22·41. The following season was not quite so profitable with 689 runs, a highest of 86 and an average of 20·87. By 1933 he was getting into his stride, now as a regular opening bat with Ted Bowley, and finding, no doubt, that his previous five years apprenticeship were coming to fruition with the excellent example shown to him by Bowley. That was the year, too, of the Sussex record first-wicket partnership of 490 runs which they shared, scored at Hove against Middlesex before a large August Bank holiday crowd; a record which still stands for Sussex and was for many years the third highest opening partnership in the County Championship. In this year John made his highest first-class score of 250 not out against Glamorgan at Hove.

From 1933 runs flowed from his bat; until 1955, with the exception of the years of the Second World War when he served in the National Fire Service, he scored more than 2,000 runs on eleven occasions, and between 1,000 and 2,000 runs six times. His best year was 1949 when he scored 2,914 runs, including 12 centuries with a highest score of 234 not out and a season's average of 60·70. By the time he finished playing at the close of the 1955 season he had scored 34,152 runs for Sussex, which is still the county record. In all first-class matches he scored 34,380 runs. He made 76 centuries and had an average of 37·69 for Sussex, and 37·45 in all first-class matches. He scored more runs and centuries in first-class cricket than any other player who has never played in a Test match; it was unfortunate in that he was playing in an era when there were such batsmen as Len

Hutton, Reg Simpson, Bill Edrich, Denis Compton, Wally Hammond and others who were playing at their best, otherwise he would have been a certainty for international honours. He was, however, selected for the M.C.C. tour of India in the winter of 1939-40, a tour which had to be cancelled before it started because of the worsening European situation before the beginning of the Second World War. John Langridge was an outstanding slip fielder, making, in his career, 786 catches, a record surpassed only by F. E. Woolley, W. G. Grace, W. R. Hammond, G. A. R. Lock and D. B. Close. He made most of his catches off the bowling of his brother James, so that on 134 occasions the scorebook showed the lengthy entry 'ct. John Langridge b. James Langridge'; his next highest number of catches was 89 off the bowling of Jim Cornford.

As a bowler he was overshadowed by his brother James, but nevertheless he was a useful change bowler, often brought on to break a troublesome partnership. In 1950 *Wisden* selected John Langridge as one of the Five Cricketers of the Year, an honour which is normally reserved for international players. James Langridge was similarly honoured in 1932.

As a first-class umpire, appointed first in 1956, the year after which he retired from playing first-class cricket, John has always been held in the highest esteem; he has umpired in some of the most important matches, including seven Test matches, between 1960 and 1963. When they have attained the age of 65 years it has been the policy for first-class umpires to retire but, in 1976, when John reached that age, he was asked to continue for another year, a policy which has been extended annually to the present year. John Langridge was a player whom any county would have welcomed to their side, and it does not require much imagination to think how grateful Sussex and England would be to have a 1949 vintage John Langridge in their sides at the present time.

John is now in his Golden Jubilee of First-class Cricket, a unique and outstanding record. We don't seem to breed this type of cricketer these days.

John Langridge will no doubt remember an occasion in the late 'forties as told by George Cox. 'We had finished the match at Hove in two days—again— and were going off on the Friday to Northampton. Because I had played football for Luton, I was staying with friends nearby and went by car, while the skipper Hugh Bartlett and the rest of the team travelled by train. When they arrived at the hotel in Northampton, Hugh led the way to the reception desk, "We're the Sussex cricket team," he said. "Oh yes," replied the girl. "How many of you are there?" Hugh said, "There are ten of us—without Cox"— the girl fainted.'

(1978)

Cricketer's notes

E. W. Swanton in Australia on the vanishing, noble art of 'walking' when you're out

There is no more melancholy aspect of Anglo-Australian Test cricket since the war than the recurring angry skirmishes in print between the cricket writers covering the tours in Australia. There have been occasions when hot words have been exchanged on a nationalistic basis when Australian teams have been in England, but the trouble usually crops up over here because of the system whereby Australian papers print selected quote-backs from those sections of the English Press which give most prominence to incidents of a controversial kind whether they take place on the field or off.

It is scarcely ever fair to the writer to take a stray remark out of context, without any qualifying phrases. Yet several of these random quotes are regularly strung together, care having been taken to pick the tastiest bits from the most highly flavoured reports, and the crude, distorted whole is given as representing the views of the English Press. Small wonder that English cricket writers are commonly thought of in Australia as 'squealers' and trouble-stirrers.

It would, of course, be possible when any incident arose to present a symposium of a different sort, arranging extracts to portray the English cricket press as a singularly well-informed, objective, generous-minded body of critics. That, it may well be thought, would not be a true picture either, though it would not be such a distorted one as the other. In any case, such is the character of much of the Australian Press, and such the love-hate relationship where burning issues are concerned, there is no chance whatever of the kinder portrayal being assembled or published.

Before passing on to a closer look at the vexed subject of 'walking', which was ventilated at such tedious length at Brisbane, let me mention one recent instance of how the composite view of the English Press was misrepresented here. There were a dozen English writers at Sydney when the umpire took the action, unprecedented in Australia, of barring Jones from bowling for the rest of the innings because of damage to the pitch in the follow-through. Though the severity of the verdict was completely unexpected it was supported by, I think, all the English critics—with only minor reservations in an odd case or two—as it was by the Australians. But the only agency quote-back that was given prominence was one critical of the umpire from one of the least well-known and experienced sources.

To those of us who, tour after tour, have been doing our utmost to give a fair, unbiased picture of events this sort of thing, constantly repeated, is exasperating.

But what, again, about this walking business which twice within a few weeks has centred around Lawry, the Victorian captain? Once he was certainly out hit wicket and accepted the benefit of a thoroughly poor decision by the square-leg umpire, who was to be seen following the course of the hit instead of looking at the batsman and the stumps. (Having scored 103 at the time Lawry went on to make a further 50.) In the second case England appealed for a catch behind the wicket on the leg-side in the first over of the First Test. C. Egar (one of the best umpires in the business) declined the appeal and Lawry went on to score a little matter of 166.

These were galling experiences for M. J. K. Smith and his side, even if in the case of the catch the fielders near the bat might have been wrong and the umpire right. Everyone knows how often doubt exists in cases of catches behind the wicket, especially on the leg-side. What gave this incident its poignancy was the modern English philosophy—adopted latterly, perhaps with some reluctance, by several of the foremost players of other countries—which ordains that when a batsman is sure he has been caught he 'walks' without waiting for the decision.

On the face of it such an attitude reflects sportsmanship of a most laudable order, and one can scarcely fail to admire practical examples of it, such as that of Cowdrey who against Australia at Leeds in 1961 walked out voluntarily following the faintest tickle which he might well have survived with his score in the nineties. One naturally respects greatly also the views of the secretary of M.C.C. who thinks that a voluntary code of this kind expresses the true spirit of cricket, and has said that he personally hopes to see English cricketers continue to 'walk', as the great majority of first-class ones certainly do today.

Yet this is a new thing, and old cricketers in the Press-box out here such as J. H. Fingleton, W. J. O'Reilly, A. R. Gover and others fortify my own conviction that before the war the batsman waited almost invariably for the decision. Jack Hobbs, for instance, regarded as the beau idéal of a sportsman, always waited: so did a man of an equally highly considered integrity in the other camp, Charlie Macartney. The following seem to me to be strong arguments against usurping the umpire's function, however admirable the motive:

(1) If a man advertises himself as 'a walker' he must do so not only when he has made plenty and it doesn't greatly matter, but in answer to a lone appeal and following the faintest possible tickle when the scores are level in a Test match with the last man in. Otherwise he has prejudiced the

umpire who may think, 'This man "walks"—I must have been mistaken.' If everyone does not conform to this standard—and there have been instances of failure in the crisis in at least one recent Test match where the batsman has got away with it—the system surely fails.

(2) If a known 'walker' fails to do so and is then given out the inference is made, notably in the Press, that the umpire has made a mistake. 'A story' is automatically constructed.

(3) No one can deprive a batsman of his right to stay there, and it is a source of friction between players when some do and some do not.

(4) The most important principle in cricket—as in other games—is respect for the umpire's decision. It takes away from his authority in doing what must always be a highly skilled and most difficult job when players act irrespective of his verdict.

All in all, I believe that in Test cricket especially the good of this new fashion has been much outweighed by the evil. Every cricketer knows that he can help (or impede) the umpire by his demeanour, and there is nothing to stop those whose conscience impels them to convey that they have hit the ball from looking prepared to go, or even giving a nod. I believe, however, that they should await the verdict. I am also quite sure that the best service all cricketers can render to umpires, be they batsmen or fielders, is to obey the verdict phlegmatically, and certainly without the slightest visible sign of disagreement. That may not be easy in Test matches with so much depending, but it is in Test matches when the eyes of the world are upon him that the cricketer's manners are most important.

(1966)

The perennial 'Shack'

John Arlott on a 'master bowler of modern cricket, essentially English'

Year after year, cricketing Hampshire has contemplated, first with an air of delighted discovery, then satisfied possession and, latterly, utter amazement, the perpetually self-renewing miracle of Derek Shackleton's bowling —both shock bowling and stock bowling, apparently automatic, yet endlessly and subtly varied and resourceful.

It is one of the most well-worn stories in cricket that, in 1948, when Hampshire were desperately in need of an opening bowler—preferably two—their entire playing strength was turned into the nets to bowl as fast as possible. From the moment he turned his arm in that 'trial' there was no doubt that the young batsman from Todmorden, who had occasionally bowled leg-breaks, was a natural seam bowler.

That was, it seems, his destiny—he has done little else for twenty years since—but does he ever regard the previous twenty-three years of his life as wasted?

Almost ten years ago I was watching a Hampshire pre-season practice match in the company of an extremely wise and experienced cricketer. 'Poor old Shack,' he said; 'he's lost his snap: he can't go on getting people out at that pace.' 'Shack' bowled on; during the next quarter-hour a large, heavy cloud moved up over the ground. His bowling began to wobble, duck, dart and dive about like a live thing and he bowled the opposition out almost as quickly as they came in. The critic grinned, rueful yet as a Hampshireman, relieved: 'He's won again.'

Early this season, a major batsman of another county team said, 'I'm afraid Shack's had it now: he's only a slow bowler, nowadays, really—good length and all that, I know, but what a nice friendly pace.' I did not recall the conversation when the batsman returned caught at short-leg, off the glove—and off Shackleton. Certainly a scud of rain had livened the pitch: there was much rain in May: and Shack used those damaged pitches well—so well that, at one point, he had taken more wickets than anyone else in the country, and Hampshire stood first in the County Championship table.

His record of a hundred wickets in each of 18 consecutive seasons is unique—and is likely to remain so: in any case, if he remains fit—and he has managed to do so for many years—it will be 19 by August.

His bowling is a triumph of economy: the first step of his walk away to his place in the field is built into the end of his follow-through on the last ball of each over. His hair is so well tended that he wastes no energy in pushing or tossing it back into place; and, apart from the shading of black and grey, it has not changed in a single detail for 20 years. The whole action is easy and near-perfect: short, light-treading run up; wrist extremely sharply cocked: delivery swing, usually from close to the stumps, very high and easy—as if his shoulder joint rotated on ball-bearings: complete —180 degree—flick-over of wrist—*that* produces not only the swing but his unexpected pace. His delivery stride used once to be a jolt but now it is an almost prim heel-and-toe of the left foot. His length, like his line, is so regular that he could reproduce it blindfold. There is the basis of fluid, persistent accuracy. To this he adds inswing and outswing, change of pace —still, when he cares to stamp his foot, the ball whips through—and, because he holds the seam quite upright and bowls it from such a straight arm, he achieves some surprising movement off the seam.

Fred Trueman at times has handled him roughly but, of all the major batsmen who have resolved to hit him off, none can claim even 50 per cent success. No bowler of our time has been at once so steady and so penetrative, so apparently guileless yet so full of artifice, has given so much in both quantity and quality.

Still, occasionally, he reminds us of his early batting promise with a useful innings—usually against pace bowling—at a crucial time: and he is a safe catcher at mid-off or mid-on. But no reasonable captain would ask him to expend in other directions energies better saved for bowling. This is, indeed the master bowler of modern cricket; essentially English—and head and shoulders greater than any of his imitators.

(1967)

League cricket

John Kay on the charm of the clash between the known and the unknown

Fifty years are but a milestone in the history of league cricket. Most of the important ones, and the three that matter most today as they did fifty years ago, are the Lancashire League, the Bradford League and the Central Lancashire League, all formed towards the end of the nineteenth century at a time when leisure and pleasure were sought and earned in a much more relaxed world. League cricket was for the 'do it yourself' breed of sportsmen. It was the desire and the intention of the founder members of the three leagues to provide competitive cricket, created by enthusiasm, controlled with discipline and flavoured by professionalism. It was Saturday afternoon cricket with the added spice of local rivalry at both player and spectator level. It provided a jumping-off ground for cricketers of ability and offered a taste of the good time for spectators who could not travel far afield in their then brief hours of leisure. The local cricket ground was their Saturday afternoon Mecca.

Much has happened in the past fifty years. Professionalism, at first designed to provide labour on the ground and at the practice nets, has undergone the most radical change of all. But it was not until after World War I that the league clubs of Lancashire and Yorkshire began to look upon professionalism with ambitious eyes and ideas. In the early days of the century the three major leagues were content to recruit their paid players from the retired lists of the English counties and their main objective in engaging these men of experience was to prepare good pitches, provide knowledgeable coaches, and take advantage of talented aid when runs and wickets were in dire demand on match days. The league cricket professional of fifty years ago was more of an artisan than an artist, but there were some great players among them and by no means all had played for their counties let alone their countries.

Sydney Barnes was one of them. To me he typified the real spirit of league cricket. He was dour, determined and demanding. He was always a difficult man to handle yet always a successful one. He gave value for money and fulfilled the very letter of his contract. His clubs and his leagues were numerous and he earned a reputation for being a 'hard' man. His ability was never in question. In the days when figures and records were by no means the be-all and end-all of cricket Sydney Barnes was the deadliest bowler of them all. He accepted praise and criticism with equal disdain. He was being paid to do a job and in the course of doing it had no thought for showmanship or 'gimmicks'. He treated league cricket as he treated life—with deadly seriousness. To Barnes cricket was never a laughing matter and his attitude was the correct one. He endowed every game with dignity and demanded that others do the same. Throughout the 1920s he continued to play league cricket with the same deadly earnestness that typified his career and he saw club after club change their attitude to professionals and professionalism. He once acidly remarked, 'They now look for clowns not cricketers!'

He was referring to the cult of showmanship that began in 1929 when Nelson signed Learie Constantine and brought a new dimension to league cricket. Constantine was undoubtedly the brightest jewel in the first glittering collection of magnificent West Indies cricketers to tour this country, and in the boom days of the cotton trade and the woollen industry the league cricket clubs of Lancashire and Yorkshire had money to burn. They turned to the overseas players and billed them as star attractions to pull in the crowds. They did just that. Most of the invaders were superb cricketers and, like Constantine, matched their playing ability with showmanship, tinging their batting with big hitting and their bowling with devastating destructiveness. The spectators loved this new look. It was the beginning of a new era and it earned for league cricket a new image as well as worldwide publicity. A game built on the solidness of team work nurtured by hard labour on and off the field changed course.

It was still primarily an amateur game with the professional outnumbered 10 to 1 in every side, but the headlines and the clamour went to the international player, often at the expense of talented amateurs, and a club was judged by the success of its professional and not its team. They were engaged to provide cricketing 'fireworks' and duly obliged, earning their money and attracting the crowds. Not all the clubs could afford the luxury living of the new cult. Many, including my own club at Middleton, stuck to their old beliefs and spent their money modestly. At a time when Learie Constantine and George Headley were carrying all before them in the Lancashire League, Middleton introduced Hedley Verity to Central Lancashire League cricket and saw him move up the playing scale until he became a Yorkshire and England bowler of great distinction. They provided Verity with an opportunity to learn—other league clubs simply offered scope to earn for professionals with world-wide reputations already established.

How did the amateurs react? In the main they enjoyed themselves in the company of the famous. To play alongside Constantine and his like was to achieve distinction and more so when the Worrells, the Weekes and the Sobers followed in the wake of the earlier West Indies cricketers. And never a summer week-end went by without some local boy upsetting the odds by collaring a famous bowler or dismissing a star batsman. The charm of league cricket lay in the clash between the known and the unknown.

Criticism of the league cricket policy in regard to professionalism has always been rife. Often it has been and still is misunderstood. Now the league game is spreading all over the country; this reminder that its real strength still rests with the amateurs is timely and truthful. Professionalism, after all, is optional in all but a very few leagues—and even then it is strictly controlled. However, the amateur remains the man who matters most in league cricket. On and off the field they play the leading part and when a man puts away his pads or hands the ball to a younger bowler there is still a job for him to do in league cricket. The game is administered and kept alive by honorary officials who work hard and often with a blinding passion and belief in the game of cricket as played on Saturday afternoons.

I can vouch for the truth of the story about the old-time Nelson supporter who, occupying the same pavilion-side seat for more than thirty years, watched Ray Lindwall make his debut with the Lancashire League club and offered him some sound advice. He saw Lindwall suffer from dropped catches behind the wicket and in the slips, and when the great Australian fast bowler showed a touch of petulance at the wastage of his labours, loudly admonished him. In tones that could be heard all round the ground he stoutly proclaimed: 'It serves thee reet. Tha should bowl at bloody wickets!' I can also confirm the attempt another famous player, a batsman of worldwide repute, made to bluff a Lancashire League umpire —an old player still enjoying life in the middle. Bowled out first ball the batsman calmly replaced the bail and remarked to the umpire: 'It's a bit windy today, Jack.' ''Tis an' all, tha'd better stick to thee cap as tha reaches yon pavilion,' answered the man in the white coat, unknown but also unflappable.

Yet there were good stories in league cricket even before the advent of the international professional. One old Central Lancashire League umpire earned undying repute in a clash with the mighty Sydney Barnes. Barnes was surprised to find himself no-balled three balls in succession and did not look kindly on his accuser. When the umpire called him a fourth time the great man was clearly incensed. 'What's the matter? I am being paid ten pounds to do this job,' said Barnes. 'Ah knows that. I'm getting ten bob, but I'm bloody gaffer and until tha toes yon line tha'll never finish thi over,' replied a determined little umpire. And I was playing in a match when a young and brash Middleton batsman hit the same Barnes for three sixes in one over and watched his admiring father invite dozens of his immediate neighbours on the popular side to the bar to celebrate an historic cricketing occasion. Such was league cricket, spectacular, crowd-pulling and salty for both players and spectators. Great days, great players—and even greater upsets with the unknown amateur ever likely to upset the odds.

(1971)

200 up

John Reason on Ernest William Swanton, known to most in cricket as 'Jim'

The First Test match against Pakistan at Lord's may not be one of the more searching examinations of English cricket, but it will have one un-suspected distinction. It will be the 200th Test match reported by E. W. Swanton, O.B.E.

According to *Who's Who*, Ernest William Swanton is now 60 years of age (b. February 11, 1907, s. of the late William Swanton). He has never been called either Ernest or William and while, like Bradman, he takes fresh guard and prepares to go on to 300 (the Swantons are a long-lived lot), this is not an inopportune moment, if I might be permitted to use one of his favourite double negatives, to consider both the man and his recollection of all the Test cricket he has seen.

The first clue to Jim Swanton is the fact that he even *knows* that this is his 200th Test match. I cannot think of another journalist who would bother to count. Swanton must be easily the best organised sports writer in Fleet Street. He fires off memoranda here, postcards there, he books hotels months in advance, his car never runs out of petrol, he answers correspondence scrupulously, he keeps carbon copies of everything, he has files of everything relevant to his job, he has kept books of his own newspaper cuttings from the year dot and his movements are as well tracked as those of Jim Bond.

I have the impression that if a computer was fed with all this information, it might grow to be about 6 ft. 3 in. tall, 16 stones in weight, with dark hair growing grey in the most distinguished manner away from a powerful face, that it might marry in middle age, build a lovely house in Barbados and buy another in Kent, and it might start to pronounce on cricket as if it had just come down from Mount Sinai.

Swanton has spent three years of his life watching Test cricket. Three whole years doing nothing else, seven days a week, twelve months a year, Sundays, Christmas Days and August Bank Holidays included, and he still thinks that the first Test match he ever reported was the best. That was England v. Australia at Lord's in 1930.

This again gives a clue to the man, this time to his feeling about cricket. Woolley made a jewel of a 41, four batsmen made hundreds and Bradman made 254. A total of 1,601 runs were scored in four days for the loss of only 29 wickets. England batted first and made 800 runs in two innings and were beaten. Australia declared at 729 for 6 in their first innings and won the match after scoring 72 for 3 in their second.

No policy of containment there. No grafting, except by the bowlers. Instead, a cataract of runs, and even then, victory and defeat. Above all, five batting heroes led by the young Bradman, who not only played his first really gargantuan Test innings, but who had the supreme sense of occasion to do it at Lord's.

'Cricket is a batsman's game,' says Swanton. He has no doubt about it. He states it as a fact. 'The City of London has never emptied to watch a bowler as it did to watch Bradman.'

Significantly, in the notes he was kind enough to give me to help me write this piece (more organisation!), he lists Best Batsmen, Best Matches, Best Captains, Best *Touring* Captains and Best Managers, but the smallest list of all is Best Bowlers. They have to take the place that one feels was ordained for them, at the bottom of the order, among the Best Performances, just before the groundsman comes on to ask one of the Best Captains (or even one of the Best *Touring* Captains) what size of roller he wants.

Bowlers may be more essential than anyone else to the winning of matches, and Laker's 19 for 90 may have been all very well in its way, but Swanton has always been fascinated by batsmanship and especially by the heroic Test innings. He regards Bradman as the best batsman he ever saw and he still regards Bradman's 254 as the best innings he ever saw. In that, he is in good company. Bradman himself regards it as his best performance. In an interview with Swanton just after the war (a scoop, no less!), Bradman explained his opinion by saying, 'I never hit the ball with anything other than the middle of the bat and I did not lift a ball off the ground until I was out.' Swanton recalls wryly, 'and even that one was going like smoke when it was caught by Percy Chapman at mid-off.'

Swanton swiftly disillusions those moderns who imagine that to score all those runs Bradman must have looked and played like the England selectors' wishful image of Colin Milburn, with a furious flurry of strokes instantly generated by a lean, hard, 11-stone body, and ten times as inevitable.

'He was a great accumulator,' says Swanton. 'He would come in, and play quietly, and after about 20 minutes, you would think he had scored about seven or eight and you would look up at the scoreboard and be surprised to see that he had got 19. He was a marvellous cutter, all the way through the ninety degrees between square and late, and he played beautifully off his legs. He did very little driving, comparatively speaking, between the covers and mid-off. His batting hadn't the romance or the bloom of a Woolley or a Compton, but I never saw him make an ugly stroke. He went on and on, over after over, hour after hour, hitting the ball with the middle of the bat. There was an inevitability about his play that brought the bowlers to despair.'

Swanton also thinks that Bradman was the best captain he ever saw. 'I remember with what hope and confidence England went out on the boat to Australia just after the war,' he says. 'We had a fine team, and it was simply bursting to play cricket after all those years. I think it was the best batting side England have had since 1930. Everyone wanted to see them. It is true that we had all the bad luck going, but the fact is that the Don could give poor old Wally [Hammond] a stroke a hole at captaincy and the whole thing gradually fell to pieces. It was so sad.'

By then, Swanton was reporting cricket for the *Daily Telegraph*. It was his first major assignment for them. He had started, by his own confession, as a rather priggish tea-maker with Amalgamated Press when he left Cranleigh in 1924 ('I played only once for the XI; I made 33 and wasn't required again,' he says with some asperity). He joined the *Evening Standard* in the autumn of 1927 as a rugby and cricket writer. He bought an AC motorcar for £120 the first week he was there. 'It was a sort of duck-egg blue,' he recalls. 'It looked quite elegant with the hood down, and quite awful with it up. I remember driving my father over to Richmond when I reported my first rugger match.'

Swanton was made cricket correspondent of the *Standard* in 1930 but the appointment only lasted two years. After that, he had to alternate with Bruce Harris, who was also the lawn tennis correspondent.

'The paper felt that they wanted a more experienced journalist to cover the M.C.C. tour of Australia,' says Swanton. 'Naturally, I was more than disappointed not to make the trip. This was the bodyline tour, and it is interesting to reflect what might have happened if I had gone. There were only three journalists writing for English newspapers on that tour. One was Jack Hobbs, who was doing it for the *Star*, the second was Warwick Armstrong and the third was Bruce Harris.

'Jack had already had a taste of bodyline and did not approve of it. Warwick Armstrong was an Australian, which was enough to damn him in any case, and the only journalist reflecting the popular view in this country was Harris. Douglas Jardine had the sense to see this and, as a result, Harris had a great journalistic success. He was giving the people the pro-bodyline and anti-Australian stuff they wanted to read. If I had gone, of course, it would have been very different. My view was the same as Jack Hobbs' and Gubby Allen's. I did not think that bodyline was in the best interests of the game, and I still don't.'

At about this time, Swanton met Ian Peebles, and they shared a flat, first at the back of Sloane Square and then in the Temple. Eventually, they were joined by Henry Longhurst and his succession of spectacular motorcars. Swanton played a lot of club cricket, and as an opening batsman, he scored 1,000 runs every year between 1928 and 1939. Twice he scored 2,000 runs and he played for Middlesex against the Universities. His first game for the Middlesex 2nd XI was Denis Compton's last. 'I remember Denis loped in to join me when our score was about 12 for 4, and we put on a hundred for the fifth wicket. I thought he was a pretty good player!'

Swanton toured America with Sir Julien Cahn's team and he raised a team himself to tour Bermuda. Unfortunately, the financial arrangements broke down, and Swanton was left with a very good team and nowhere to go, so he took them to Jersey and R. C. Robertson-Glasgow christened them the Arabs. Swanton has run the side ever since, and it has helped to keep him in touch with the important business of actually playing the game.

Swanton stayed with the *Standard* until 1938 when, with commissions amounting to a meagre £200, he bought himself a first-class ticket on the Balmoral Castle and went to South Africa to cover the M.C.C. tour, chiefly as a broadcaster. He started radio work in 1934 on the old Empire Programme and after he had done his first outside broadcast, on the match between Surrey and Lancashire at the Oval in 1938, he persuaded the B.B.C. to commission some work for the South African tour. He also persuaded the South African radio authorities to do the same, starting with a quarter of an hour a day and finishing with two hours a day. As they paid him by the day, Swanton was the only man to find the timeless Test at the end of the tour no hardship at all. It went on for ten days, and as a result, he showed a modest profit on the tour.

When the war broke out, Swanton and Peebles joined up with the Bedfordshire Yeomanry. They were briefly billeted in a house 200 yards from my own home, and then went to Norfolk, which they defended against the Fuehrer with fewer and fewer guns. They were much more severely exercised in a game of cricket at Ingham, where they suddenly found themselves surrounded by Edriches. In 1941, Swanton played some League cricket for Liverpool, and then embarked for the Far East, via America, the Cape and Poona. They arrived at Singapore on January 29, 1942, they went into action the following day, and they were all either killed or captured a fortnight later when Singapore surrendered on February 15. Swanton was wounded in the arm ('the only time I have been on the heroin kick!') and spent 3½ years as a prisoner of war in 12 different camps. He worked on the Burma railway and on the bridge over the River Kwai and he survived an attack of polio. He also thought a great deal about the hereafter. 'If you are not going to do it in those circumstances, you never will.'

When he was released, he spent a year in Pusey House, in Oxford. This is a religious institution, and he was admitted as a layman. 'I was recuperating,' he says. He does not admit as much, but I think he also considered going into the Church. If he did, he obviously decided against it, but he has retained a close affinity with the Anglo-Catholic position. This interest, his Army training, his cricket, and his sympathy for schools and schoolmastering are easiest to see in his character.

Swanton returned to journalism with the *Daily Telegraph*. He concedes that his memory of cricket before and after the war is clearer than his memory of the game in the last few years. He remembers Bradman, Woolley and Duleep at Lord's in 1938, and Headley's two hundreds at Lord's a year later. He remembers Lindwall and Miller as the game's first Everest after the war. 'They were a great pair, and we were foolish enough to let them have a new ball every 55 overs, so the Don held all the cards.' He remembers Compton's 184 'made in a funny yellow light at Trent Bridge, and his 145 at Old Trafford after he had been hit on the head'. He pauses to philosophise about Compton. 'Of all the English batsmen I have seen, Denis had more of the smack of genius than anyone since Jack Hobbs. Mechanically, Len was a magnificent player; so was Wally Hammond; so was Peter May; so was Ted Dexter; but Denis had an instinct which seemed to put him apart. The greatest tragedy was that he lost six years just as he was coming to the top, and then was cut short by that knee trouble.'

He remembers Walcott at Lord's and Worrell at Trent Bridge in 1950, and Hutton's 169 and 205 against the West Indies in 1953. No doubt he remembers Hutton's 364 against Australia, too, but he does not put it on his list. He remembers Washbrook's 97 at Leeds in 1956 and Graveney's 165 ten years later. He remembers Dexter's at Lord's and Old Trafford, Cowdrey in Melbourne and May in Sydney and the pair of them against the West Indies at Edgbaston. He remembers Barber's 185 at Sydney and Sobers all through 1966. With them all, he remembers the exact score, the place and the year.

His memory of bowling is not nearly so precise. He remembers it as such and not as a series of statistics. Verity at Lord's, Grimmett and O'Reilly at Trent Bridge, Lindwall and Miller wherever they bowled, Ramadhin and Valentine, Bedser at Melbourne and Trent Bridge, Tyson and Statham, Laker at Old Trafford, Trueman at Georgetown and Hall at Leeds.

He is certain that Gary Sobers is the greatest player that he or anyone else has ever seen, and says, 'The greatest change in cricket since the war has been the emergence of the West Indies as a major force.' Swanton is now the West Indies' most ardent champion; perhaps because he has a strong sense of occasion, and now that he has a home in Barbados, would like to take some small part in cricket administration. It is curious that he has never been asked to do so in this country, although he has done more to preserve national newspaper coverage of cricket than anyone else. Summer football and the expansion of minority sports are constantly eroding the space allotted to cricket in the newspapers but the blanket coverage of cricket in the *Daily Telegraph* never wavers. In a strange way, I am sure that it acts as the cricket conscience of Fleet Street (it has even persuaded the new *Times* to expand its own cricket effort enormously) and the game owes a lot of that to Swanton.

The sports writer he admired above all others was the late Bernard Darwin, who always wrote sense and who always wrote it beautifully. Swanton likes fine writing, but not at the expense of content. What you say is always more important than how you say it, but Fleet Street is prone to get those priorities upside down. Admittedly, it is easy to do so. It is immensely diverting to take a professional delight in cosseting words. Unfortunately, it takes a great deal more intelligence and application to make those words discerning and well-informed. Darwin did both.

Apart from county cricket, which irks him regularly, Swanton has never been a particularly critical writer, and he himself has often been criticised for this. He prefers to stick to the classic formula of, What happened? Why did it happen? How did it happen?

He thinks that the three worst Test matches he has seen were England v. Australia at Leeds in 1953, England v. Australia at Brisbane in 1958–9 and England v. West Indies at Bridgetown in 1954, but in each case, he softens his criticism of individuals by immediately pointing out their virtues.

Hutton had to do with two of those matches and so did Bailey and in all three matches the common factor was the negation of batting. Consciously or otherwise, Swanton finds that unforgivable. Of Hutton, when England made 128 in a full day's play in the West Indies, he says, 'When Len's cautious self came uppermost, we were in trouble . . . but he redeemed himself by his remarkable personal performances in the fourth and fifth Tests.'

Of Bailey, when England made 106 in a full day's play at Brisbane, he says, 'He had a misconception of his role; there were times when he batted like a caricature of himself.' However, Swanton goes on at once to talk of Bailey's great Test match value as a bowler and fielder. At Leeds, England deprived Australia of victory by what Swanton regards as dubious means. 'Our method of forcing a draw rankled a bit.'

Apart from this understatement of criticism, Swanton sometimes seems to go out of his way as a writer to hold himself aloof from controversy. His attitude is, 'A writer often carries the reputation of his country for sportsmanship, particularly when he is working abroad. He is tempted to be critical when his country is losing. That is usually the worst time to criticise. Controversies are invariably exaggerated, and it is difficult to keep them in the right perspective. It is better to present the whole game, and I have tried to do that as well as I can.'

(1967)

The best series ever

E. W. Swanton bemoans the missing link in his cricketing life

If I am asked what, in all the cricket of the last half-century, I am sorriest to have missed the answer is automatic. It is the Test series between Australia and West Indies of 1960–1 which began with the tied Test at Brisbane and ended with the motorcade through the streets of Melbourne wherein Frank Worrell and his team were accorded a parting ovation which surely has no parallel in sport.

It's much too much to hope that the rubber between the two countries which will be under way in Australia by the time these words are being read can match that of fifteen years ago. The stars could not be so favourably disposed twice in a generation—or, if a more practical reason is preferred, it must be allowed that Australia cannot command a captain from her present resources with anything approaching the quality of a Benaud. Nevertheless the auspices are not unfavourable—if the passions of all concerned can be kept under leash.

Happily that 1960–1 series had a distinguished recorder in Jack Fingleton, whose book *The Greatest Test of All* covers not only the tie at Brisbane but the remaining four Tests which, it may be remembered, ended thus:

2nd Test (Melbourne): Australia won by 7 wickets
3rd Test (Sydney): West Indies won by 222 runs
4th Test (Adelaide): Drawn
5th Test (Melbourne): Australia won by 2 wickets.

Considering that at Adelaide Australia survived only after a last-wicket stand of nearly two hours, at the start of which was a hotly-disputed 'catch' which would have given West Indies the match by 200-odd runs, it is easy at this distance—as indeed it was at the time—to conclude that the moral honours went to the losers. However, this time for once the game, for all who followed the fortunes of the rubber, really did mean much more than the result.

Fingleton in the Foreword to his book told how the cricket 'breathed new and lusty life into the ailing spectre of a once great game. . . . What was the principal cause of this stupendous transformation? To me the answer is clear. The principal cause was the simple, the unsophisticated, the generous, the essentially carefree and *good* cricketing behaviour which Frank Worrell and his happy band gave to Australia from the moment their tour began. Good behaviour evokes good behaviour. It is difficult among the carefree to be a prophet of doom, indecent among the generous to behave meanly, impossible, if you are an Australian international, to play timidly when courage and challenge form the hallmark of your opponents' game.'

Summing up the tour from afar I wrote in the *Daily Telegraph*:

'The prime moral for all concerned with the welfare of cricket is, of course, that the game is as fascinating a pastime as it ever was. The crucial thing is the attitude of the players. The basic Laws don't need fiddling with when a five-day match, without the benefit of any sort of public holiday, can attract 270,000 people.

'It is hard to overpraise Richie Benaud's contribution to the series. He has always been an intelligent and courageous, as well as a highly-talented, cricketer. He has acquired during the last two years a fully-developed sense of the responsibility for the well-being of cricket that goes properly with the job of Test captain.

'However, it is not the Australian side of the picture that is the extra-ordinary one. With few exceptions—and their 1956 English tour was one—Australia's cricket has generally been virile and combative. Above all, they have rarely failed to take up any gage thrown down by the enemy.

'The really significant thing is the overall performance of the West Indians. Their cricket virtues have been admired by all, over the years, but certain apparently intrinsic limitations of temperament have too often counter-balanced them.

'Brilliant, yes—but are they 'stickers'? If you get on top of them can they fight back? In a crisis won't they lose their heads? Such questions have always surrounded West Indian cricketers. They have been asked so often that they must have doubted the answers themselves.

'It is the measure of the achievement of this team that in Australia, before the toughest (but not the least generous) public of all, they have dissolved all such doubts. They have met adversity with brilliant counter-attack, they have 'stuck it' when necessary, they have kept their heads in critical situations at least as well as their opponents.'

The predominant feeling one had was of relief because international cricket had been going through a dreadfully bad time. The Australian tour of England in 1956 had been a failure on any computation; the M.C.C. tour of Australia in 1958–9 had been no less so. The visit of M.C.C. to West Indies in the following 1959–60 winter certainly had shown Test cricket in a better light. And now came Worrell as a leader with the mission he saw so clearly of presenting his own race to the world as ambassadors and sportsmen.

I quoted the verdict of Ron Roberts, our correspondent covering the tour (who died so tragically young only a few years later):

'Worrell has immense natural dignity. No cricketer since Hammond has had such sheer presence as he takes the field. The petty things of cricketing life seem to be below Worrell. The will to win at all costs is somehow dis-tasteful to him. The game, not the result, means more.

'Worrell has been the producer and mastermind of this show but he has also had in the wings a most able director, Gomez, with that jutting jaw like the prow of a battleship, has not tried to run the party. For all his own deep knowledge and feeling for the game he has tactfully let Worrell take care of the cricket. But his presence in the background has been extremely reassuring to his captain.'

Gerry Gomez, of course, was the West Indian manager. I concluded:

'It should be emphasised to a public even wider than that of cricket that here was a perfect blending in harmony between the two predominant races forming the West Indian nation. Could the point be noted even in Cape Town and Pretoria?

'What do the immediate gains add up to? In the first place Australia, whose cricketing economy has been nearly as rocky as our own, have now the prospect of another regularly stimulating visit beside that of M.C.C. Before this they had not considered the West Indies as serious Test opponents.

'On the £ s. d. side, the fifth Test produced a record turnover of £39,000 and the West Indies—who actually lost money on their last visit to Australia—will this time take home more than £25,000.

'As a revivifying influence on cricket the tour has been priceless, and I will not weary our English cricketers by reiterating the obvious. For them this indeed is the moment of truth.'

(1975)

A legend in his own day— Frank Tyson

John Arlott writes on one who beat the best by sheer speed

A letter from Frank Tyson has brought the news that he will be back in England next summer—and aroused a string of memories. Already he is something of a legend; already, too, there are young men who ask 'How fast was he?'

The ranking of fast bowlers by comparative speed is almost impossible but among the genuinely fast, there are gradations of speed. At the top stand those who, with unquestionably legitimate actions were—usually for only a short period—capable of beating the best batsmen of their time by pace alone. They are not necessarily the most skilful, nor the most successful and often they have been inconsistent, but they are a class apart. There is a fair evening's debate in compiling the list but, if the qualification of a fair action is strictly applied, it will not be a long one. Frank Tyson's name, however, must stand high in it.

Perhaps, we became used to him and, at times, forgot what a rare asset English cricket—as a playing force and a spectacle—possessed in him. Often a crowd seeing him bowl for the first time let out a gasp of amazement: so, undoubtedly did batsmen.

Frank Tyson expressed himself in fast bowling. His body was a glorious fast-bowling engine. His shoulders, arms, chest, back, hips, legs were mightily made and he employed them all in a perfect unison: in the huge final bound his whole trunk heaved forward and the arm came down like a flail. He spent his energy prodigally in it, in the knowledge that he would not have to labour at it after the spark was gone. When he received the news that he had passed his degree examination he went out and came back with a bottle of champagne, opened it, poured it and said, 'This is not to celebrate just this degree but that I don't *have* to bowl fast—I can go on until I don't want to, or can't, do it any more—then I can go and teach for a living.' In the end he did that: but in the meantime he bowled gloriously and unforgettably.

Three occasions in his career stay in my mind. In the first over of his first first-class match—for Northants against the 1952 Indians—he bowled a ball that touched Pankaj Roy's bat and flew to Fred Jakeman at slip so fast that he had no time to move his hands to it before it hit him on the knee and felled him. There were experienced cricketers in that slip field—Jock Livingston, George Tribe, Desmond Barrick and Norman Oldfield—but after that ball they, and the wicketkeeper, moved quite five yards deeper. His studies kept him away from Northants until a year later, and the match against Ian Johnson's Australians. Again in the first over he had Colin McDonald l.b.w. to a full toss he never saw: and then bowled Graeme Hole with his bat only halfway down. Hole was an established Australian Test batsman but in 1955, in three consecutive Test innings—two at Sydney and one at Melbourne—Tyson beat and bowled him by pace alone, and bowled him out of Test cricket for ever.

So perfect was his body-swing that he could bowl his fastest off an approach of only three yards; he used his run to give rhythm and avoid wrench; but, even so, the force of his plunge through on to the left leg in the deliver stride was so violent as to fracture his ankle and, for all the care he took over his condition, he suffered a number of strains.

He appeared only once in 1952, played half a season in 1953, little more in 1956, and at the end of 1960 he retired. He made his first Test appearance against Pakistan in 1954, the year he won his county cap, and his last, against New Zealand, in 1959, the year before he retired. He only played one full Test series—in Australia in 1954–5—and virtually won it. In the five matches he took 28 wickets at 20·82: but the significant figures are those for the three Tests which England won to take the rubber—25 at 14·2. He has always maintained that success was the product of his partnership with his fellow Lancastrian and friend Brian Statham. Certainly, with a genuine respect and liking for one another, they made a truly complementary pair and if, as Tyson wished—when he felt himself frustrated by the slow wicket at Northampton—they had bowled together for Lancashire they must have been a shattering force in county cricket.

Frank Tyson was not merely a fast bowler: in his last season he often reduced his pace and cut the ball skilfully, while his batting was useful and his out-fielding capable. But anything less than truly fast bowling left him unsatisfied and he had only one season in league cricket before he went to Melbourne as a schoolmaster and, after extending his teaching experience here, he will probably return to Australia.

In the meantime there will be much to discuss, including the remarkable coincidence that every one of his great bowling performances, including his last outstanding analysis for Todmorden, in the Wood Cup, occurred on the day after a dinner with Burgundy as the staple wine.

(1967)

OBITUARIES

A. C. Bannerman

He wore down great bowlers

A great personality in the cricket world has been removed by the death of Alexander Chambers Bannerman, who died in Sydney last month in his sixty-sixth year. His career in great matches was both long and distinguished, and after his active participation in the game ceased he did valuable coaching work in Sydney for many years. He will, of course, always be remembered on account of his wonderful defensive powers as a batsman, for as a stonewaller he would be classed in the same category as Barlow and Scotton. Like his two great English contemporaries, he was often most tedious to watch, but there can be no doubt that, like them, he rendered the teams for which he played far greater service than score-sheets suggest, for he stopped and wore down much excellent bowling which might well have proved fatal to men with less sound defence, or less patience.

(1924)

McCabe—a master

Jack Fingleton on a classical batsman who engendered immense power with a minimum of effort

Stanley Joseph McCabe, of warm memory, began his cricket career on the concrete pitches of Grenfell, N.S.W. He took it a considerable step further on the splendid turf pitches of St Joseph's College, Hunter's Hill, Sydney, where he was for several years a notable if not outstanding member of the school first eleven.

It was back in Grenfell, after his schooldays, that McCabe came under the notice of E. A. Dwyer, then a N.S.W. selector and later an Australian one for many years. Dwyer was a member of a Sydney team that played at Grenfell, a sheep and wheat-growing district, and when a second N.S.W. team needed a player, Dwyer recommended McCabe and he was duly summoned to Sydney. The district said the wrong McCabe went to Sydney. They considered Leslie McCabe, an elder brother, the better cricketer. But the story is apocryphal. Dwyer knew which McCabe he wanted.

McCabe, like Sir Donald Bradman and W. J. O'Reilly, settled in Sydney to further his cricketing prospects. A teacher's posting letter sent O'Reilly back to the 'bush' and so denied him the 1930 tour of England but Bradman and McCabe continued on in Sydney without interruption. Whereas Bradman, however, had an immediate and meteoric rise to the top, McCabe worked his way there by a slower process.

He got useful and always attractive scores for N.S.W. in the Sheffield Shield but in batting deeds, to that time, he was subjugated in N.S.W. cricket by Bradman and Archie Jackson. But his rich promise was always evident.

After Ryder's team had been soundly whipped by A. P. F. Chapman's team in Australia in 1928–9, the Australians decided, wisely, to put their trust in youth. Under Ryder, Bradman, Jackson, Fairfax and a'Beckett had shown the value of that policy and the selectors, Ryder, Dr C. E. Dolling and R. L. Jones, had decided to jump even further ahead with their team to England. Ryder, to his consternation, when the selectors met to choose the touring team during a N.S.W. v. Victoria match in Sydney, found that his co-selectors meant him to be jettisoned, too, in the general policy, with W. M. Woodfull as captain.

Ryder had one success. He was due to bat the next day and he induced his fellow-selectors to hold the team over for one day. Ryder, in difficult circumstances for him, made a notable century. But his co-selectors were adamant. Ryder was out—McCabe was in.

McCabe was a successful if not unduly prominent member of that side in which Bradman dominated the series, making scores of 131, 254, 334 and 232. There was also Ponsford. McCabe, like some of his fellows, was engulfed by the Bradman dynasty but he surged to immortality in 1932–3 in Australia when, in Sydney against the devastating body-line bowling of Larwood and Voce, under the direction of Jardine, McCabe hit an incredible 187 not out. On a sunny Saturday morning, he sent the Sydney crowd into ecstasies of disbelief and joy as he flayed both Larwood and Voce on the leg-side. McCabe's heroics of that innings, in many minds, disproved the Australian contentions that bodyline was unsporting and hampered stroke-play. But McCabe was first to admit that everything went his way. Neither he nor any other Australian ever again attacked Jardine's methods with such brilliance.

McCabe hit 137 against England at Old Trafford in 1934; he hit 112 against England in Melbourne in 1936 and he hit 232 against England at

Trent Bridge in 1938. He hit 149 against South Africa at Durban in 1935–6 and made 189 not out against South Africa at Johannesburg, also in 1935–6. His Trent Bridge and Johannesburg innings rank with his Sydney one against England as three of the greatest of all time.

I had the extreme privilege of playing in all three games and was on hand to put on record for posterity the remark made by Don Bradman on the Trent Bridge balcony in 1938. Players on tour seldom watch a match. They involve themselves in many dressing-room chores. Bradman called back to some of his fellows, 'Come and see this. Don't miss a minute of it. You'll never see the like of it again.' McCabe made 71 of 78 for the last Australian wicket that day. He made his last 78 in 22 minutes.

He pulverised and demoralised the English attack. Once he swayed on to his back foot, seeming to play a defensive stroke. He lifted Ken Farnes, the England fast bowler, high over the leg fence.

One hesitates to say which innings was McCabe's greatest. That at Johannesburg, another one of sheer bowling massacre, was played on a broken pitch in the dark light of a pending storm. McCabe so demoralised the Springboks with his onslaught that the South African captain, Herbert Wade, appealed successfully against the light from the field. Yet in retrospect and considering the opposition possibly McCabe's Sydney innings was his greatest.

Over the years in which he played his genius had limitations imposed upon it by Bradman's tremendous influence. McCabe batted after Bradman and after Ponsford, and sat for hours at The Oval with the pads on in 1934 while Ponsford made 266 and Bradman 244.

McCabe was a classical batsman who engendered immense power with a minimum of effort. His footwork was impeccable. He once said he learnt more about footwork in an innings at The Oval by Jack Hobbs (McCabe was fielding in the covers) than he did in the rest of his career. McCabe was a master of the pull, which he played to any ball a fraction short, and the drive in all directions. He played all his strokes with consummate grace.

McCabe was not disposed to take himself seriously as a bowler yet the records will show that he captured many dangerous Test wickets. He used the new ball with ability, on a good length, and was faster off the pitch than many thought. He bowled, too, an odd ball—a seeming type of fast legbreak which came, if anything, from the off, or straight through. He loved to recall how Duleepsinhji appreciated his bowling. 'Duleep didn't half love to bat against me,' would recall McCabe, with a twinkle. In his early days, he was a superb over-field. Of his later playing years, he was a slip catcher above the ordinary.

There was a lovely photograph which showed the grace of McCabe, as he was playing forward to Allen, who is in full flight after bowling the ball. It does McCabe's majesty full justice. I was in runs and McCabe would often chidingly—and with merit—reproach me for not backing up properly. I was certainly a little slow off the mark. But I had the answer to him. 'It was never any good looking for singles with you, Napper,' I replied. 'You are much too slow—and anyway you only believe in hitting fours.' It wasn't too far wide of the mark. It was Alan Kippax who christened him 'Napper'. He bore a strong resemblance to Napoleon.

That, in a sense, was McCabe the cricketer. His manner and character never changed. He abhorred humbug. He was the warmest and most loyal of friends and there was not deceit nor conceit in his nature. He was a true friend and a humble, great Australian.

(1968)

Lord Nugent—an elder statesman

Lord Nugent, G.C.V.O., M.C., was 77 when he died at Midhurst on April 27: yet the news of his death came to those who knew him well as a deep shock, not only because he always looked so fresh and full of health but because he was someone who commanded a very special degree of affection.

He was, of course, a man of many worlds: of the Court chiefly, of the theatre and the arts generally, of the army, which was his profession, and of sport. In all these spheres he was universally admired, for though he had a strong mind of his own he mingled a transparent sincerity with a winning tact and charm. These virtues were particularly forthcoming when as Comptroller to the Lord Chamberlain (an office he held for twenty-five years), to quote *The Times*, 'he managed the delicate and controversial conduct of stage censorship with consummate skill'.

Tim played in the Eton XIs of 1913 and 1914. Picking up his cricket after the war (in which serving in the Irish Guards, he was wounded and won the Military Cross) he played a lot for Household Brigade and the wandering clubs. That might well have been the extent of his impact on the game if in the 'sixties both M.C.C. and Surrey had not seen in him the ideal committee man and President. As President of M.C.C. he is said to have accepted every invitation he received. He travelled much as the game's chief figurehead, and was the first President to visit the M.C.C. team in Australia.

As an elder statesman of cricket his opinion was continually sought, and his wisdom will be much missed both at Lord's and The Oval. Readers of *The Cricketer* will recall several delightful light pieces from his pen. In this regard, as in all others, he was ever ready to oblige.

E. W. Swanton (1973)

Jim Sims—a rare and endearing character

Cricket lost a fine cricketer and a real character when J. M. Sims, the former Middlesex and England player, died at Canterbury on April 29. 'Simmo', as he was known to his colleagues in his playing days, will be remembered for his high standards of sportsmanship and particularly for his sense of humour and the delivery of his speech, which came out of the corner of his mouth.

Jim was quite devastating on his day with his leg-break and googly—the old 'wozzler', as he called it. He used to revel on a dry, dusty pitch because he bowled his leg-break so quickly. I would compare his pace with that of Chandrasekhar, who caused so much trouble last winter in India and who has a similar dip in his flight.

I played most of my career with Jim and so much of the fun which I had was contributed by him. There is a wealth of stories one could tell about him.

Once against Gloucestershire he was bowling to that magnificently aggressive batsman, Charlie Barnett, and I was fielding at mid-off. Jim had not had the best of luck and the fielding had not been of a very high standard. He came up to me during one over and said out of the corner of his mouth, 'I think I'll bowl Charlie a long-hop, Denis, he might hit it down deep square-leg's throat.' This he carried out to perfection, for Charlie laid back and cracked it straight to Alec Thompson on the square-leg boundary. Unfortunately Alec, who was not renowned for his fielding, moved in too far and the ball dropped over his head and hit the fence.

Jim had the sun in his eyes and could not follow the flight, so he came up to me and said, 'What 'appened, Denis?' I told him that regrettably Thompson had misjudged it and the ball had dropped over his head for four. After a moment's silence he muttered, 'Should have hit him on the bloody head'—and with that unforgettable smile was off to bowl the next ball.

I have been at the wicket on numerous occasions with Jim, who was no mean batsman and did for a time in the early 'thirties open the innings for Middlesex. He could 'prop and cop' effectively, and when the occasion warranted he could give the ball a powerful thump.

In one match at Lord's when I was going pretty well it was essential for Jim to play up the line. He beckoned me up the wicket and said, 'Don't do anything silly, Denis. I'll show 'em the maker's name all right.' As usual, it came out of the side of the mouth and, in fact, his manner of speaking was so infectious that I used to find myself talking to him in the same way.

He was a great help to me throughout my career, as he was to so many other Middlesex players. Even after his retirement in 1953 he did much, as coach and scorer, for the welfare of Middlesex.

One tends to forget his fine record of 1,582 first-class wickets—eight times he took 100 in a season and in 1948 all ten in an innings in a festival match at Kingston—because he was such a rare and endearing character. There has been no-one quite like him in my experience. I, and many others, will miss him greatly.

Denis Compton (1973)

Ian Peebles on Reg Bettington ; surgeon, golfer and one of the most memorable and rumbustious of university cricketers

In the season of 1920 Oxford University Cricket Club was surprised and delighted to find their resources greatly enriched by an unexpected addition. Reg Bettington had come up to New College the previous autumn from King's School, Paramatta, an unknown quantity so far as his English contemporaries were concerned.

He was an instant success in college circles and just the current idea of 'Young Australia'. Enormous, prodigiously strong, with a sunny, friendly disposition, his contemporaries were soon aware that they had in their midst a very notable athlete as well as a most exceptional young man.

By the accident of time and season his first prominence was as a rugger player, but it is chiefly as a cricketer that he is so clearly remembered as an undergraduate. The first sight of this newcomer in the Parks must have filled the captain's heart with joy, for there has never been a better-looking 'googly' bowler. A fine high-stepping, bouncing run led to a rhythmical wheeling action, and the ball left with a snap of the fingers which could be heard on the boundary line on a still day. Once he had taken a look at English pitches he also found his true form as a batsman, which was rude and rough, and extremely effective.

Oxford already had a very fine leg-spinner in Greville Stevens, and they made a well-balanced pair. Greville was not only well qualified to judge his partner but also in a perfect position to do so. He has no doubts that Reg at that time, in regular practice, was the best of his type in the country. It was an opinion probably shared by Jack Hobbs who was fully stretched when they met at The Oval. Greville says of this occasion that here was the only bowler he ever saw make 'The Master' look almost ordinary. Allowing for the passage of time, and a margin of poetic licence, it is certainly further than any other 'googly' bowler ever got.

It was a personality as big and generous as his presence which made Reg one of the greatest of all figures in university cricket. His size, his good nature, and a blunt Australian turn of phrase attracted the full spate of the several considerable wits in a lively side. He was early named 'The Doctor' —and a number of less respectful but equally affectionate nicknames. This and other badinage he received in the spirit it was given. His only recorded riposte was to an impertinent sally from Stevens. He gathered the speaker's 14 stone as a babe in arms and threw him out of the dressing-room window.

There are countless tales of similar feats. One of my favourites is of his arrest on Boat Race night. According to witnesses he was happy but perfectly sober when, with a group of friends, he sought admission to a restaurant. An officious commissionare tried to prevent them and mistakenly started to push Reg. Entering into the spirit of the thing, Reg gave him a playful push in return, at which the official shot backwards to wind up reclining amongst the potted palms and aspidistras. When the dreadful charge of 'drunk and disorderly' was preferred an impressive list of cordials was read out as being the night's consumption. It went from Martinis by easy stages to finish with port and brandy. At that the accused spoke his only word of remonstrance: 'Naow port,' he said.

But he had a sharp eye for the proprieties. When on tour he struck a somewhat notorious 'hearty' being objectionable in a pub whilst wearing the blazer of a famous club; he advanced on him. 'What's your name?' he demanded, and received an understandably meek reply. 'You're a disgrace to the club,' said 'The Doctor', at which the offender slunk from this awesome presence without further ado.

He became a famous surgeon, a most successful golfer, and, indeed, met success in every sphere he touched. He remained the same all his days: kind, able, unaffected, an enormous personality which stemmed from a fundamentally gentle and modest nature. Few cricketers have inspired so much admiration and unalloyed affection as he in the vast number of people who knew him and played with him.

He had a shrewd eye for a cricketer. When he captained New South Wales he was given a new bowler. After the day's play he drew the attention of his immediate circle to the novice standing at the bar. 'There's the best bowler in the world,' he said. The new boy's name was O'Reilly. When, in the next match, he was to be left out for lack of a place, Reg himself stood down. He was that sort of chap.

(1969)

Last gallant steps of Hedley Verity

There are worse wars than those of the Roses—the last one, for example, when Hedley Verity died of wounds in Italy. John Bapty followed it up.

July 31, next Saturday, is the day on which twenty-five years ago Hedley Verity died of wounds, a prisoner of war in Italy. He had been reported wounded and missing after the Eighth Army's first attack on the German positions at Catania in Sicily on July 19, 1943.

Not until September 1, 1943, did the news of his death reach his home in the Aire Valley, and then some of us recalled that the first day of September, 1939, was that on which he had spun the ball for Yorkshire for the last time in championship cricket.

The game was with Sussex at Hove. Verity had seven wickets for nine runs in the six overs he bowled in an innings which held only 33 runs. After Yorkshire had got, for the wicket of Hutton, the 30 runs required for nine-wicket victory—Wilfred Barber made the boundary shot which gave Yorkshire their last pre-war runs—Brian Sellers and his men, champions for the third season in a row, turned to the grim journey home.

A hurriedly-chartered Southdown motor coach was there to take them across the tide of evacuation from London, along second-class roads on which the fantastically valuable white lines were being painted, and through the first blackout to Leicester, and on the following morning—the Saturday morning—to Leeds where under the old New Station clock they parted for the last time.

In Verity's pocket on that coach was the military training manual that had been with him for more than a year, since, in fact, a talk with D. R. Jardine, one of his firmest friends, had convinced him of the need for preparation.

On that coach, too, was Norman Yardley, a century-maker at Hove, who had his first full season with the county behind him. Yardley, like Verity, was destined to be commissioned in the 1st Battalion, The Green Howards, and to be with them through the East into Italy. He last spoke to Verity on that baleful morning in Sicily.

A letter dated August 23, 1943, came to me from Yardley. He answered questions about Hedley . . . 'We have great hopes that he has been evacuated by the Boche. He was most certainly wounded while leading his Company. A search has been made of the area and there is no trace of him—and no trace of any grave. Another thing that makes us think he was wounded and is prisoner is that his batman stayed with him, has never been seen since, and so he is presumed to be a prisoner. I saw Hedley about an hour before the attack and had a word with him as I went past. He was very fit and in good spirits.'

The batman was Private Tom Rennoldson, a Durham man, who had never seen a first-class game of cricket. Time-expired and returning as a reservist, he had, in November, 1940, become Verity's batman, to serve him through Northern Ireland, India, Persia, Irak, Egypt, Syria and, finally, Sicily, where, as he told me, 'The captain put away his cricket gear for the last time and I took it to the P.R.I.'

Verity's company led the attack on the German strong point on July 19, 1943, and at his home at Bridlington after the war when he had been returned to England from a P.O.W. camp in Austria, Rennoldson told me of it:

'We were up against it and we went right into it. They set the corn alight and gave us everything they had got. We were trapped.

'It would be, as near as I can tell, between half-past three and half-past four in the morning when the captain was wounded in the chest. Some of our fellows smothered the fire in the corn, and there we stayed until the morning and the Germans came.

'They made me leave the captain and go to their headquarters where I found a nice young fellow—an officer—who spoke English. I told him that I had been compelled to leave my captain behind on the field. He said, "I will go with you"—and he did, though for him there was the danger that our men might attack again over that ground.

'When the German saw the captain he said, "We must find something to carry him on." Near the farm we got hold of a broken mortar carrier. The German officer packed it with sheaves of corn and we—the German and I —took the captain in on it.

'In the afternoon they moved him to a field hospital where, as they prepared for the operation, a grenade fell out of the pocket of the captain's bush shirt. The Germans told me to "unprime it", and there, in the improvised operating theatre, I removed the detonator and made the grenade safe.

'After that I got a tin of soup from the Germans and made some for the captain. I stayed with him until late that afternoon and the captain said he would try to keep me with him; but that was the last time I saw him. I was ordered away with the others who were not wounded.'

From the field hospital at Catania, Verity was taken through Messina and Reggio to Naples where the Germans handed him to the Italians who moved him to Caserta where on July 31, after another operation, he died.

His grave at one time had a stone with a white rose. Frank Smailes, who was on the coach from Brighton on September 1, 1939, and Phil King, a Yorkshireman who had played with Worcestershire before the war, fixed that. They met in Italy—one a captain and one a sergeant—in April, 1944, and hitch-hiked to Caserta to stand by the grave.

But now, of course, the grave is in the Military Cemetery at Caserta, and there it is occasionally visited by Yorkshire cricket folk. There was a white rose on it in 1954, for then, Hutton, M.C.C. captain, and a party in which there were cricketers from Surrey, Middlesex and Australia, as well as Yorkshiremen, left the *Orsova* when she called at Naples on the way to Australia.

Abe Waddington, who had bowled for Yorkshire in the decade before Verity's, was with them on the rush by car to Caserta, and it was his Yorkshire tie, with the white rose on blue, that was left on the stone so white under the Italian sun.

In 1946, the first season after the war, Hedley's name often turned up in the talk as we travelled about the country, mostly by train in times of petrol rationing. It was bound to do, for there was not a ground we visited which had not a link with him and his left-arm in one way or another.

I remember Sellers on a trip from Canterbury to London speculating on the part there might have been for Verity (38 a couple of months before he was fatally wounded) in Yorkshire's re-building, and it can be said here and now that Yorkshire's post-war story would have been a very different one had there been no early morning attack in Sicily by the 1st Battalion The Green Howards on the morning of July 19, 1943.

(1968)

Above: Geoffrey Boycott who, like two other distinguished Yorkshire opening batsmen, Herbert Sutcliffe and Sir Leonard Hutton, has scored 100 first-class centuries.

Opposite: Surely the supreme all-rounder? Garfield Sobers, in 1970. As a bowler he was capable of producing three different styles in a session, and his virtuosity in batting could humble the finest of bowlers.

Above: Ian Botham in Bombay, February, 1980—all-round sportsman, as cricketer, soccer player, fisherman and marksman.

Opposite top: The power, balance and control of the Australian fast bowler
Dennis Lillee.

Opposite bottom: Clive Lloyd, at Lord's, June, 1980. A magnificent West Indian
batsman and now captain of Lancashire.

Clive Taylor : 'His death was stupefying, for he avoided the occupational hazards of journalism, which are excess in most if not all things.' Ian Wooldridge (not for the first time) gets it right

The death of Clive Taylor, at the age of 50, has deprived the cricket Press box of a master craftsman and the game of one of its most rational and constructive critics. He died in Dorset on April 19 following an illness contracted while touring India last winter.

He would have detested a solemn or sanctimonious obituary notice, for he was the calmest and most pragmatic of men. He will be painfully missed by many reporters and cricketers, for he was a loyal, generous and amusing friend who could spot a phoney down the length of a cricket ground.

A reasonable club cricketer whose batsmanship reflected an idolatry of Len Hutton, Clive Taylor's outstanding talent was for reporting cricket in almost flawless yet graphic English at immensely high speed. In this he was without peer in the world.

The pressure, imposed by the early deadlines of the mass-circulation *Sun* newspaper, meant that he had to complete his report of a day's action in a Test match in England exactly 30 minutes before the close of play. Frequently he wrote 1,000 words inside 25 minutes, rarely changing a phrase and invariably thanking the young man who had to dictate it by telephone to his office. Next morning you could only marvel at its judgment and style.

It was a remarkable achievement, born of a rigorous newspaper training supplemented by extensive reading, an intense love of cricket and an appreciation of the Hemingway dictum about never confusing movement with action.

He rarely attended cocktail parties or Government House receptions, regarding them as an insufferable waste of time, and would leave any conversation the moment it turned to golf, which he found intolerably boring. Thus he unwittingly displayed the fierce independence which was the hallmark of his work.

Trained in local newspapers, the *Morning Advertiser*, and Reg Hayter's sports reporting agency, Clive Taylor could have written cricket with distinction for any England-language publication. That he chose to continue working for the *Sun*, despite frequent offers to move elsewhere, bemused many people who did not quite understand him.

Above all he was loyal to the *Sun*'s sports editor, Frank Nicklin.

Secondly, that loyalty was rewarded by a freedom to write as he pleased for a newspaper not noted for its restraint. He avoided insularity, chauvinism, vulgarity and cheap sensation and never wrote gratuitous scandal. Only the greatest professionals could have got away with it.

Born in London, he lived near Bridport, Dorset, which he adored so much that he would drive home on the rest days of Test matches in Nottingham or Manchester merely to spend a few hours there with his wife, Elsa, and daughter, Lynn.

The *Sun* proudly billed him as The Man the Players Read, and this was true. Sometimes they could not have liked what he wrote, for he was uncompromising and a fearless campaigner against bad manners and cheating. He never ducked an issue, from apartheid to throwing, and stood by what he wrote without fear or embarrassment.

Many tributes have been paid to Clive Taylor, but the truest was probably that of John Woodcock, cricket correspondent of *The Times*, 'Clive,' he said, 'could have done any of our jobs only better.'

His death was stupefying, for he avoided the occupational hazards of journalism, which are excess in most if not all things. He died at the height of his powers and will be missed more than a little.

(1977)

P. A. Gibb : he died at his station—not behind the wicket—but at a bus depot where he worked as a driver

Paul Anthony Gibb, who played eight times for England as a wicketkeeper and/or batsman between 1938 and 1946, collapsed and died on December 7 at Guildford bus station, where he was employed as a driver. He was 64. A 'private' man, he had needed some persuasion from his colleagues before accepting the invitation to the Melbourne Test Centenary celebrations earlier in the year. He lived alone in a caravan at Shamley Green.

Born at Brandsby, near York, on July 11, 1913, Paul Gibb worked for cricket-loving millionaire Sir Julien Cahn upon leaving St Edward's School, Oxford, and toured Canada, the U.S.A. and Bermuda with Cahn's side in 1933. His debut in first-class cricket was for Scotland against the 1934 Australians, and he scored 157 not out on his debut for Yorkshire (v. Notts) the following year, when he also went up to Cambridge, to gain the first of four Blues, making 122 in the Varsity match in his last year, 1938. The Manchester washout and then injury prevented him from making his

Test debut that season (when he recorded his highest score, 204 for Cambridge v. Free Foresters, and also carried his bat for 80 in the Cambridge innings of 163 against the Australians) but he toured South Africa with the 1938–9 M.C.C. side, and played in all five Tests.

His Test debut was memorable. Opening with Bill Edrich, Gibb made 93 in the first innings and 106 in the second at Johannesburg, sharing stands of 184 and 168 with Eddie Paynter, who succeeded in making a pair of hundreds. In the final Test, the notorious ten-day event at Durban, Gibb's 120 in England's 654 for 5 in the final innings included only two fours and, lasting 451 minutes, was the slowest century then ever made for England. His scoring rate was 15·96 runs per hour. Edrich (219) proved a worthy partner in a Somme-like attrition, their record second-wicket stand realising 280.

After the war, during which he flew Coastal Command Sunderlands and Catalinas, Gibb, bespectacled, prematurely bald, and with a passion for ice cream, played one more season for Yorkshire, in 1946, and twice in the Test series against India. That winter he went with M.C.C. to Australia, but played only in the first Test, at Brisbane, before ill-health contributed to his having to give way to Godfrey Evans. With the appreciable overall Test record of 581 runs, average 44·69, Gibb was to play no more for England—or Yorkshire. But he was lured back to first-class cricket in 1951 by Essex, as a professional now, a factor which caused his M.C.C. membership to be placed in abeyance. He made four centuries for his adopted county in 1951, and after retirement in 1956 he joined the first-class umpires' panel. In the early 1960s he settled for a time in South Africa, scene of his big Test scores, and coached at schools there. Among his pupils at Hilton College, Durban, was a young Mike Procter.

Returning to England, Paul Gibb worked in a London store before applying to the Alder Valley Bus Company for a job as driver. And in that capacity the frail, inoffensive former Test cricketer was to see out his days almost completely incognito.

David Frith (1978)

There will never be another

E. W. Swanton on Henry Longhurst: 'They always printed [his] article in the same place on the back page. More than a thousand'

Henry Longhurst's association with cricket, once he was freed from compulsory games at St Cyprian's, Eastbourne, and Charterhouse, was confined to a little mellow watching and pithy comment now and then from the hospitable confines of a Lord's box. But I suppose that among the wide readership of *The Cricketer* are several thousand golfers who at least will excuse this brief valedictory word about an old friend.

Moreover there is a fellowship—and a philosophy—about the world of games which, to me at least, especially links cricket and golf. To Henry's generation and mine a code attaches to the playing, and if at this some of the youngsters may sneer so much the worse for them. In all he wrote about golf, and in all he said to his vast following on television, Henry conveyed that the full expression of the game lay not only in its infinite skill and subtlety but in a tacit acceptance of civilised values. About the happenings in great championships and the tribulations of the week-end golfer alike he wrote and talked with the sympathy of one who knew the difficulties from experience: and, of course, he had in abundance the saving grace of humour.

In the early 'thirties we were not only colleagues on the *Evening Standard* but fellow-occupants with Ian Peebles of 8, King's Bench Walk, in the Temple, having cunningly rented the rooms, without having the slightest legal pretensions, from a retired barrister. It was in his early years as a journalist that Henry perfected the art of the short golf essay—something he reckoned might be read in five sedentary minutes in the loo before the Sunday morning round—for he was also simultaneously golf correspondent of the *Sunday Times*. This post he held, including the war period, for forty years.

During the Kemsley, as opposed to the Thomson, era they always printed the Longhurst article in the same place on the back page, and he took a natural pride in the fact that more than a thousand of these appeared in successive issues. When soon after the war the B.B.C. discovered the great pull of cricket and golf on television we often found ourselves handing over to one another: from Lord's to St Andrew's, or wherever, and vice-versa. Perhaps the story bears re-telling of how on one such occasion, seeing the golf picture succeed that of the Test Match, I handed over to Henry and after a brief moment remarked to my neighbour at the commentary point,

'. . . and I bet he's got his gin bottle up there in the tower'. This slanderous aside went out live because some ass of an engineer had omitted to make the switch, and it caused much consternation in the B.B.C. hierarchy. I assured them that Henry would only be amused—as he was. As his obituarist, James Dow, remarked in the *Sunday Times* the only things that gave him trouble were his putter and his liver.

It is not too much to say that on both sides of the Atlantic Henry 'made' TV golf. He said all that was needed with point and brevity, and when the picture told it all he said nothing. He was a master of what among our fraternity became known as 'the golden pause'. After a long struggle against illness the pause has become a silence, for which the world of game is the poorer. I don't believe that sport does not produce 'characters' any more, but there will never be another Longhurst.

(1978)

Charles Hallows—a household name in the North

by Sir Neville Cardus

Charles Hallows, who died on November 10, was renowned in the 1920s in every North-country home of cricket. He succeeded to the great Lancashire county tradition of opening batsmen—Hornby and Barlow, MacLaren and Ward, MacLaren and Spooner, then after the 1914–18 war, Makepeace and Hallows, Hallows and Watson.

In the summer of 1928 in consecutive games Hallows and Watson opened a Lancashire innings with scores of 200, 202, 107, 118, and accomplished first-wicket partnerships during this same season twelve times amounting to 100, four of those to 200.

Charles Hallows, nephew of James Hallows, a superb all-round player in the MacLaren high noon, first came into the Lancashire XI in 1919, and soon established himself. He was a left-handed batsman who combined great obstinacy with recurrent strokes of rare style, ease, and mastery. His straight-drives were classic. But, in his period, Lancashire batsmen put forward their finest strokes according to the plan of campaign mapped whenever Lancashire won the toss on a good wicket.

The plan envisaged 300 runs on the first day, enough, as a rule, to give scope for pushing home to victory by bowlers as top-class as Parkin, McDonald, Richard Tyldesley, Hopwood.

Harry Makepeace was the tactical power behind the throne. If the occasion happened to be Lancashire v. Yorkshire at Old Trafford—gates closed at 11 a.m. first day—and if Lancashire had won the toss in dry weather, the Makepeace dictate was: 'Now, lads, wicket's lovely. No fours before lunch!'

In those years a score of 300 in a day was considered tedious. I often 'slated' Lancashire, in my reports, for such 'slow' play; I often 'slated' Hallows if he scored a century in four, or three-and-a-half, hours. I did not know, in the 1920s and 1930s, what was coming to us.

Today, Charles Hallows would be my first or second choice, were I a selector, as opening batsman for England.

In 1928 he compiled 1,000 runs in a single month—May. In his career he scored 55 centuries, two in one match. But only twice was he chosen to play for England in Test matches—at Old Trafford in 1921, when he batted merely to put an end to a draw with Australia; and in 1928, at Lord's against West Indies, when, in first, he scored 26. Hobbs and Sutcliffe barred the front entrance of the England innings for years.

Before radio and television blew the bubble of cricketers' reputations, the name of Charles Hallows was a household word in the North. He played in great company—Rhodes, Macaulay, Sutcliffe, Leyland, Makepeace, Ernest Tyldesley, Parkin, Percy Holmes.

In a Lancashire v. Yorkshire engagement of Hallows' epoch you would see a dozen Test cricketers in action—seven or eight in the same Lancashire XI.

Hallows stood erect in the several circumstances of comparison. Also, he could break a partnership by left-arm bowling of graceful rhythm. I think he had the potentiality of a spin bowler. He preferred to go in first for Lancashire, to defend with a quite fascinating, sometimes exasperating, compound of dourness and lithe, effortless power and brilliance of stroke-play.

(1973)

F. H. Grisewood

Frederick Henry ('Freddie') Grisewood, the well-known broadcaster, who died at Grayshott, Hampshire, on November 16, 1972, at the age of 84, played once for Worcestershire in 1908 against Oxford University at Oxford, scoring 1 and 6 not out. In the same year, while up at Magdalen College after being in the Eleven at Radley, he scored 47 and took 2 for 15 in the Freshman's Match, his side winning by 271 runs. Mr Grisewood, however, did not represent his University in first-class cricket.

J.D.C.

Percy Holmes

J. M. Kilburn wrote of him: 'Neither unduly downcast in failure nor ostentatiously elated in success'

Percy Holmes, who died on September 3rd at the age of 84, was one of the most enjoyable of cricketers. He gave pleasure to those who watched and to those who played in his company. His own satisfaction in batting and fielding, and with the cricketing life of his time, was never obscured by an assumed indifference.

He came early to Yorkshire's notice through precocious success at club level, but his establishment in first-class cricket had to be postponed until after the First World War.

In 1919 he won his county cap, scored 1,887 runs and began his historic association with Herbert Sutcliffe. When he left the Yorkshire team in 1933 he had made over 30,000 runs, completed 67 centuries and shared in a world-record opening partnership.

For so accomplished and consistently successful a batsman his international appearances were remarkably limited. He played for England against the fearsome Australians at Trent Bridge in 1921, but not again until he toured South Africa in 1927-8 and only once more in England, as late as 1932. He was the victim of circumstances more than of any inadequacy in himself. Denied an immediate success he had no opportunity to try and try again.

There was no denying his quality. He looked a batsman of uncommon talent, sound in method and enterprising in manner. Swift footwork made the hook and the late cut his characteristic strokes and all his batting carried an air of briskness and eager anticipation. He signed himself with a little flourish of the bat at the end of his forward strokes and he was the most accommodating and trustworthy of partners in running between wickets.

His approach to the crease and his preparations to receive the ball had a military precision. He marched rather than walked, back straight, head held high. His general practice was to wear only a right-hand batting glove and his flannels and pads were invariably neat and clean. For fielding, when the grass was dry, he preferred light, rubber-soled footwear and he was as tireless on the boundary edge as he was alert in the slips.

He was accepted everywhere as a good companion in cricket, neither unduly downcast in failure nor ostentatiously elated in success. Yorkshire called him 'Wappy' in acknowledgment of one of his favourite hostelries near Huddersfield and when he chanced to be first to the reception desk, as the team were booking in for an away match, he created a composite nickname that Yorkshire applied to themselves for years. 'Register us,' he said, 'as Percy Holmes and his Circus.'

The crown of his career as an individual batsman was an innings of 315 not out at Lord's, chanceless and containing 38 fours. In partnership his day of days was at Leyton in 1932 when he and Sutcliffe opened the Yorkshire innings with 555. Holmes, hampered by lumbago, contributed 224 not out.

This was his last big innings and will be for ever his memorial. This most unselfish of cricketers was happy to share success.

(1971)

The gentle stalwart

Peebles on Woodfull

Bernard Shaw once pointed out that whilst there are many people with average eyesight there are comparatively few with normal vision. By the same token, if the popular image of the tough, taciturn, hatchet-faced, uncompromising warrior is the criterion, there have been few 'typical' Australian captains in the last fifty years. Bill Woodfull was just as far removed from this legendary figure as a man could be.

Woodfull was a well built, athletic looking man who bore an unmistakable air of the academic world to which he belonged. His features, familiar to all cricketers, were set in a thoughtful but friendly cast, his voice was quiet and never, on any recorded occasion, raised. His movements were deliberate rather than graceful, all these attributes compounding to give a quiet, likeable personality, but transparently one of courage and unfailing dependability. Woodfull's career as a cricketer accurately bore out this impression. The salient characteristic of his leadership was his anxiety to shoulder the full responsibility of his post. Wherever things were most awkward there the captain would be found, and seeking to stay there.

The steadfast sense of duty which dominated his whole character had solid foundation in his ancestry and early environment. He was the son of a methodist clergyman who inculcated in him not only the ethics of Christian behaviour, but also principles of orthodox batsmanship and, perhaps not so inconsistently, the legitimate deception of the 'googly'.

In 1921 the family moved from Maldon, whence Woodfull derived his second name, to Melbourne, and there he made his first appearance in State cricket. From modest beginnings he very soon started a lasting legend in association with W. H. Ponsford. The difference in his style from that of the other legendary heroes of his land, Trumper and Macartney, was about as great as men could achieve whilst still handling the same implement. His backlift was so slight as to be almost imperceptible, a feature of his play which early earned him the soubriquet of 'the worm killer'. It is notable that this affectionate but somewhat derogatory title rapidly gave way to the altogether more respectful and appropriate 'unbowlable'. Throughout his career he guarded his stumps more successfully than any batsman before or since.

Whilst his name was already well established in his own country, his first visit to England in 1926, was a success but not in any sense a triumph. In 1928-9 the fact that his side were thoroughly trounced by A. P. F. Chapman was the sort of challenge which naturally aroused his staunch spirit to full exertion, and he made three centuries in the series.

Despite this success his appointment as captain of the 1930 side to England came as a surprise, for it had been confidently expected that Jack Ryder, who had weathered the storm of defeat, would be entrusted with the ship he had done so much to restore and refit. The decision of Ryder's co-selectors may have been harsh, but, with due respect to its victim, it was to be eminently justified.

Woodfull's span saw immediate success, bitter defeat and dissension, and then final victory. These varying fortunes he met with the same unwavering modesty and courage. Basically a pacific man, he found himself in the forefront of the heated 'bodyline' controversy in which he strove to exert a restraining influence. His one protest, made in the moment of personal and severe physical hurt resulting from a system of which he heartily disapproved, was his oft-quoted reply to Sir Pelham Warner's sincere and well-intended regrets. It seems, in perspective, a mild and dignified protest and quite undeserving of the resentment it evoked at that time. When he tartly observed that one side was playing cricket and the other was not, anyone knowing the man would recognise that it was said in genuine affront at the course of events, not in petty resentment of his own, not inconsiderable, pain of the moment, which he was wont to bear without complaint.

Having emerged from a regettable situation with at least as much dignity as any other participant, he dealt with its rather embarrassing aftermath in 1934 with the same bland, unassuming certainty. As victor he retired after captaining his country in 25 Test matches, a greater consecutive number than any predecessor. Of those he won 14, drew 4, and lost 7. In all he played in 35 Test matches.

His figures in those matches, of which five were against the South Africans and five against the West Indies, are impressive—an average of 46 for 54 innings with seven centuries. His highest score was 155 against England at Lord's in 1930; but perhaps it may serve to endorse the earlier statement that he always sought the most dangerous challenge to point out that he twice carried his bat through a Test match innings. These were both occasions of sore adversity for his side; at Brisbane in 1928–9 he made 30 out of 66, and at Adelaide, in 1932–3, he battled through an innings of 193 to finish undefeated with 73. His figures in State cricket are well known and remarkable, bearing, as does his Test match career, a curiously similar pattern to those of his illustrious partner Ponsford.

Strangely enough there sticks in the writer's mind a moment of triviality which was revealing of the man. Delivering a most carefully prepared speech on an august occasion he suffered the orator's greatest agony by completely muffing the point of his story of the evening. He paused, then laughed unaffectedly at his own embarrassment and got, by way of consolation, a louder and warmer laugh than the best turn of point could possibly have brought.

It was a pleasant but chastening experience for the young cricketer to play against Woodfull. The somewhat guillotine-like movement of the bat presented an impassable barrier but, if it led to any belief that the lack of momentum robbed it of offensive power, this illusion was quickly dispelled. Any scorable ball was pushed with surprising force, or deflected with immaculate timing, and invariably shrewdly placed to best advantage. He would, characteristically, have time amidst these activities to say an encouraging word to the young, of either side. This was to be expected in the nature of the man for, when all was said and done, those who knew him said that his heart really belonged to his chosen profession of educating the young. He must have been a very good schoolmaster.

(1965)

Ron Roberts died at 40. Michael Melford remembers him

Ronald Arthur Roberts, whose distinguished writing on cricket gained him a world-wide reputation, has died at the age of 40.

All over the cricket world the death of Ron Roberts will be sorely felt—not only by his colleagues who worked with him and respected him as an accomplished journalist with a profound love of cricket. While still in his twenties he had the enterprise and vision to leave his job in Taunton and set off for Australia to report as a freelance the South Africans' 1952–3 tour of Australia.

Against all predictions it turned out to be a close and interesting series. He acquired more work than he can have foreseen and did it so well that his talents were swiftly recognised. His contacts grew, his capacity for work was enormous and he became a highly successful one-man business.

Winter and summer he went where cricket was played, and he reported many series overseas for the *Daily Telegraph* and the *Sunday Telegraph*. Through these, and the private tours which he began to organise himself with what seemed, perhaps deceptively, extraordinary nonchalance and lack of worry, he became one of the best known figures on the international cricket scene, immediately greeted as a friend in such widely separated places as South Africa, Rhodesia, India, Pakistan, Hong Kong, Singapore, Australia and New Zealand. Last autumn he arranged Yorkshire's tour of the United States, Canada and Bermuda and went on it himself.

His great contribution, for which he will be remembered gratefully in many places, is that he took on his tours players from all countries, not just from England. By playing in the same side, they made friendships and achieved an understanding which often proved of immense value when they were on opposite sides in sterner contests later.

(1965)

The man who made history

*Sir Frank Worrell died at 42 and C. L. R. James (who else?) recalls how he
initiated a regeneration in Test cricket*

Dying at the tragically early age of 42, Sir Frank Worrell had already
written his name imperishably in the annals of cricket. In practice and
theory combined, C. B. Fry dominated the first twenty years of the century;
similarly Sir Donald Bradman before 1948; after 1960 in Australia Frank
Worrell succeeded to the proud position.

Worrell was no accident. The merchant-planter class of Barbados made
cricket into the popular artistic expression and a social barometer of the
West Indies. That was the environment which moulded the future Worrell.
He was a prodigy, at the age of 13 playing for his school against cricketers
like Martindale, whose pace at the time was too much for most English
batsmen. Barbados selected him as a slow left-hander, but, sent in as a
night-watchman, he at once earned his place as a batsman. Before he was
20 he had scored 300 runs in a first-class match. But the Barbados social
discipline was very firm. Even when playing for the island as a schoolboy
he had to attend school every morning until play began.

He could not adjust to Barbados and went off to make his home in
Jamaica. Early in 1948 he scored 294 runs in three Tests against G. O.
Allen's team, and for the next few years probably had no equal anywhere.
In the winter of 1949 he went to India with a Commonwealth team. In
1950 he came to England with the West Indies team and that winter he
was again in India with a Commonwealth team. There was no memory of
anyone scoring runs in every class of cricket with such grace and power.
Of many historic innings he himself preferred 223 not out and 93 not out
in an unofficial Test at Kanpur in 1949–50. To his mastery of bat and ball
Worrell, in 1950–1 substituting for the ailing Ames in India, led his side
with notable skill. In Australia in 1951–2 he alone of the three Ws lived
up to their reputation. During that tour Worrell's form did not advance
and against India and against Australia in the West Indies, he was demon-
strably ineffective both with bat and ball: curiously enough, whether
scoring or failing he remained a stroke-player without peer. In England
in 1957 Worrell recaptured form. He played through the innings at Nottingham for 191 not out; bowling now fast-medium at Leeds he took seven
for 70. After an absence of two years from first-class cricket, against
England in the West Indies in 1959–60 Worrell at once played an innings
of 197 not out. He did little else of note in the series but at its end was

appointed captain, the result of a successful attempt to dislodge the mercantile-planter class from automatic domination of West Indies cricket.

Worrell as captain entered a decadent Test cricket. Captains sought to ensure the avoidance of defeat, batsmen to remain at the wicket, bowlers to avoid being hit. Worrell made the tremendous decision to restore to Tests the spirit of the game he had learnt in Barbados. Already experienced in India at building a team of disparate individuals, he was able to weld his West Indians from dispersed areas into a disciplined unit. Having rapidly created his instrument, Worrell initiated a regeneration. Benaud, the Australian captain, met him halfway and the result was the most exciting Test series in living memory.

In the M.C.C. tour to Australia in 1962–3, Test cricket seemed to sink back into the doldrums and everyone awaited with anxiety Worrell's team to England in 1963. They repeated the renaissance begun in Australia. George Duckworth believed that 'no more popular side has ever toured in the old country', and in the words of the Lord Mayor of London, 'A gale of change has blown through the hallowed halls of cricket.'

This was no casual achievement. Behind the singular grace and inherent dignity of his manner, Frank Worrell was a man of very strong character. He has himself confessed his strange inability to feel at ease in the society of Barbados. His relations with the West Indies Board of Control earned him the title of a 'cricket Bolshevik'. What is by now obvious is that he was possessed of an almost unbridled passion for social equality. It was the men on his side who had no social status whatever for whose interest and welfare he was always primarily concerned. They repaid him with an equally fanatical devotion.

It was typical of his particular origins that in 1958, planning his future after cricket, Worrell studied sociology at a university to emerge with a degree in 1959. He was a combination of most unusual gifts. His unobtrusive skill, his reserve and his dignity on the field made him a great favourite with the British public who saw in him the embodiment of qualities which they admired: after the 1963 tour he was knighted. But with the Australian public it was the same. The population of Melbourne turned out in 1961 to give Worrell's team a send-off 'the like of which is normally reserved for Royalty and national heroes'. Australia presented the Worrell Cup so as to ensure the memory of a historic tour.

His captaincy will stand on his record and on the evidence of the men who played with him and against him. But it is my duty to record that he had an altogether exceptional acuteness and intelligence of mind. I had long conversations with him and in 1963 I wrote publicly as follows:

'Worrell is one of the few who after a few hours of talk have left me as tired as if I had been put through a wringer. His responses to difficult questions were so unhesitating, so precise and so took the subject on to unsuspected but relevant areas, that I felt it was I who was undergoing examination. No cricketer, and I have talked to many, ever shook me in a similar manner.'

If his reserve permitted it, this remarkable intelligence could be seen in his views of West Indian society. To us who were concerned he seemed poised for applying his powers to the cohesion and self-realisation of the West Indian people. Not a man whom one slapped on the shoulder, he was nevertheless to the West Indian population an authentic national hero. His reputation for strong sympathies with the populace did him no harm with them, and his firm adherence to what he thought was right fitted him to exercise that leadership and gift for popularity which he had displayed so notably in the sphere of cricket. He had shown the West Indian mastery of what Western civilisation had to teach. His wide experience, reputation, his audacity of perspective and the years which seemed to stretch before him fitted him to be one of those destined to help the West Indies to make their own West Indian way.

When all this has been said, it must never be forgotten that Frank Worrell was a great cricketer on the field of play. His greatest years had been between 1948 and 1951 but it was characteristic that as a captain he re-mobilised himself and personally led the renaissance in Australia in 1960-1. He began the season with 1, 37, 65 not out and 68 not out, 82, 51, and 0 (absent hurt), 65 and 65 (first Test), 0 and 0 (second Test), 18 and 53, 22 and 82 (third Test), 71 and 53 (fourth Test). It was Worrell who set the tone for Sobers and Kanhai and the whole team, and the words of A. G. Moyes on his batting in the third Test should be recorded: 'Technically, he was the finest player in the West Indies side and in this innings he simply could not be faulted. If ever a man deserved a century it was Worrell that day, for he entered the arena when three had fallen for 22 and right from the start he batted with a superb mastery that reduced Davidson in a couple of overs to mediocrity.' He was a notable personality of our century and it was cricket which had made this West Indian what he was.

(1967)

'Great little Lancastrian'

Eddie Paynter died at his home in Keighley, Yorkshire, on February 5, aged 77.

Cyril Washbrook, the former Lancashire captain and England opening batsman, pays this tribute to his friend and county colleague:

'I count myself fortunate indeed to have played with Eddie Paynter and to have enjoyed his close companionship before war brought an abrupt end to his first-class playing career in 1939. Success came to him by what we, in Lancashire, call sheer guts and a scant regard for the reputation, however forbidding, of opposing bowlers. His 16,555 runs for Lancashire at an average of 41·59, and the even more impressive figure of 59·23 from 1,540 runs in 20 appearances at Test level, are ample proof of his standing in the game.

'Eddie could hardly be described as a correct, or even stylish batsman, being a complete law unto himself in his method of playing all types of bowling. He never flinched, nor showed any signs of fear in facing the world's fastest bowlers but, being small in stature, he often played the short-pitched delivery or bouncer with both feet off the ground to achieve the necessary extra height to play the ball down. He never worried about attempting to read leg-breaks and googlies from the bowler's hand, being content to play from the pitch. He hit the ball hard and often, with every loose delivery receiving the full treatment.

'From the beginning of the 1937 season until the outbreak of war in 1939, I had the great privilege of opening the Lancashire innings with Eddie. We were fortunate to enjoy a very good understanding in our running between the wickets and rarely missed an opportunity of taking the quick single. Quite apart from keeping the scoreboard moving, the frustrating necessity for the bowlers constantly to change their line of attack against the left and right-hand batting combination frequently had a general unsettling effect on opposing counties.

'This feature was never more clearly demonstrated to Lancashire's advantage than in our match against Sussex at Hove in 1937. Eddie's score at lunch was 127 and I, considerably slower, had scored 68. As many will recall, in those days, a new ball could be taken after 200 runs had been scored, which occurred in the second over after lunch. By five o'clock that afternoon, Eddie was relaxing in the bath after going on to score 322 out of a Lancashire total at close of play of 640. The slowest scoring rate of the day came in the last hour's play, by which time Eddie was enjoying a quiet drink at one of the bars around the ground. Those who condone the pedestrian rate of scoring so frequently witnessed in the first-class game today may care to take note.

'In his last full season and despite his wonderful playing record, he found himself passed over by the selectors for the final Test against the West Indies at The Oval. One of the batsmen brought into the England XI was Walter Keeton of Nottinghamshire who, by chance, were playing Lancashire at the time the team was announced. Eddie's reaction was typical of him—"I'll show 'em tomorrow", and he did—with a century.

'Just two years ago, this great little Lancastrian and I were invited to join the party of ex-internationals, whose playing careers spanned more than fifty years, at Heathrow to board a 400-seater jumbo bound for the Centenary Test celebrations in Melbourne. For Eddie, it was the very first time he had ever set foot in an aircraft, but how thrilled he was by this entirely unexpected opportunity to meet so many old friends once again and relive times past.'

Editor : Paynter wrote his name into the annals of Test history during Douglas Jardine's tour to Australia in 1932–3. In the fourth Test at Brisbane he developed tonsillitis but discharged himself from a sick bed and, though still ill and weak, played a superb innings of 83 which guided England into a first innings lead, a situation which had seemed most unlikely when eight men were out for 271 with England still 69 behind. He also achieved the distinction later on, of making the winning hit which enabled The Ashes to be regained.

He scored 45 centuries—the first in 1931 against Warwickshire at Old Trafford—and in the 1938–9 series in South Africa hit 653 runs (average 81·62) which remains the highest aggregate for a series between the two countries in South Africa.

He shared two record partnerships against the 1938 Australian team, 222 for the fourth with Walter Hammond at Lord's and 206 for the fifth with Denis Compton at Trent Bridge, where he finished with 216 not out.

His many batting achievements were the more remarkable for the fact that he did not receive his first chance in the Lancashire XI until he was 25. He had to wait more than ten years to establish a regular place in the side but as *Wisden* observed when making him one of their Five Cricketers of the Year in 1938 . . . 'the real turning point of his career occurred the following summer, 1932, when he scored 152 against Yorkshire at Bradford. That innings probably placed him in the forefront of Lancashire cricket.'

(1979)

Father of modern cricket-writing

Sir Neville Cardus, who died in a London hospital on February 28, at the age of 85, was among the most imaginative of writers and founder of modern creative cricket journalism. There cannot have been many cricket enthusiasts whose early passions were not ignited by Cardus's prose in books or newspapers; *The Cricketer* too was often privileged to feature his work. The following tribute by John Arlott appears by kind courtesy of the *Guardian*:

'The father of literate sports-writing is gone. Sir Neville Cardus objected—with fair reason—to being described as a cricket-writer. He was a writer; and, whether that was cricket, music or life—his own or anyone else's—he wrote Cardus. He stocked his mind out of his reading—from tuppenny "bloods" to Dickens—and the concerts, music halls and plays he could afford to see in Manchester at the turn of the century, and fused it all with the flame of enthusiasm.

'He made his deepest mark as a cricket-writer because his other subjects had all been regularly treated by outstanding writers. Cricket, sport in general, had not had that benefit. So, when, in June 1919, W. P. Crozier, then news editor of the *Manchester Guardian*, suggested that the convalescent Cardus should spend a few days writing about cricket from Old Trafford instead of Manchester news in the office, the young man advanced on a vulnerable position. Within a year, "Cricketer"—his *nom de plume*—was positively selling newspapers through the most imaginative reports the game had known. *A Cricketer's Book*, a selection of his writings, was put out by as distinguished a publisher as Grant Richards, and this found him a new, small but discriminating public. Afterwards—like a novelist embarrassed by a youthful slim volume of verse—he was somewhat shamefaced about the "greenery yallery" excesses of his early days. The fact remains that he was the first writer to evoke cricket; to create a mythology out of the folk-hero players; essentially to put the feeling of ordinary cricket-watchers into words. They warmed to him and created for him a following which never faded.

'On other subjects he wrote well; in cricket he initiated a literature. Just as there can never be a greater cricketer than W. G. Grace—because he created the whole technique of modern cricket, which no one can do again—so there can never be a greater cricket-writer than Neville Cardus. He created cricket-writing. Others perform what he showed them: there is not one of his juniors who has not been influenced by him; and few who have not, shamelessly, copied him.

'His *Autobiography* and its sequel *Second Innings* demonstrate beyond doubt his skill as a writer. Ten cricket books and seven on music complete his output. He was, though, in his own mind, above all, a *Manchester Guardian* man—"a dear tyrant, the 'MG'. I have never been able to break free from it." He was not simply proud but excited and grateful to be that paper's cricket correspondent and music critic. He went to Australia to broadcast and to write for the *Sydney Morning Herald*; when he came back he worked for a year on the *Sunday Times*; but he felt the tie and returned to the *Guardian*.

'He wrote, always in pen, in a flowing hand, with barely an alteration. After a performance at Covent Garden a hire-car driver would collect his copy from the nearby restaurant where he had written it and transport it to the office—"I cannot bear the idea of going to Gray's Inn Road".

'Neville Cardus was pre-eminently a man who enjoyed—reading, writing, listening to music, eating, talking, drinking, watching, travelling— his gusto was immense. Sex, he said, was a late-blooming pleasure. He married Edith—"because I always said if I married anyone it would be her". She it was who, when he was a boy, guided him to and lent him the books on which his culture was founded.

'She was amazed to find herself Lady Cardus; he was at heart equally staggered by his knighthood, though outwardly blasé—"It is so useful, it gets me a table at the Savoy". He was proud to dine with the chairman of the Hallé in a house where, as a boy, he had delivered the washing—and he told his host as much: proud, too, at being made president of Lancashire.

'He retained zest and enthusiasm to the end. Although he was, he said, "a delicate child" he was generally well (apart from diplomatic ailments which enabled him to avoid a boring engagement) and he could not bear to contemplate illness. He was 85: he had called his last book *Full Score*; he was not a greedy man. Indeed, he was a most generous one. He cherished his few enemies almost as enthusiastically as his many friends. His public life is published: less well known is his kindness to an unknown beginner in the craft he had created; his generosity, his unstinting delight in some- one else's success; gratitude is part of the regret.'

(1975)

Dai Davies

An appreciation by Wilfred Wooller

The sudden death of Dai Davies, one month short of his eightieth birthday, marked the last of the great characters who served Glamorgan cricket in the erratic decade when the Welsh county was finding its first-class feet.

Dai Davies was the first genuine Welsh professional. He arrived on the first-class scene at the age of 29, when he was an established Llanelli club player of merit, in a way which heralded his typical flair for drama. In 1923 he was woken up at 10 a.m. by his mother after being on the night shift to play cricket 'somewhere or other'. This turned out to be for Glamorgan at St Helen's, Swansea, where he arrived to be refused admission to the pavilion because he was unknown. He eventually got on to the field against Northants when the score was 40 for 0. Dai Davies was never a man to do anything by halves. When he was put on to bowl he took a wicket in his fourth over and got two more before lunch. He came in to bat when Glamorgan were struggling at 131 for 7 and hit 58 runs. He opened the batting in the second innings, scored 51, and Glamorgan won a rare victory.

Dai was destined to become one of the great Welsh cricket characters. He was a 'tumultuous' after-dinner speaker who brought a real Welsh Hwyl into his dissertations, and he would have made a magnificent preacher after the manner of the great Welsh pulpit orators. He stayed in cricket all his life and after an active playing career became one of the outstanding Test umpires of the decade or so after the war, and umpired in 23 Tests involving every major cricket nation. In August 1951 he dismissed the immortal Len Hutton for 'obstructing the field' when South African wicketkeeper Russell Endean scrambled around him to make a catch which Hutton flicked out of his way.

Dai hit 15,000 runs before his career ended in 1939 and scored more than 1,000 runs on six occasions. His highest score of 216 came in his last season at Newport, in 1939, when Dai was angered by a Somerset crawl of 385 runs. He decided to stay at the wicket as long as Monmouthshire miners were down the pit staging a stay-down strike. As he passed the 200 mark nearly nine batting hours later the call came from the pavilion, 'The colliers are up, Dai!' He developed his own dour dependable style and became an excellent three or four in a strong pre-war line-up.

Jack Hobbs referred to him as one of the greatest cover points in the game. At military medium with a suitable sense of presentation he took 271 wickets and held 192 catches.

Dai was a Welshman and very proud of his national heritage. It was his custom when batting with Emrys Davies to talk in Welsh, and this not only confused the opposition in moments of normality but even more so in moments of crisis because Dai, after the manner of Denis Compton, was apt to rush up the wicket for a quick single shouting in Welsh, 'No, go back!'

(1976)

Bert Oldfield

Ray Robinson recalls a master of glovework and safety

A fusion of skill and style distinguished the wicketkeeping of William Albert Stanley Oldfield, who died at 81 in Sydney on August 10, with some of his feats still unequalled. Matching his bland sportsmanship, a constant quest for perfection rewarded Bertie with the distinction of being the first 'keeper to reach 50 Tests and to play in 54 without missing one through a hand injury.

Oldfield is the only wicketkeeper who dismissed 90 Englishmen in Tests (38) and had 15 wickets in a series in England before Tests were lengthened to five days. He was first to bring off 38 wickets for one bowler, Grimmett, who said he could never have achieved his degree of success without Bertie.

When a German shellburst near Ypres in 1917 buried a squad of stretcher-bearers, Oldfield was dug out unconscious, the only survivor. Well-muscled for a man barely 5 ft. 6 in., he was nicknamed 'Hercy', short for 'pocket Hercules', in the Australian Imperial Forces tour in 1919.

Amid tensions of Test cricket his politeness was reflected in a chapter being headed The Gentleman in Gloves. Batsmen knew better than to assume from his courteous greeting that he would be lenient with a snick or stumble. They had not invented 'walking' before the Second World War, yet his 130 wickets were obtained with fewer appeals than crowds expect. Sir Jack Hobbs believed Oldfield never appealed unless he believed the umpire would uphold it. Umpire Frank Chester recalled having been ready to signal Hobbs out leg-before in an Oval Test but neither leg-spinner Mailey nor Oldfield appealed.

Bertie asked N.S.W. slipfielders hearing a noise as ball passed bat not to appeal until he held the catch aloft.

Hobbs was victim of his widest catch, running to leg slip at Sydney for a glance off Gregory's fast inswinger, and of his most spectacular leg-side stumping, off Ryder, medium-pace, at Melbourne. Yet captain W. M. Woodfull thought his finest 'keeping was on the 1926, 1930 and 1934 tours of England, when he was in his thirties.

Kneading emulsion into his gloves and safeguarding his joints with finger-stalls, tape and two sets of inner gloves took Oldfield an hour before each day's play. The courtier of keepers based his balance and footwork on orthodox heels-down stance and tried to convert Godfrey Evans from his tilted wait on the balls of his feet. He kept his finger-ends low without touching the grass.

Hobbs thought him the neatest of all 'keepers and team-mates O'Reilly and Ponsford ranked him the best they knew. They nicknamed him 'Cracker'. He has since been excelled in glove-speed and safety only by Don Tallon, whom Sir Donald Bradman ranks as the finest of all.

Oldfield's peaceful passing snaps the last Australian link with wicket-keeping as it used to be. Nobody else has stumped 52 Test batsmen. Out-cricket is a changed art since 1947's drastic imbalance of new balls began the eclipse of slow spinners in most countries. Whereas Bertie stumped 40 per cent of his victims, Evans stumped fewer than one-quarter of his Test wickets, Grout one-eighth, Knott, one-thirteenth and Marsh one-twentieth.

Of Oldfield's 130 Test wickets against England, South Africa and West Indies all except 39 were taken up at the stumps, a tribute to his reflexes. Five of his stumpings were off medium-pacers Ryder, Kelleway, McCabe and Hurwood. He stood back only to the fastest bowlers. For 17 years he was one of the first names in selectors' lists.

Thickened joints on the first fingers of his left hand were the only traces of having taken thousands of balls in 245 first-class matches, more than 100 grade games and dozens of earlier junior games on matting stretched over concrete.

Oldfield's only absence from a Test through injury was for a skull fracture when at the age of 38 he edged an attempted hook at an offside bouncer from Larwood at Adelaide in the Bodyline series.

Grout 187 and Marsh 160 have passed his Test total but he is the only Australian 'keeper who has exceeded 600 wickets.

English crowds saw more of his polished glovework than by any other Australian 'keeper this century—five visits, including the A.I.F. Before the third he married at 35. He was in line for a unique record of the only man to play in every Anglo-Australian series between the two World Wars until errors against G. O. Allen's team at 42 cost him a place in Bradman's 1938 tour team. Problems in detecting Fleetwood-Smith's left-arm googly and topspinner undermined his confidence. Though he figured in a number of run-outs as batsman as well as 'keeper, Oldfield was the first gloveman to score 1,000 in Tests, total 1,427 (av. 22). Five centuries in first-class games included 132 at Kimberley, 123 against Warwickshire and 129 for N.S.W. against Victoria.

In the Second World War the Army used his knowledge of sportsgoods as a major in the Amenities Service. He wrote *The Rattle of the Stumps* at 60, coached schoolboys in Ethiopia at 69 and was awarded the M.B.E. at 76. He died the morning of a lunch date with Harold Larwood.

Herbert Sutcliffe, 81, who batted all day for four of his Test centuries against Australia with Oldfield crouching behind him, wrote from a Yorkshire nursing home to the Australian's widow Ruth: 'Like me, he was a Christian. We will meet in the holy of holies where I am sure Bert will captain the team.'

(1977)

The Duke of Norfolk

*Colin Cowdrey salutes 'the cricketer's friend', who died on January 31, 1975,
aged 66*

'This boy has ability, but we only see him at his best playing football or cricket.' Much to the dismay of his mother this was the standard report from the headmaster of the Oratory School on young Bernard, Duke of Norfolk, who had succeeded to the title at the age of nine. The predicted ability became plain for all to see in his series of administrative triumphs as Earl Marshal, but his interest in sport ran deep and sustained him right to the end.

He owed his love of cricket to his father, who laid out the ground at Arundel Park and took our Duke to his early matches, notably at Hove, Lord's and The Oval. Furthermore his mother was a Yorkshirewoman and the family owned Bramall Lane, Sheffield. So he developed when young a close link with Yorkshire cricket. But his first loyalty was to Sussex, to whom he gave unique service for some forty years as president and patron.

Blessed with an eye for a ball and a good cover-drive, he insisted that cricket should always be an attacking game. He had no time for defensive batsmen, maiden overs, ringed fields bent on saving runs, and players who nursed averages. Cricket was a game for enjoyment and I had the feeling that good cricket, especially cricket on his own lovely ground, brought him more fun than anything else in the world.

Just before I learned of my call to Australia [1974–5], Billy Griffith and I lunched with him at Arundel. He was not well but we talked cricket and hoped for better things from Brisbane. Little knowing that I would be flying to Australia the following week, he ventured with a mischievous twinkle in his eye: 'Mr Thomson looks very fast to me, even for young 42-year-olds!'

If his presidency of M.C.C. in 1957–8 was inevitable his appointment as manager of M.C.C. in Australia in 1962–3 took the cricket world by surprise. It seems that Ted Dexter was the selectors' choice as captain provided that the right manager could be found, a man both wise and strong enought to guide his mercurial temperament and so harness his undoubted gifts. Such a man proved elusive and it was a result of this dilemma that the twin partnership of Norfolk and Bedser was forged.

I am sure I can speak for all the players when I say that no manager could have gone to more trouble to care for them. We found him the kindest and most considerate man. As a speech-maker he was in a class of his own and the Australians came to love and respect him. In later years he had a special affection for the West Indies, taking a side to Jamaica in 1957 and another to the eastern Caribbean in 1970. In a period of convalescence, enchanted by Tobago he yearned to take further tours to help cricket in the smaller islands but alas he was never well enough.

In 1970 we persuaded him to play in Dominica and I am sure that this was his happiest day playing cricket. The crowd was packed to capacity in the lush tree-ringed setting of the Botanical Gardens. Amid scenes of feverish excitement we won in the last over by five runs. Within a few seconds the little pavilion was surrounded by several thousand deliriously happy Dominicans chanting 'Nor-foak'. He climbed on a chair, silenced them with an imperial wave of the hand, produced the sort of speech which only he could have done, culminating in a very funny story which left them laughing and dancing with delight. The chanting broke out again: 'You our friend, Massa Dook!' I know how they felt. He was more than cricket's Duke; he was the cricketer's friend.

(1975)

Howard Marshall

Rex Alston writes: Howard Marshall, who died on October 27, aged 73, was the first man to bring cricket into our homes. His rich, melodious voice, his journalistic ability, and his knowledge and love of the game (he was an

Oxford Authentic) enabled him to convey over the air a feeling for cricket which endeared him to millions.

Commentary style and presentation have changed over the years, but the principles which Howard worked out—'always follow the ball' and 'vary the pace to suit the action'— still stand, and those who followed him salute him as one of the great pioneers. I was fortunate to be learning the commentary trade as he was forsaking regular broadcasting for a business career: no man could have been a more helpful adviser or a better model.

Howard, a big, friendly man, was the most versatile of all the early broadcasters. Rugby football, at which he nearly played for England, boxing, and State occasions all came easily to him, and his radio war despatches from North Africa and Western Europe, especially his memorable description of the D-Day landings, set a pattern for colourful on-the-spot reporting. But he will be remembered primarily as the first Voice of Cricket.

(1973)

Leslie O'B. Fleetwood-Smith

He became a down and out. Here is a brief and affectionate chronicle by Ray Robinson

Leslie O'Brien Fleetwood-Smith, the former Australian Test bowler, died in Melbourne on March 16 at the age of 60. He had made an inspiring comeback from the precincts of Skid Row for two years before illness ended his life.

At his previous stay in St Vincent's Hospital, Melbourne, last year doctors called the famous googly left-hander the 'miracle man' when he survived a prostate operation, Hong Kong 'flu, bronchitis and supervening pneumonia and septicaemia.

When his second marriage broke up the cricket world was shocked to read of a court appearance giving the impression that he had become a park-bench deadbeat. On a charge of having insufficient means of support a good-behaviour bond was granted by a magistrate who could see beyond the shabby surface.

He acknowledged that the court appearance spurred him to pull himself together and make a fresh start in the late 50s. After the heady heights of bowling for Australia against England's batting idols, before packed crowds, he had failed to settle to regular employment as a salesman whose round involved calling on hotelkeepers for orders. 'Too many friends, too many social drinks,' he recalled with a twisted smile.

In 123 first-class matches Fleetwood-Smith's 597 wickets cost fewer than 23 runs each, a run less than Richie Benaud's and only half a run more than Grimmett's. 'Chuck's' striking rate was exceptionally quick, a wicket every 41 balls. He hit the stumps of almost one-third of his 42 victims in 10 Tests.

'Batting is different now,' he mused. 'I don't see anyone batting like Ponsford or McCabe used to. I don't bring Bradman into it, because he was something apart from the others. In Britain an English bowler asked me: "How do you bowl to this man?" I told him: "Now, what have you to complain about? You only come up against him every fourth year. We have him all the time, every summer." The Englishman said: "Yes, but how do you bowl to him?" Over my shoulder as I walked away, I said: "Sorry, old chap, but that's not my worry . . . not just now, anyway." '

Sipping lemonade, Fleetwood-Smith reflected: 'A great English batsman I can never forget was Hammond. In a double-century against Victoria in 1932 he blazed 32 off a couple of overs from me. As he intended, that cooked my chance of Test selection then, but I managed to get on the 1934 tour of England with Bill Woodfull skipper. As third-change bowler at Bristol I came up against Hammond and got a wrong'un past to bowl him. As he walked by me Wally said: "A good one, too early." Next meeting at Folkestone I bowled a succession of top-spinners to Hammond. Oldfield stumped him off the last one, which he expected to turn from the off. Wally told me: "I didn't think you'd give me another one." So we finished all square.'

Friends who rallied to him when he appeared in court early in 1969 watched him bringing off a comeback which nobody had prophesied. We should have known it was not beyond a man who, in The Oval Test wherein Sir Leonard Hutton made the Anglo-Australian record 364, could bowl 87 overs in England's mammoth innings. When we parted, with a handshake as firm as his grip on the ball, neither of us guessed that another onset of bronchial congestion would end his life less than two months later.

(1971)

Scholars, schoolmasters and cricketers of distinction

E. W. Swanton puts on his clinical and psychological glasses to diagnose H. S. Altham and R. C. Robertson-Glasgow. They died within a few days of each other

It is axiomatic that a game reflects the character of those who play and those who serve it. By this token cricket is made infinitely poorer by the deaths within a few days of one another of H. S. Altham and R. C. Robertson-Glasgow. In personality so unalike, they had so much in common that they were inevitably close friends. Both were scholars, Raymond—or 'Crusoe' as he was generally known in the cricket world—literally so of his college, Corpus. Both were cricketers of distinction, both schoolmasters, though 'Crusoe's' health was the cause of his turning quite early from teaching to games-writing. That, of course, was a talent they shared in a high degree, and uniquely wide as was the scope of Harry Altham's contributions to the game it is probably as a historian that he will be best remembered.

Both in their separate styles were in the highest class of after-dinner speakers, and while in later life 'Crusoe' was on doctor's orders forbidden to indulge his wit and whimsical fancy in this way Harry's astonishing zest led him to undertake more than he should have done. It was not in his nature to ease up. He hated to say no to any request in connection with cricket, and I suppose that the manner of his death, after speaking at a cricket dinner, will have been very much as his friends would have foretold.

Both were devoted in particular to Oxford cricket and the Parks, where in the spring those University sides whose captains were wise enough to invite them were sure to profit from their advice. In the 'thirties their visitations often coincided, and the fortunate undergraduates might turn from the kind, encouraging, dedicated coaching of the one to the light-hearted, not to say at times ribald, comment of the other.

H. S. A., of course, was the complete mentor, but 'Crusoe' was a great help to bowlers, especially the faster ones of his own kind, as many a now middle-aged cricketer will testify. Both perhaps were altogether at their best and happiest with the young in any sort of context. Harry's interest in and encouragement of the Winchester racket players was second only to his involvement in the cricket: and to how many has he not brought an appreciation of things ecclesiastical by his tours of Winchester Cathedral, of which he was perhaps the leading authority? Who of St Andrew's School, Pang-bourne, in the grounds of which 'Crusoe' lived for the last twenty years of his life, will not remember his brilliant, highly individual conduct of the Litt. Soc.?

Both, incidentally, have been among the most distinguished contributors to *The Cricketer* ever since the paper was founded in 1921. As all the cricket world knows Harry's *History* first appeared in serial form in this paper in the early 'twenties: how he found time for the research and the writing, leading the busy life of a Winchester don, and playing for Hampshire and the Harlequins in August, is one of the minor miracles. His 'Then and Now' essay in the issue of last November will have given many modern players an insight into the changes of the last fifty years. I need scarcely say how much we will all miss 'Crusoe' Talking at Random. His piece in the March number must have been almost the last thing he wrote.

Since both fulfilled for me every test of friendship over a span of well over thirty years I am endeavouring from a distance to augment with these personal memories and impressions the obituaries that will be appearing elsewhere in this issue. I first got to know Harry on the cricket field playing against him when the Harlequins came to the Saffrons on their August tour.

He managed and led the Harlequins, and to observe him in either capacity was an education to a young cricketer. Much fun, infinite good humour, but always the fullest rigour of the game: no half-hearted performer, inclined to slackness, would have lasted a second match with him.

In 1937 Harry asked me, to my great joy, to undertake the new work on the second edition of *A History of Cricket*, and since then we had been associated closely not only in the subsequent editions but in other ventures, not least *The World of Cricket* (to be published in October), to which he has contributed some superb biographical sketches of the great. I had not supposed he would want to be plagued with much work on this new venture, until I found him almost offended at not having been asked to do more. In the end, to the inestimable advantage of the book, he has written some 30,000 words. Such was his energy and unimpaired enthusiasm.

I am not sure that when he retired from regular teaching at the end of the 'forties he did not become even busier than before. His life revolved now around the twin foci of Winchester and Lord's. The Treasurership of M.C.C., involving ex-officio membership of all committees, made the most exacting demands, as also did the M.C.C. Youth Cricket Association. This was very largely his brainchild, the germ of the idea coming, I believe, from a correspondence in the *Daily Telegraph* following the triumphal tour of the 1948 Australians. It is one of my regrets that I was never able to get to Lilleshall for one of the coaching courses run by the M.C.C. Y.C.A. of which he was the inspiration right up to his death.

The tragic key to 'Crusoe's' life was the acute mental depression that plagued him in black, inevitable cycles, alternating with the moods of exaltation and mental brilliance when all his best work was done, and when he was the most scintillating company in the world. This half of him was all that most were permitted to see, and it is by this that he will be remembered. 'Crusoe' batting, arms crossed, with a surf-board on the sands at Jersey, 'Crusoe' going in number 11 to save the match for Somerset at Fenner's, entering the field from the press-box at square-leg where he had been shaping his light report for the *Morning Post*, and being stumped by a mile: above all perhaps, 'Crusoe' on many a summer's evening among the tankards at Vincent's holding forth with a spontaneity wonderfully diverse on any subject under the sun. 'Here's Crusoe', everyone would say whereever cricketers gathered, 'now for some fun!' He never disappointed, but few knew at what cost. He, like Harry Altham in a rather different way, was very much the victim of his friends.

(1965)

Wilfred Rhodes died aged 95 in 1973. Bill Bowes knew all about him

Wilfred Rhodes, Yorkshire and England cricketer, perhaps the greatest all-rounder in the history of the game, died in a Dorset nursing home on July 8, aged 95. He had outlived his wife, daughter, and son-in-law with whom he had lived for many years in Bournemouth after becoming totally blind. Apart from his affliction he had kept in excellent health, physically and mentally alert, and never happier than when talking cricket or going to 'watch' a Test match. 'I see they've taken new ball,' he said on one occasion.

'You see?' said his companion in surprise.

'Aye,' said Wilfred, 'It makes a different noise on t'bat.'

I introduced Yorkshire slow left-arm bowler Don Wilson many years ago with the remark, 'And if you want to know anything about bowling this man will tell you everything you want to know.'

Wilfred smiled his pleasure at what was a truth rather than a compliment and said to Wilson, 'I don't know about that, young man, but I'll tell you one thing I've noticed, you're bowling a bit too short.'

Wilfred seemed to guess from the ensuing silence that Don was looking at him in amazement, and he continued.

'Aye, I can tell where they've hit t'ball when I hear t'fieldsmen's feet, especially when they hit it in my direction and they're hitting it in my direction too often. It means they're square-cutting and a slow bowler should never be square-cut or pulled.'

Born at Kirkheaton, near Huddersfield, on October 29, 1877, Rhodes played his first game for Yorkshire in 1898 after a professional engagement in Scotland. It was the realisation of an ambition he had cherished all his life.

I had a letter from a Mrs Nora Marsden of King's Heath, Birmingham, the other day and she told me her father, Mr Crow, retired in 1919 after being a schoolmaster in Kirkheaton.

She writes: 'One day Mr Rhodes senior called to see my father and said, "Can you do anything to change my son? He has nowt in his head but cricket." My father wisely replied, "Leave well alone, he'll probably make his name in sport." '

It was wise advice, but Wilfred's chance to make a name with Yorkshire came as a result of an argument between Lord Hawke and Sir Stanley Jackson. Lord Hawke favoured a left-arm bowler called Albert Cordingley, Sir Stanley favoured Rhodes and a toss of the coin settled the issue.

His skill and highly developed cricket brain brought immediate success with 154 wickets in his first season and more than 1,000 in five years.

He had that supreme ability of being able to get batsmen out in the air. His flighting of the ball was so cleverly hidden that Bert Strudwick, one of the best wicketkeepers the game has known, said, 'Wilfred was the most difficult man of all to take. I kept wicket to him hundreds of times but he was always making me snatch for the ball before it arrived or hitting in my gloves before I expected it.'

He had spin and immaculate control, an economical and graceful three-pace bowling action and, always in evidence, a cricket brain.

From a No. 11 batsman he made himself a No. 1 for Yorkshire and England. With George Hirst at The Oval in 1902 he shared a last-wicket partnership to give England a dramatic victory and, a year later, shared with R. E. Foster a record tenth-wicket partnership of 130. With Jack Hobbs at Melbourne in 1911 he shared a record opening partnership of 323. He was a safe catcher of the ball, too, and his records stamp his greatness.

He helped the other players too, acted the general in the field and was always consulted by the wise captains. I once asked him about one famous England captain, 'Was he good?'

'Aye, Bill. Very good, he allus did as he wor told,' came the astonishing reply.

In my first County Championship match against Essex I watched Wilfred take nine wickets for 39 runs.

I fielded at mid-on and as batsman Laurie Eastman came to the wicket Wilfred called to me, 'Go back a bit for this chap, Bill.'

I went back. 'Too far,' said Wilfred. 'Come in a bit.'

I came in. 'Now a bit to your right. No, too far, come back a bit. Now in a yard. Nay, nay, nay!'

Despairing of ever getting me where he wanted me, Wilfred walked across and scratched a big cross with his spikes.

'See lad,' he said. 'Stand theer.'

Three balls later Eastman hit one so hard if I'd been a foot either side of that mark I should never have seen it. As it was I had to catch it or it would have gone clean through me. Fortunately I caught it. Wilfred so to speak had put a fieldsman on a sixpence.

He walked across and the only thing he said was, 'You see, lad, always go where th'art put . . . go wheer th'art put.'

When Wilfred retired in 1930 he went as coach to Harrow school but he was far too advanced for schoolboys who wanted elementary principles and enthusiasm rather than instruction in the three lines of defence—left leg, bat, and right leg swinging round.

Wilfred was at his best among cricketers who understood his language and I doubt anyone ever talked with him, or watched him, without learning something.

Some other tributes

Sir Donald Bradman : I believe his greatest triumph was the uncomplaining fortitude with which he accepted the tragic affliction of his declining years. To the intense admiration and pleasure of his countless friends and admirers he was able to see and enjoy cricket through his mind's eye almost to the end. The world was enriched by his example. If ever a man deserved a century from life he did.

Sir Leonard Hutton : He taught me much that stood me in good stead during my own cricket life, especially about Australian conditions.

Brian Sellers : He was a very great gentleman and the greatest cricketer that Yorkshire ever produced. It was always a pleasure to meet him.

Herbert Sutcliffe : His influence over the younger players, of which of course I was one, was very great. He was a magnificent man.

E. W. Swanton : His blue eyes and fresh complexion might suggest the Pennine moors, but there was a vein of iron in his cricket soul.

Sir William Worsley : He was an immense personality, a man of quiet and yet enormous charm.

Eleven major records

Most wickets in first-class cricket: 4,187

100 wickets in a season most times: 23

'Double' of 1,000 runs and 100 wickets in a season most times: 16

Most County Championship appearances: 763 (1898–1930)

Oldest Test player: 52 years 165 days, England v. West Indies, Kingston, 1930

First- and last-wicket records (323 with J. B. Hobbs and 130 with R. E. Foster) for England v. Australia

Most appearances for England v. Australia: 41 (with Hobbs)

Most wickets for England v. Australia: 109

Only player to achieve 'double' of 1,000 runs and 100 wickets for England v. Australia

Seventh-wicket record (254 with D. C. F. Burton v. Hants, 1919) for Yorkshire

Most wickets in a season (240) and career (3,608) for Yorkshire

He scored 39,802 runs (including 58 centuries) in first-class cricket.

(1973)

INDEX

Dates in brackets refer to the original date of publication in *The Cricketer* (where known).

Waterloo, Battle of, and a match at Lord's, 32–3
Watson, F., 155
Webbe, A. J., 11, 24
Weekes, E. D., 63, 127
Wellings, E. M., on Titmus, 112
Wellington, Duke of, 32, 33
White, Crawford, on Dexter, 79
Wilson, Don, 178
Wilson, F. B., 2
Wilson, L. B. (R. G. Barlow's grandson), 48
Winser, Leigh, 39–41, 42
women cricketers: Netta Rheinberg on, 103–5
Wood, Arthur, 29, 30, 31, 43, 44
Woodcock, John, on Viv Richards, 63; on Jeff Thomson (1975), 114–16; on Clive Taylor, 152

Woodfull, W. (Bill) M., 20, 21, 142, 171, 175: Peebles on, 158–60
Woods, Sammy M. J., 26, 91
Wooldridge, Ian, on Doug Walters (1966), 105–7; on Clive Taylor (1977), 151–2
Wooller, Wilfred, on Dai Davies (1976), 169–70
Woolley, Frank E., 27, 28–9, 40, 120, 129, 132
Worrell, Sir Frank M., 63, 95, 127, 133, 134–7: James on, 162–4
Worsley, Sir William A., 72, 180
Wrathall, Harry, 25, 26

Yardley, Norman W. D., 72, 149
Young, Jack A., 112, 113

Zaheer Abbas, 67, 100